Far West Record

Minutes of The Church of Jesus Christ of Latter-day Saints, 1830-1844

Edited by
Donald Q. Cannon, Lyndon W. Cook

Deseret Book Company
Salt Lake City, Utah

Printed in the United States of America
First Printing February 1983

Library of Congress Cataloging in Publication Data
Main entry under title:

Far West record.

Minutes of various kinds of church-related meetings held by the Church of Jesus Christ of Latter-Day Saints from 1830-1844.

Bibliography: p.

Includes index.

1. Mormon Church—History—Sources. I. Cannon, Donald Q., 1936- . II. Cook, Lyndon W. III. Church of Jesus Christ of Latter-Day Saints.

BX8611.F37 1982 289.3 82-23476

ISBN 0-87747-901-1

Contents

Preface

The Far West Record is an early Church minute book containing the proceedings of many general Church meetings and high council minutes from 1830-39.[1] Essentially, there are only two general Church minute books for the Joseph Smith period, namely, the Far West Record and the Kirtland Council Minute Book.[2] The Far West Record contains one hundred eighty-one handwritten pages of minutes in the hands of two notable recorders: Ebenezer Robinson and Hosea Stout.[3] The brown ledger measures 8½ inches by 13 inches. The ink is mostly brown, and two-thirds of the sheets are blank. Located in the office of the First Presidency, in Salt Lake City, the original has not been available for historical research; nevertheless, a typescript as well as a microfilm copy of the original have been made available to serious researchers since about 1960.[4]

Efforts to publish the entire ledger began in 1974; permission was granted in February 1977. A prime source document for preparing the seven-volume *History of the Church,* the Far West Record provides information on a wide range of Church activities in five different states, particularly Ohio and Missouri.

The complete, unedited text of the Far West Record, as it appears in the original, is presented in this volume. Every effort has been made to publish a faithful copy of the document. The original spelling, punctuation, and paragraphing have been retained. The occasional use of a bracket denotes the insertion of a letter or word by the editors. Footnotes supply important historical, biographical, doctrinal, organizational, and procedural commentary to the manuscript. Biographical data for most of the people mentioned in the Far West Record will be found in the

Biographical Appendix, alphabetically arranged. Other items in the appendixes supplement the text.

The following abbreviations will be used in the text and the notes:

History of the Church	Joseph Smith, Jr. *History of The Church of Jesus Christ of Latter-day Saints*, ed., B.H. Roberts, 2nd ed. rev., 7 vols. (Salt Lake City: Deseret News, 1932-51).
Journal of Discourses	*Journal of Discourses*, 26 vols. (1854-1886) Liverpool, England.
Evening and Morning Star	*The Evening and the Morning Star*, June 1832-July 1833. Independence, Missouri. December 1833-September 1834, Kirtland, Ohio. *Evening and Morning Star*, June 1832-September 1834, Independence, Missouri, and Kirtland, Ohio [Kirtland, Ohio, January 1835-October 1836].
Messenger and Advocate	*Latter Day Saints' Messenger and Advocate*, October 1834-September 1837, Kirtland, Ohio.
Times and Seasons	*Times and Seasons*, 1839-1846, Nauvoo, Illinois.
Elders' Journal	*Elders' Journal of The Church of Latter Day Saints*, October-November 1837. Kirtland, Ohio. *Elders' Journal of The Church of Jesus Christ of Latter Day Saints*, July-August 1838. Far West, Missouri.

Journal History	Journal History of The Church of Jesus Christ of Latter-day Saints, Church Archives, Salt Lake City, Utah.
The Scriptory Book of Joseph Smith	The Scriptory Book of Joseph Smith Jr—President of the Church of Jesus Christ of Latterday Saints in All the World, Far West April 12th 1838 (1838), Church Archives.
Kirtland Council Minute Book	The Kirtland Council Minute Book (1832-37), Church Archives.
Kirtland Revelation Book	The Kirtland Revelation Book (1831-34), Church Archives.
Nauvoo High Council Minutes	Nauvoo High Council Minutes (1839-45), Church Archives.

---

[1]Also included in the Far West Record are minutes of two High Council meetings (dated 1 and 15 June 1844) in Nauvoo, Illinois. These minutes constitute three pages of the document.

[2]While there are several other Church record books for the Joseph Smith period (e.g., Kirtland Revelation Book, Scriptory Book of Joseph Smith, and Nauvoo High Council Minutes), only the two records referred to above served as "general" minute books.

[3]The Far West Record does not contain the original minutes as taken by the twenty-four clerks whose names appear in the document. The ledger served as a book of final recording for minutes taken earlier. Robinson and Stout were the recorders of the minutes, not the actual clerks.

[4]The first typescript of the Far West Record was made about 1930.

Acknowledgments

Initial interest in the Far West Record as an important source of early Mormon history was generated in a Church history class at Brigham Young University in 1971. While the editors considered publishing the record book in 1974 (when they first met as professor and research assistant), they did not submit a formal proposal to edit and publish the document to the Church Historical Department until 1976. In February 1977 permission was granted to prepare the manuscript for publication.

We are indebted to many talented individuals for assisting with this project. Research materials used in this work were taken from the Church Archives, Historical Department of The Church of Jesus Christ of Latter-day Saints, Salt Lake City, Utah; Special Collections and Manuscripts, Harold B. Lee Library, Brigham Young University, Provo, Utah; Manuscripts Division, J. Willard Marriott Library, University of Utah, Salt Lake City, Utah; History Division, Library-Archives, Reorganized Church of Jesus Christ of Latter Day Saints, The Auditorium, Independence, Missouri; and Missouri State Historical Society, Columbia, Missouri. We thank the kind, able staffs at these libraries.

We give special thanks to Leonard J. Arrington, director of the Joseph Fielding Smith Institute for Church History, Brigham Young University, for his help in securing permission to publish the Far West Record as well as his encouragement and enthusiasm during the preparation of this volume.

We kindly remember the cooperation of James L. Kimball, Jr., at Church Archives. He has gone well beyond the second mile in helping us locate important materials used in this book. Chad

Flake, Scott Duvall, Dennis Rowley, Hyrum Andrus, Haybron Adams, Donna McGee, and A. Dean Larsen of the Harold B. Lee Library, and Madelon Brunson and Patricia Roberts at the RLDS Library-Archives have also greatly assisted us in our work. Others who have contributed significantly are Richard L. Anderson, Dean C. Jessee, Larry C. Porter, LaMar C. Berrett, Milton V. Backman, Jr., Max H. Parkin, and Davis Bitton.

Finally, we appreciate the painstaking efforts of Steven Bergstrom, Steven Knowles, Karen Sundell Costello, Kaylene Porter Harding, Cindy Compton, and Cheryl Clement, who assisted in the research, typing, proofreading, and final preparation of the book.

Introduction

At a time when the Church has achieved international recognition as a keeper of historical and genealogical records, the Far West Record has special relevance. This pioneer effort in early Church record-keeping was faithfully performed in the spirit of D&C 21:1, wherein the Lord said: "Behold, there shall be a record kept among you."

Mindful of the unsophisticated nature of recording and preserving documents in the early nineteenth century as well as the difficult and extensive travels of the Saints from New York to Utah, it is undoubtedly providential that we have the Far West Record today. The secretaries or clerks who kept the minutes of meetings contained in this ledger did not have shorthand skills, and, except for some knowledge of orthography, were essentially untrained. Yet, while their reports are occasionally incomplete, they are largely lucid, conceptually well-rounded, and probably fairly accurate summaries of what actually transpired.

The Far West Record contains minutes of various kinds of Church-related meetings (general conferences, high council and priesthood quorum meetings, and special councils) for the period 1830-44. But while the record chronologically spans the entire Church career of Joseph Smith, it is not a continuous, unbroken history of events in Church history for that same period.

The Far West Record is a record book into which original, loose pages of minutes were copied. (Some had been around for at least eight years.) Although several different clerks had taken the minutes, it was undoubtedly John Whitmer who had preserved them. Whitmer had been ordained Church historian in

April 1831. Except for good continuity in minute-keeping during the later Missouri period, the Far West Record turns out to be a potpourri of minutes taken at various meetings held in New York, Ohio, Indiana, Missouri, and Nauvoo, Illinois. For this reason the title is somewhat of a misnomer. Nevertheless, a full 80 percent of the total entries are from the Missouri period.

The ledger was given to the high council at Far West, Missouri, for their own minutes in 1838. But at some point in time it was decided that many loose pages of minutes of earlier years would occupy the first pages. The modern title of the record book was attached to the document by association after the Saints had settled in Utah. It was from the title page of the book that the name "Far West Record" was derived. This title was used in Church inventory of historical documents in 1855.

A study of the Far West Record demonstrates that Joseph Smith was respected and revered by early Church members as an inspired prophet. A perusal of its pages amply shows that he was an astute and wise counselor as well as a dynamic and charismatic leader.

Although the Far West Record does not contain the text of any revelation received by Joseph Smith, at least thirty-four different sections of the Doctrine and Covenants are referred to in the minutes of meetings (see index). A study of the record book provides information about the background and setting of some revelations (for example, sections 1, 32, 38, 82, and 133), precise dating of revelations previously unidentified (for example, section 57), the degree of acceptance and implementation of the instructions found in the revelations by members and leaders, and important insights into the nature of revelation.

In terms of tracing the early development of Mormon doctrine and polity, the Far West Record is critical. During this early formative period, theology was essentially undefined, and quorums of Church government were searching to find their proper places. Despite the forces of new scripture and the presence of a modern prophet, popular notions and forms of evangelical Protestantism significantly influenced the Church during its first decade. Consciously seeking not to become creedal, Mormonism was, nevertheless, attempting to define its boundaries and standards in doctrine and Church government. The Far West Record richly documents many of these early issues. Is disease of the devil? Should medicine be administered to the sick? How can one detect false spirits? Who can receive revelation for the Church? Who has authority to organize a stake? Can one hold a Church office without keeping the Word of Wisdom?

The Far West Record was an important source used by early Church historians in preparing Joseph Smith's history. And while B. H. Roberts occasionally footnoted the published version of the Prophet's history with citations from the Far West Record, professor Richard L. Anderson has proposed that any revision of the seven-volume *History of the Church* should properly include additional material from this record.

Historically, the Far West Record is significant in understanding the law of consecration, the United Firm, the organization of stakes, mission calls, priesthood assignments and ordinations, the growth of testimony among members as well as their frustrations and disappointments, excommunications, dates and places of meetings and conferences, business enterprises, Church-state relationships, and land purchases. The lists of names that are included within the minutes of nearly all meetings of this record provide important data for the historian, biographer, and genealogist in establishing chronology and outlining profiles of early Mormons.

Significant information on Church courts of both a general and specific nature is also found in the Far West Record. Many procedures implemented during this early period (some by revelation) soon became established precedents—many have remained to the present time. While the court was used to discipline violaters of the law of chastity, the ordinary function was to work out petty differences between members. The charge of "unchristian-like conduct" was a catch-all for a wide variety of infractions ranging from refusing to pay a debt to licentiousness.

Each quorum of the priesthood could try its members for wrongdoing, and these decisions could be appealed to the bishop's court or high council court.

The organization of high council courts in 1834 marked an important milestone in Church tribunals. The high councils held wide judicial and administrative powers during this early period, and while their authority would subsequently diminish, members of these early councils (ordained high priests) were clearly recognized as "general authorities." Although these early high councils rarely convened to hear criminal cases, Church courts did adjudicate controversies that today would be settled by civil courts. An important feature of the high council court was that the rights of the accused were protected by at least half of the participating high councilors.

Because courts decided administrative as well as juridical matters, they naturally convened more frequently during Joseph Smith's lifetime than they do today. Yet, early Mormon history reveals a democratic spirit that actually encouraged uninhibited criticism of Church policy and procedure and a certain freedom in questioning the actions of one's neighbor. These notions and the fact that Church courts often acted as civil courts effectively multiplied the number of cases that came before them.

In terms of possible discipline, other options were available in addition to disfellowshipment, excommunication, and exoneration. In the case of brethren, misconduct could result in some form of restriction of priesthood privileges: one could be "stripped" of his priesthood office; "silenced" (restrained from preaching); or have his preaching license taken away. If misconduct on the part of sisters was not sufficient to warrant excommunication or disfellowshipment, they were usually restricted only in partaking of the sacrament. Recalcitrant Church leaders, after being "cut off" (excommunicated), were often delivered over to the buffetings of Satan. (Of particular importance in the Far West Record are the excommunication trials of Oliver Cowdery and David Whitmer.) However, it should be pointed out that whatever the charge, a humble confession was, almost without exception, rewarded with forgiveness and the hand of fellowship without any period of waiting. (See Appendix B.)

The Far West Record is an important source in helping us understand the growth of the Church and the changes that have occurred in one hundred and fifty years. Church meetings during the 1830s and 1840s were nearly always held in homes, sometimes in schools, but rarely in meetinghouses built for worship. During this period the brethren could "apply" to be ordained to a priesthood office, and minutes in the Far West Record show that men were sometimes rejected as members of the high council because they were "too noisy" in meeting, and in one case because they were merchants.

Strongly influenced by American Protestantism, early Church customs reveal a contrast with present practices. Yet, this contrast between past and present helps one comprehend today's Church. Change has been, is now, and will be an integral part of The Church of Jesus Christ of Latter-day Saints. Studying the Far West Record, today's Church member can more easily understand and accept the rapid changes associated with a rapidly expanding international Church.

The Conference Minutes,

and

Record Book,

of

Christ's Church

of

Latter Day Saints

Belonging to the High Council of said Church, or their successors in office, of Caldwell County Missouri;

Far West: April 6, 1838.

1830

June 9, 1830

Minutes of the first Conference[1] held in the Township of Fayette,[2] Seneca County, State of New York. by the Elders of this Church, June 9th 1830.[3] according to the Church Articles and Covenants

Elders Present:[4]

Joseph Smith, junior	David Whitmer,
Oliver Cowdery,	John Whitmer,
Peter Whitmer,	Ziba Peterson

Ezekiel 14th read by Joseph Smith jr. and prayer by the same Articles and Covenants[5] read by Joseph Smith jr. and received by unanimous voice of the whole congregation, which consisted of most of the male members of the Church. Samuel H. Smith was then ordained an Elder under the hand of Oliver Cowdery, & Joseph Smith seignior and Hyrum Smith were ordained Priests.

The following persons were then seated repectively & received their licences,[6] Viz:

Elders of this church.	Priests of this Church
David Whitmer	Martin Harris
John Whitmer	Hyrum Smith
Peter Whitmer	Joseph Smith sen
Ziba Peterson	
Samuel H. Smith	Teachers of this Church
	Hiram Page and
	Christian Whitmer.

Exhortation[7] by Joseph Smith jr. and Oliver Cowdery, conference adjourned to the 26th September 1830, to be held in the same place. Br. Oliver Cowdery appointed to keep the Church record and Conference minutes until the next conference.[8] Prayer by all the Brethren present[9] and dismissed by Br. Oliver Cowdery. The above minutes were taken at the time of this conference by Oliver Cowdery. Clerk.

---

[1]Although these minutes were copied into the Far West Record at Far West, Missouri, in 1838, they are the minutes of the first conference of the Church in this dispensation.

[2]The place where this conference was held, as also the organization of the Church on April 6, 1830, was a log structure located on the Peter Whitmer, Sr., farm in Fayette, New York. (See Richard Lloyd Anderson, "The House Where the Church was Organized," *Improvement Era,* April 1970, pages 16-25.)

[3]See *History of the Church* 1:84.

[4]Many precedents for present-day Church procedure were established in these early conferences, such as the listing of those present.

[5]The "Articles and Covenants of the Church of Christ," originally Doctrine and Covenants 20 and 22, were faithfully read and followed at each of the early conferences.

[6]One of the important functions of the early conferences was the issuing of licenses. In order to properly identify missionaries and other Church officers, official licenses were issued. In conjunction with the licensing process, the Church also issued certificates that verified one as a member in good standing. This practice was established in the Articles and Covenants, Doctrine and Covenants 20:63-64. For additional information, see Donald Q. Cannon, "Licensing in the Early Church," *Brigham Young University Studies* 22 (Winter 1982): 96-105.

[7]The word *exhortation* is used frequently in the Far West Record. In the early nineteenth century, exhortation meant a discourse designed to encourage or admonish earnestly. The word is not presently in colloquial usage. See *Oxford English Dictionary* and *Webster's Unabridged Dictionary*.

[8]Oliver Cowdery and other prominent Church leaders served as clerks in the early Church conferences. Minute-taking and other clerical functions were considered to be of great importance.

[9]Obviously all conferences were opened and closed with prayer. In this instance, the congregation prayed in unison.

September 26, 1830

Minutes of the second Conference held by the Elders of this Church according to adjournment, Sept. 26. 1830.[1]

Elders

Joseph Smith jr.
Oliver Cowdery
David Whitmer
John Whitmer
Peter Whitmer
Samuel H. Smith
Thomas B. Marsh.

Br. Joseph Smith jr. appointed leader of the Conference by vote.[2]

Brother Joseph Smith jr. was appointed by the voice of the Conference to receive and write Revelations & Commandments for this Church.[3]

The fifth chapter of Isaiah read by Br. Joseph Smith jr. & prayer by the same. Articles & Covenants read by br. Oliver Cowdery and remarks by Brother Joseph Smith jr.

No. of the several members uniting to this Church since the last Conference, thirty-five, making in whole now belonging to this Church sixty-two.[4] Br. Newel Knight ordained a priest under the hand of brother Oliver Cowdery and prayer by the same.[5] Prayer by all present. Exhortation by all the Elders respectively. Singing and prayer in behalf of Br. Oliver Cowdery & Peter Whitmer jr. who were previously appointed to go to the Lamanites.[6]

Conference adjourned to January 1. 1831.[7] to be held at this place. Br. David Whitmer appointed to keep the Church records until the next Conference. Prayer by br. Oliver Cowdery. The foregoing minutes were taken at the time of this Conference by Oliver Cowdery.

[1]This conference was held in the Peter Whitmer, Sr., home. See *History of the Church* 1:110, 115-18.

[2]In the appointment of Joseph Smith as the leader of the conference, one sees the application of the principle of common consent. See Doctrine and Covenants 26.

[3]Joseph Smith was appointed to be the *one* to receive and write revelations. See Doctrine and Covenants 21, 28, 43.

[4]From this information one can determine that there were twenty-seven members at the first conference. For additional information on the number of Church members, see *History of the Church* 1:76-77.

[5]Another important function of early Church conferences was the ordination of men to priesthood offices.

[6]For information on the early mission to the Lamanites, see Doctrine and Covenants 28, 30, and 32.

[7]This conference was actually held on January 2, 1831, at the Whitmer home.

1831

January 2, 1831

Conference convened according to adjournment[1] but there were no minutes taken, save a commandment received, giving directions to the Saints, see Book of Commandments, page 80.

---

[1]This is the conference referred to in footnote 7 of the previous conference. Doctrine and Covenants 38, directing the Saints to remove to Ohio, was received during the conference.

April 9, 1831

At a special meeting of the Elders of the Church of Christ held at Kirtland Geauga Co Ohio, April 9. 1831. to do Church business &c. agreeable to a commandment received March 8 1831. John Whitmer was appointed to keep the Church record & History by the voice of ten Elders.[1] Conference adjourned until the first Saturday in June next.

John Whitmer, Clerk.

---

[1]See Doctrine and Covenants 47. Previous to this time both Oliver Cowdery and David Whitmer had been responsible for the records of the Church. At this time the Lord officially gave this responsibility to John Whitmer. In effect, he became the first Church historian. His history, known as The Book of John Whitmer, has recently been published with scholarly notes. (See F. Mark McKiernan and Roger D. Launius, eds., *An Early Latter Day Saint History: The Book of John Whitmer* [Independence: Herald Publishing House, 1980].)

June 3, 1831

Minutes of a general Conference held in Geauga County Ohio June 3. 1831.[1]

Elders Present.

Joseph Smith jr.
David Whitmer
John Whitmer
Samuel H. Smith
Hyrum Smith
Joseph Smith, sen.
Parley P. Pratt
Thomas B. Marsh
Sidney Rigdon
John Murdock
Lyman Wight
Levi Hancock
Orson Pratt
Edward Partridge
Ezra Thayer
Newel Knight
Northrop Sweat
(denied faith)[2]
Emer Harris
Joseph Wakefield
Ezra Booth
(denied the faith)
John Corrill
Seymour Brunson
Isaac Morley
Harvey Whitlock
Zebedee Coultrin
Jacob Scott
(denied the faith)

Elders Present

William Carter
(denied the faith)
Sylvester Smith
Simeon Carter
Calvin Bebee
Solomon Hancock
Wheeler Baldwin
Edison Fuller
(denied the faith)
Burr Riggs
(was cast out)
Ebenezer Abbott
(denied the faith)
Reynolds Cahoon
Solomon Humphrey
John Woodard
(denied the faith)
Joseph Brackenberry
(died on a mission
to preach)
Newel Knight
Joseph Coe
William Mitchell
Ebenezer Page
Alpheus Gifford

Priests[3]

Martin Harris

Caleb Baldwin
(cut off recd back & reordained a Priest)
James Durfee
Major N. Ashley

Teachers

Hezekiah Peck
Hiram Page
Christian Whitmer

Daniel Stanton
Solomon Chamberlain
Lorin Page
Jacob Sherman
(cut off)
Benjamin Bragg
(denied the faith)
William Smith
Stephen Burnett
Isaac Bebee
Benjamin Johnson
Samuel Day
Thoret Parsons
Jacob Chamberlain

Conference opened by br. Joseph Smith jr. in exhortation & prayer. Prayer by br. Sidney Rigdon & exhortation by the same. Exhortation by most of the Elders present.

Brs. Lyman Wight John Murdock Reynolds Cahoon Harvey Whitlock & Hyrum Smith were ordained to the high Priesthood[4] under the hand of br. Joseph Smith jr.

Exhortation by brs. Lyman Wight & Harvey Whitlock

Brs. Parley P. Pratt Thomas B. Marsh Isaac Morley Edward Partridge Joseph Wakefield Martin Harris Ezra Thayer Ezra Booth (denied the faith) John Corrill Samuel H. Smith Solomon Hancock Simeon Carter Wheeler Baldwin Jacob Scott (denied the faith) Joseph Smith sen. John Whitmer Joseph Smith jr. & Sidney Rigdon were ordained to the High Priesthood under the hand of br. Lyman Wight.[5] The Bishop (Edward Partridge) then blessed those who were ordained in the name of Christ according to commandment br. John Corrill & Isaac Morley were ordained assistants to the Bishop under the hand of Lyman Wight.

Exhortation by br. Sidney Rigdon & Joseph Smith jr. closed by prayer by br. Sidney Rigdon.

John Whitmer Clerk

[1]See *History of the Church* 1:175-77 and Doctrine and Covenants 44. Although the term general conference is used here, this was not a general conference in the same sense that the Church holds general conference in April and October now. See Jay R. Lowe, "A Study of the General Conferences of the Church of Jesus Christ of Latter-day Saints, 1830-1901," Ph.D. dissertation, Brigham Young University, 1972. The word *conference* had at least two meanings in the early nineteenth century:

1. A meeting of the officers and elders of the Church.
2. An association of branches or churches in a given geographical area. This developed after about 1835 and was a forerunner of the mission district. Other American religions such as the Methodists, Mennonites, and Congregationalists also held conferences. (See S. George Ellsworth, "A History of Mormon Missions in the United States and Canada, 1830-1850," Ph.D. dissertation, University of California, 1951, pages 150-51.)

[2]When this conference was held, in June 1831, all of these men were members in good standing. However, in 1838, when these minutes were copied from loose pages into the Far West Record, the recorder inserted the notations in parentheses "(denied the faith)" or "(cut off)," thus indicating that these people had left the Church.

[3]The conference minutes in this period listed those present by priesthood office, as, for example, elders, teachers, priests, followed by the names of the office holders.

[4]The office of high priest.

[5]Note that Joseph Smith was ordained by the man whom he had previously ordained (Lyman Wight).

The term "High Priesthood," as used by Joseph Smith and others during his lifetime, is not generally understood today. Current usage simply equates high priesthood with Melchizedek Priesthood. While a complete appreciation of the early usage of the term may be impossible, it is clear that for several years the office of high priest was the highest priesthood office in the Church, only high priests held the high priesthood (not elders, seventies, or apostles), and all elders, if worthy, could be ordained to the high priesthood. The "President" of the high priesthood presided over all the high priests, and since the office of high priest was the highest office in the Church, the president of that order was naturally the presiding ecclesiastical officer in the Church. (See Lyndon W. Cook, *The Revelations of the Prophet Joseph Smith: A Historical and Biographical Commentary of the Doctrine and Covenants* [Provo: Seventy's Mission Bookstore, 1981], pages 136-37.)

June 6, 1831

June 6th 1831

Brother Simonds Rider Selah J. Griffin Daniel Stanton Peter Dustin Sidney Gilbert & William W. Phelps were ordained Elders of this Church according to the Church Covenants under the hand of Joseph Smith jr.

August 4, 1831

Minutes of a special Conference held in Kaw township Jackson County Missouri by special commandment[1] of the Lord August 4, 1831.[2]

Elders Present	Elders Present
Joseph Smith jr.	William W. Phelps
Oliver Cowdery	Martin Harris
Peter Whitmer	Frederick G. Williams
Ziba Peterson	Newel Knight
Sidney Rigdon	Joseph Coe
Edward Partridge	Sidney Gilbert
Isaac Morley	Ezra Booth (denied the faith)

The conference opened by singing "Glorious things &c[3] Prayer by br. Edward Partridge, Exhortation to obedience to the requisition of Heaven by delivering a charge in the name of ~~the Lord~~ Christ to the Bishop, Rulers & Members of the Church planted in their inheritances in the land of Zion,[4] by br. Sidney Rigdon.

Confession of br. Ziba Peterson of his transgressions which was satisfactory to the Church as approved by unanimous vote.[5]

Exhortation by br. Joseph Smith jr. to acts of righteousness and keeping the commandments of the Lord with promise of blessings.

Thirty-one members present, who with the Elders partook of the sacrament.[6]

Closed by prayer by Oliver Cowdery. Oliver Cowdery, Clerk.

---

[1]See Doctrine and Covenants 52, 57. These revelations directed the Saints to hold a conference in Missouri.

[2]See *History of the Church* 1:199. This conference was held in the home of Joshua Lewis, a convert of the Lamanite missionaries to Missouri.

[3]Many of the meetings were opened by congregational singing.

[4]The members referred to here are the members of the well-known Colesville Branch, who arrived in Independence July 25, 1831. Just prior to this conference Sidney Rigdon consecrated the land of Missouri for the gathering of the Saints, and Joseph Smith dedicated the temple site at Independence.

[5]See Doctrine and Covenants 58:60.

[6]It was customary in the early conferences to partake of the sacrament.

August 28, 1831

August 28, 1831.[1]

At a Church meeting held in Kirtland, Ohio, Oliver Cowdery was ordained to the High Priesthood by the voice of the Church & command of the Lord under the hand of br. Sidney Rigdon[2]

John Whitmer

---

[1]Joseph Smith arrived in Kirtland, Ohio, from Missouri on August 27, 1831. (See *History of the Church* 1:216.)

[2]At the June 3, 1831, conference, Joseph, Sidney, and others had been ordained to the high priesthood, and now Oliver, upon his return from the Lamanite mission, was also ordained. Note the use of the minute book to record ordinations.

September 1, 1831

Minutes of a Conference held in Kirtland Geauga County Ohio, Sept. 1. 1831.

Elders Present

Joseph Smith jr.	Ezra Thayer	Emer Harris
Oliver Cowdery	Joseph Smith	William W. Phelps
Sidney Gilbert	Joseph Coe	Frederick G. Williams

Br. Newel K. Whitney was ordained an agent[1] unto the Disciples in this land under the hand of br. Oliver Cowdery. Upon testimony given satisfactory to this Conference it was voted that our brethren Edison Fuller & William Carter be silenced from holding the office of Elders in this Church. By request of br. Lorin Page the Conference received his licence as a Priest.[2]

Oliver Cowdery, Clerk of Con.

---

[1]As an agent, Whitney and others transacted business for the Church. While the business was essentially temporal, i.e., related to the mercantile establishment, this was an ecclesiastical position. See Doctrine and Covenants 63:45.

[2]Here three brethren were subjected to two forms of discipline not presently used in the Church. Elders Fuller and Carter were "silenced," i.e., not allowed to function as elders, while Lorin Page gave up his license to act as a priest.

September 6, 1831

Minutes of a Conference held in Nelson Portage County Ohio, Sept. 6, 1831.[1]

Elders present: Joseph Smith, jr. Oliver Cowdery, Christian Whitmer, Sidney Rigdon, Sylvester Parker, (denied the faith)

Upon testimony satisfactory to this conference it was voted that Ezra Booth be silenced from preaching as an Elder in this Church.[2]

Oliver Cowdery Ck. of Con.

---

[1]Nelson Township, organized in 1817, is located in Portage County about five miles east of Hiram. John Whitmer and Lyman Wight built a branch of the Church there in February-March of 1831. It is possible that the brethren held their meetings in the home of Charles Hulet, an early convert and resident of Nelson.

[2]See *History of the Church* 1:215.

September 12, 1831

Minutes of a Conference held in Kirtland Geauga County, Ohio Sept. 12, 1831.[1]

Elders Present.

Joseph Smith jr.	Sidney Rigdon
Oliver Cowdery	Frederick G. Williams
John Whitmer	Ezra Thayer
	Sidney Gilbert.

Upon sufficient or satisfactory testimony to this Conference, it was voted that our brethren George Miller,[2] a Priest in the church of Shalersville,[3] John Woodard an Elder in the Church of Orange, and Benjamin Bragg a Priest in the Church of Warrensville, be silenced from ministering in their respective offices.

Oliver Cowdery. Clerk of Conference.

---

[1]Joseph Smith moved with his family on this day from Kirtland to Hiram and took up residence in the home of John Johnson. See *History of the Church* 1:215.

[2]This is not the George Miller who figured prominently in Nauvoo and the trek west. See Biographical Appendix.

[3]The branches are referred to as the "Church of Shalersville," etc.; this is similar to New Testament usage. These branches were located in northern Ohio.

October 1, 1831

Minutes of a Conference held in Geauga County Ohio, October 1, 1831. Nine Elders present. The duty of the Elders was declared by the Spirit to go forth and warn the inhabitants of the earth of the things known in the Church of Christ in these last days. Br. Joseph Coe & William W. Phelps were ordained to the High Priesthood under the hand of Br. Joseph Smith jr.

William W. Phelps. Clerk of Conference

August 24, 1831

Minutes of a Conference held in Kaw, Jackson County Missouri, August 2 1831.[1]

Elders Present.

David Whitmer
Hyrum Smith
Edward Partridge
Martin Harris
Harvey Whitlock
Simeon Carter
Samuel Drollenger
Isaac Morley
John Corrill.

Opened by singing & prayer by br. Hyrum Smith. br. Edward Partridge made certain remarks from the 3rd Chapter of Malichi. br. Whitlock made remarks upon the second coming of Christ, br. Hyrum Smith gave an exhortation spoke of Zion[2] & the gathering of the saints into her. &c. & read a part of the 102 Psalm. Br. John Corrill & David Whitmer exhorted to acts of righteousness & sacrifice all for Christ. Br. Isaac Morley exhorted to prayer for Joseph Smith jr. and Sidney Rigdon for the Bishop Edward Partridge and himself &c.

A move was then made by br. Edward Partridge to have Selah J. Griffin tarry a while after arriving in this land if the Spirit so direct him, which was agreed to by the Elders present. Br. William E. Mclellin[3] was admited to be ordained an Elder by the voice of the conference. Glorious things was then sung. Closing prayer by Br Edward Partridge.

John Corrill, Clerk of Conference.

---

[1]This conference is out of chronological sequence. The date given here is obviously in error inasmuch as Hyrum Smith and David Whitmer did not arrive in Missouri until after this time. See Journal History, August 13, 1831. The correct date of the conference is August 24, 1831.

[2]"Zion" means Jackson County, Missouri.

[3]William E. McLellin arrived in Independence on August 18, 1831, having traveled 450 miles from Paris, Illinois, to see the Prophet. (See letter from William E. McLellin to Samuel McLellin, August 4, 1832, RLDS Library-Archives, Independence, Missouri.)

September 29, 1831

Minutes of a conference held in Amherst[1] Lorane Co Ohio. Sept 29 1831. Elders Present. Oliver Cowdery Sylvester Smith & Joel Johnson upon testimony satisfactory, it was voted, that Chauncy Odle an Elder in this Church, be silenced as a preacher in this Church

Newel K. Whitney Clerk of Conference

---

[1]Amherst, Lorain County, is located about fifty miles west of Kirtland. By February 1832, the town had six sawmills, one grist mill, two stores, and a number of mechanics of all kinds. See letter of Wesley Perkins, a skeptical non-Mormon, to Jacob Perkins, February 11, 1832, Manuscripts, Harold B. Lee Library, Brigham Young University, concerning Mormon activity in Amherst.

October 10, 1831

Minutes of a conference held in Kirtland Geauga Co. Ohio; Oct. 10, 1831.

Elders Present.

Oliver Cowdery	
Samuel H. Smith	Burr Riggs
Sidney Rigdon	Orson Hyde[1]
Martin Harris	Joseph Smith[2]
William W. Phelps	Frederick G. Williams.

Before whom was presented a difficulty wherein brs Joseph Smith Ezra Thayer & F.G. Williams were implicated, the said Ezra being absent it was motioned, seconded & carried by vote that br. Oliver Cowdery be dispatched as a speedy messenger to apprise him of the matter and bring him before this conference immediately. Prayer by br. Sidney Rigdon who addressed the Elders in the name of the Lord.

After hearing the relations of all the parties, the conference requested them to withdraw while they should investigate the testimony & pass their decision.

Decision of the conference. The Conference decided, that Br. Ezra Thayer's family remain where they are untill Spring. And Br. Frederick G. Williams family be provided with a comfortable dwelling by this Church. And that Br Joseph Smith see to the management of the farm & to the distribution of its productions as the Lord's agent according to commandment of the Lord[3] And that Brs Smith and Thayer be reproved by this conference, for the unwise course they have taken in this affair & that br Thayer be sharply rebuked for the disrespect with which he has treated this conference & that William W. Phelps be appointed to reprove them in the presence of this conference according to vote as the spirit shall direct him.[4] Lastly that the agent of the church[5] be instructed by this conference to lay the case of F G Williams' family before the church and see that they are provided with a comfortable dwelling according to the commandment of the Lord. Closed. prayer by William W. Phelps

Orson Hyde Clerk of Conference

---

[1]Orson Hyde was baptized on Sunday, October 2, 1831. In this conference, eight days later, he is listed as an elder. Apparently no waiting period was required for ordination to the priesthood.

[2]Joseph Smith, Sr.

[3]See unpublished revelation, May 1831, to Frederick G. Williams, Joseph Smith, Sr., and Ezra Thayer, Kirtland Revelation Book, pp. 91-92. According to this revelation the farm was owned by Frederick G. Williams.

[4]Note the great concern to do all things as directed by the Spirit.

[5]Newel K. Whitney.

October 11, 1831

Minutes of a conference held in Hiram Portage County Ohio Oct 11. 1831[1]

Elders Present

Joseph Smith Jr
Oliver Cowdery
David Whitmer
John Whitmer
Peter Whitmer Jr
Reynolds Cahoon
William W Phelps
Luke Johnson

Certain points were discussed by br Joseph Smith Jr, who said that the Elders present were to tarry untill the Morrow & hold a meeting so that the members might understand the ancient manner of conducting meetings as they were led by the Holy Ghost Also said that this was not perfectly known by many of the Elders of this Church. Exhortation by br William W Phelps

Br Oliver Cowdery then made a move that this conference take into consideration the propriety of appointing six Elders to visit the several branches of this church setting them in order[2] and also make known the situation[3] of brs Joseph Smith Jr and Sidney Rigdon And accordingly brs David Whitmer and Reynolds Cahoon were ~~chosen~~ appointed,[4] the other four remain to be chosen hereafter[5]

It was decided by vote that the general conference meet on the 25 Inst at the dwelling house of br Sirenes Burnett in orange Cuyahoga County brs David & Reynolds were then ordained to their office or appointment and br Stephen Burnett an Elder under the hands of John Whitmer conference closed in prayer by br Joseph Smith Jr

John Whitmer

---

[1]See *History of the Church* 1:219. This conference was held in John Johnson's home.

[2]Conferences took care of supervisory responsibilities later performed by the high council.

[3]The "situation" refers to the financial straits of Joseph Smith and Sidney Rigdon, as they needed money to continue the new translation of the Bible. (See Robert J. Matthews, *"A Plainer Translation," Joseph Smith's Translation of the Bible* [Provo: Brigham Young University Press, 1975].)

[4]Reynolds Cahoon notes that he was to obtain both money and property. See Reynolds Cahoon Journal, Church Archives, Historical Department of The Church of Jesus Christ of Latter-day Saints, Salt Lake City, Utah, hereafter referred to as Church Archives.

[5]The remaining four brethren were Simeon Carter, Orson Hyde, Hyrum Smith, and Emer Harris. See *History of the Church* 1:219.

October 21, 1831

Minutes of a special conference held in Hiram Portage co Ohio Oct 21, 1831[1]

Elders Present

Joseph Smith, jr	Sidney Rigdon
Oliver Cowdery	Frederick G. Williams
John Whitmer	Luke Johnson
Peter Whitmer	Stephen Burnett

Prayer by Sidney Rigdon who called in question the case of two brs William Cahoon and Peter Devolve who were accused by some of our brethren of offering abuse to br. Newel K. Whitney's little child.[2] Br. Frederick G. Williams arose and said that he was at a meeting with the Kirtland brethren when br. William Cahoon was present who spoke at considerable length by the Spirit of the Lord as he supposed, and also br. Peter Devolve declared that he was filled with the Spirit of God, but had confessed previous that he did offer abuse to the child, but not to the satisfaction of her parents.

Therefore voted by this conference that it is their undoubted opinion taking into consideration the testimony before them. It is therefore voted that this Conference send our beloved brethren Joseph Smith jr. and Sidney Rigdon unto the Church in Kirtland to lay before them the decision of this Conference, call before them these two brethren cause them to make sufficient acknowledgement of their sins, or be dealt with according to the law of this Church. Closed in prayer by Joseph Smith jr.

Oliver Cowdery Clerk of Conference.

---

[1]*History of the Church* 1:219.

[2]The child was Newel K. Whitney's daughter, either Sarah Ann (age six) or Mary Elizabeth (age three). The nature of the abuse is not known, but Joseph Smith and Sidney Rigdon went to Kirtland to settle the difficulty.

October 25, 1831

Minutes of a general Conference held at the dwelling of br. Sirenes Burnet in the Town of Orange,[1] Cuyahoga County, Ohio, October 25. 1831.[2]

Names of those ordained to the Highpriesthood

Joseph Smith jr.
Oliver Cowdery
John Whitmer
Hyrum Smith
Sidney Rigdon
Samuel H. Smith
Simeon Carter
Reynolds Cahoon
Martin Harris
Joseph Smith sen.
Wheeler Baldwin
John Smith[3]
(license taken)
(not of the Prophet's lineage)

Elders

David Whitmer
Peter Whitmer
Silvester Smith
Luke Johnson
Burr Riggs
(cut off)
Silvester Parker
left the Church
Orson Hyde
Daniel Stanton

Joseph Brackenbury
(Died)
William E. Mclellin
Major N. Ashley (cut off)
Stephen Burnett
Edmund Durfee
Joel Johnson
Levi Jackman
Emer Harris
Frederick G. Williams

Priests

Lyman Johnson
Edward Johnson
(denied the faith)
Benjamin Carpenter
(not fellowshipped)
Ruggles Eames

Teachers

William Smith
Uziel Stephens
Hiram Griffith

Deacons[4]

Titus Billings
Sirenes Burnett and
John Busk

Prayer by br. Simeon Carter, Glorious things, were then sung Br. Sidney Rigdon arose & said that he wished to make a few observations connected with the object of our assembling ourselves together, When God works all may know it, for he always answers the prayers of the Savior for he makes his children one, for he by his Holy Spirit binds their hearts from Earth to Heaven, And in this thing God has taught his children to sing a new song even about Zion which David Spoke of, &c, God always bears testimony by his presence in counsel to his Elders when they assemble ~~themselves~~ in perfect faith and humble themselves before the Lord and their wills being swallowed up in the will of God

Brother Joseph Smith, Jr. said we have assembled together to do the business of the Lord and it is through the great mercy of our God that we are spared to assemble together, many of us have went at the command of the Lord in defience of every thing evil, and obtained blessings unspeakable in consequence of which, our names are sealed in the Lamb's Book of life, for the Lord has spoken it. It is the privilege of every Elder to Speak of the things of God &c, And could we all come together with one heart and one mind in perfect faith the vail might as well be rent to day as next week or any other time and if we will but cleanse ourselves and covenant before God, to serve him, it is our privilege to have an assurence that God will protect us at all times

Br. John Whitmer said that a certain clause in the Church Covenants[5] was to much neglected he feared by the brethren read accordingly.

Brother Frederick G. Williams enquired if it were the business of this conference to take into consideration the situation of the families of the absent Elders. Br. Sidney Rigdon said that he supposed that it was, saying, I bear testimony that God will have a pure people who will give up all for Christ's sake and when this is done they will be sealed up unto eternal life.

Br. Joseph Smith jr. said that the order of the High-priesthood is that they have power given them to seal up the

Saints unto eternal life.[6] And said it was the privilege of every Elder present to be ordained to the Highpriesthood.

Brother Emer Harris said that he was determined to be for God & none else & with his assistance to do his will[7]

Br. Orson Hyde said that he covenanted to give all to the Lord and be for his glory and as to all his works his heart responded a hearty Amen.

Br. Hyrum Smith said that all he had was the Lord's and he was ready to do his will continually.

Br. Frederick G. Williams said that he renewed again the covenant before the Lord to give all to him.

Br. Wm. E. Mclellin said that he had the greatest reason to rejoice of any present and that he also would be subject to the will of God even unto death.

Br. Sylvester Smith said that he had the testimony that it was the will of the Lord to seal his saints, and also covenanted to give all to the Lord.

Br Reynolds Cahoon said that he could not obtain to express his heart but said that he gave all to God. also reminded the brethren of the constant care of the Savior for them.

Br. Peter Whitmer jr. said, ~~ever since~~ my beloved brethren ever since I have had an acquaintance with the writing of God I have[8]   eternity with perfect confidence

Br. Samuel Smith said that ever since he had set out to serve the Lord, not to regard the favor of man but the favor of Heaven.

Br. Martin Harris said that he was anxious that all should be saved &c. also read two verses in the book of Revelations, also covenanted to give all for Christ's sake.

Br. John Smith said that he felt through grace to do the will of the Lord notwithstanding his extreme old age, also felt to covenant to give all to the Lord.

Br. Daniel Stanton said that he had a long time since covenanted to do the will of God in all things, and also said that it was his desire to be sealed with the Holy Spirit of promise.

Br. David Whitmer said that he felt to declare to this

conference that he had consecrated all that was his to the Lord, and also was desirous to do all for the glory of God.

Br. Simeon Carter said that he was thankful that he had been spared & preserved to go to the land of Zion according to the Commandment of the Lord, for he received it as from his mouth & also thanked the Lord that his feet had troden upon the consecrated ground which was the inheritance of the saints. Testified that the book of Mormon was true. Mourned because of the falling away[9] since he took his journey to the Land of Zion.

Br. Joseph Brackenbury said that he blessed the name of the Lord that he could bear testimony of the truth of the book of Mormon, and also consecrated all to God before he was baptized, he was also determined to go on to the end of his life.

Br. Levi Jackman said he gave all his ability to do the work of the Lord.

Br. Major N. Ashley said that it was by the help of the Lord that he had been preserved, yet his greatest fear was for those who were weak in the faith.

Br. Wheeler Baldwin said that he rejoiced while he heard those give their testimony who had been up to the land of Zion, said he had many times been directed by the Spirit of God, also felt to do the will of the Lord in all things, &c.

Br. Joel Johnson said that he had professed religion for a number of years, also felt to bear testimony of the goodness of God, and to consecrate all to the Lord.

Br. Edmund Durfee said that he had professed religion for a number of years, yet now felt to bear testimony of the goodness of God, & also to consecrate all to the Lord.

Br. Joseph Smith[10] said that he had nothing to consecrate to the Lord of the things of the Earth, yet he felt to consecrate himself and family. Was thankful that God had given him a place among his saints, felt willing to labor for their good.

Br. Luke Johnson said that he was determined to be for God and none else come life or death, also remembered his covenant that he would consecrate all that he had to the Lord.

Br. Hyrum Smith said that he thought best that the information of the coming forth of the book of Mormon be related by Joseph himself to the Elders present that all might know for themselves.

Br. Joseph Smith jr. said that it was not intended to tell the world all the particulars of the coming forth of the book of Mormon, & also said that it was not expedient for him to relate these things &c.[11]

Br. Frederick G. Williams laid before the Conference the case of Sister Marsh & family who were somewhat destitute.

Br. Titus Billings said that he was surprised that the case of Sister Marsh should be brought to this Conference, as she and her family were provided for as well as her brethren around her.

Br. Joseph Smith Jr said that he intended to do his duty before the Lord and hoped that the brethren would be patient as they had a considerable distance. also said that the promises of God was that the greatest blessings which God had to bestow should be given to those who contributed to the support of his family while translating the fulness of the Scriptures, also said until we have perfect love we are liable to fall and when we have a testimony that our names are sealed in the Lamb's Book of life we have perfect love & then it is impossible for false Christs to deceive us. also said that the Lord held the Church bound to provide for the families of the absent Elders while proclaiming the Gospel.[12] further said that ~~the~~ God had often sealed up the heavens because of <u>covetousness</u> in the Church. said that the Lord would cut his work short in righteousness and except the church receive the fulness of the Scriptures[13] that they would yet fall.

Adjournment moved for by the moderator until evening.

The Clerk begged the privilege of laying before the Conference in the evening the necessity of sending certain Elders to visit the Churches and obtain means for the support of

br. Joseph Smith jr. & those appointed to assist him in writing & copying the fulness of the Scriptures, as was concluded upon in a conference held in Hiram, Oct. 11. 1831.[14]
Conference adjourned, Prayer by br. Wm. E Mclellin.
Oliver Cowdery Clerk of Conference.

---

[1]Orange, Cuyahoga County, Ohio, is located fifteen miles south of Kirtland. Large numbers joined the Church in this area. There were at least sixty-five members in this location by November 1830. (See John Murdock Journal, Church Archives.) The brethren would often meet in the home of Sirenes Burnett, father of Stephen Burnett.

[2]*History of the Church* 1:219.

[3]This is not Joseph Smith's uncle. See Biographical Appendix. The note "not of the prophet's lineage" was added by Andrew Jenson.

[4]*History of the Church* 1:219 indicates that there were four deacons present.

[5]Doctrine and Covenants 20.

[6]Here, in 1831, the Prophet addresses the conference on the subject of sealing people up unto eternal life. (See Doctrine and Covenants 68:12.) In this revelation high priests were authorized to seal, when directed by the Spirit, which many subsequently did. See, for example, Reynolds Cahoon Journal, Church Archives.

[7]These expressions are both statements of intent and declarations of belief. They are similar, in part, to testimony bearing in fast meetings now, and constituted a part of their worship service.

[8]Space left in original.

[9]This "falling away" occurred in Kirtland. (See *History of the Church* 1:220.)

[10]Joseph Smith, Sr.

[11]For Joseph's refusal to disclose the particulars of the coming forth of the Book of Mormon, see Doctrine and Covenants 5:7.

[12]Note that the Church was to provide for the families of absent elders preaching the gospel.

[13]The new translation or inspired version. (See Doctrine and Covenants 104.)

[14]See page 16.

October 25, 1831

Conference commenced[1] according to adjournment opened by singing prayer by br. Orson Hyde, singing again.

Brs. Orson Hyde Simeon Carter, Emer Harris & Hyrum Smith were appointed & ordained, agreeable to a motion of the

Clerk, to visit the Churches agreeably to the Conference of Oct. 11. 1831.

Br. Sidney Rigdon said it was the privilege of those Elders present to be ordained to the High Priesthood, telling them that if they then should doubt God would withdraw his Spirit from them.

The following Elders were then called seated & ordained by the Clerk, Viz: David Whitmer Peter Whitmer jr. Silvester Smith Luke Johnson Burr Riggs, Orson Hyde, Daniel Stanton Joseph Brackenbury William E Mclellin, Major N. Ashley, Stephen Burnett, Edmund Durfee Levi Jackman, Emer Harris, Frederick G Williams, several brethren were then called by the Clerk who were desirous to preach the gospel.

Br. Joseph Smith Jr, was appointed to examine these brethren, presenting themselves for ordination, after prayer said that he had a testimony that each had one tallent and if after being ordained they should hide it God would take it from them; exhorted them to pray continually in meekness Said that those who had been previously ordained Priests would be ordained Elders, & the others would be ordained Priests; the clerk then by appointment ordained br Lyman Johnson an Elder and brs Calvin Stodard, Ezekiel Rider, William Scobey, Uziel Stephens, William Smith William Cahoon, Albert Jackman, Stephen Strong, Calves Willson, Luman Gibbs, Eleazer Willis Michael B. Welton Gideon Carter Priests.

Conference adjourned until 8 o'clock A.M. on 26th.

Oliver Cowdery, Ck of Con

---

[1]Second session of conference on October 25, 1831.

October 26, 1831

Conference convened according to adjournment.
Opened by singing "go on ye pilgrims,"
prayer by br. David Whitmer

Br. Sidney Rigdon then made certain remarks on the privileges of the Saints in these last days. Remarks to those who were ordained to the Highpriesthood last evening[1] saying that the Lord was not well pleased with some of them because of their indifference to be ordained to that office, exhortation to faith and obedience setting forth the power of that office.

Br. Orson Hyde said that he received the rebuke in meekness. The same by brs. Stephen Burnett, Joseph Brackenberry, Levi Jackman & Frederick G. Williams.

The Clerk said that the directions which himself & his br. David Whitmer had received this morning respecting the choice of the twelve[2] was that they would be ordained & sent forth from the Land of Zion.

Voted that this Conference appoint another General Conference in Amherst Lorrain County on the 25th January 1832.

Voted that brs. Sidney Rigdon Oliver Cowdery Hyrum Smith & Orson Hyde speak this day to the congregation which shall assemble.

Closed. Prayer by br. Sidney Rigdon.

Oliver Cowdery, Clerk.

Orange Cuyahoga county Ohio Oct. 26. 1831.

---

[1]The fifteen brethren listed on page 25.

[2]The Twelve Apostles. (See Doctrine and Covenants 18.) The Twelve were not called until February 1835.

November 1, 1831

Minutes of a conference held in Hiram, Portage Co Ohio, Nov 1 1831[1]

Elders Present

Joseph Smith Jr	Sidney Rigdon
Oliver Cowdery	William E. Mclellin

David Whitmer	Orson Hyde
John Whitmer	Luke Johnson
Peter Whitmer Jr	Lyman Johnson

Br Sidney Rigdon appointed moderator & Oliver Cowdery Clerk br Oliver Cowdery made a request desiring the mind of the Lord through this conference of Elders to know how many copies of the Book of commandments it was the will of the Lord should be published in the first edition of that work. Voted that there be ten thousand ~~struck~~ copies struck.[2] Adjourned until after noon.

John Whitmer

Preface received by inspiration[3]

Conference commenced according to adjournment by Sidney Rigdon appointed Moderator & Oliver Cowdery, Clerk

Br. Joseph Smith jr. said that inasmuch as the Lord has bestowed a great blessing upon us in giving commandments and revelations, asked the Conference what testimony they were willing to attach to these commandments which should shortly be sent to the world. A number of the brethren arose and said that they were willing to testify to the world that they knew that they were of the Lord.

Revelation received relative to the same.[4]

Conference ~~adjourned according~~ adjourned until morning,
Oliver Cowdery Clerk of Con.

---

[1]See *History of the Church* 1:221. This important conference had been convened to make necessary decisions and arrangements for the printing of the revelations given through Joseph Smith. This ultimately led to the publication of the Book of Commandments.

[2]Their first effort to publish the revelations was a serious one. Publishing 10,000 copies was a major undertaking for a small church. (See Doctrine and Covenants 1.) At a meeting of the Literary Firm on April 30, 1832, the number of copies was reduced to 3,000, possibly because of the cost. (See page 46.)

[3]The importance of these meetings and the business the elders were engaged in is underscored by the fact that the Lord intervened and provided

the preface by means of revelation. This preface is now section 1 of the Doctrine and Covenants.

[4]In addition to receiving the Lord's preface (Doctrine and Covenants 1), they received two more revelations: (1) the testimony that appears in *History of the Church* 1:226 and in the Explanatory Introduction to the Doctrine and Covenants and (2) the revelation contained in Doctrine and Covenants 67.

November 2, 1831

Conference convened according to adjournment. Nov. 2, 1831[1]

Br. Oliver Cowdery appointed Moderator & John Whitmer Clerk.

Opened, Prayer by br. Oliver Cowdery

Br. Lyman Johnson was then ordained to the High priesthood under the hand of br. Sidney Rigdon.

The Revelation of last evening read by the Moderator the brethren then arose in turn and bore witness to the truth of the Book of Commandments. After which br. Joseph Smith jr arose & expressed his feelings & gratitude concerning the Commandment & Preface received yesterday.

Conference Closed. prayer by br. Oliver Cowdery.

John Whitmer

---

[1]Date added by Andrew Jenson.

November 8, 1831

Minutes of a Special Conference held in Hiram, Portage Co. Ohio, Nov. 8. 1831.

Elders Present.

Joseph Smith jr. Christian Whitmer
Oliver Cowdery Sidney Rigdon

John Whitmer	William E. Mclellin
Peter Whitmer	Luke Johnson

Br. Joseph Smith jr. appointed Moderator & John Whitmer Clerk.

Opened, prayer by br. Joseph Smith jr.

Remarks by br. Sidney Rigdon on the errors or mistakes which are in commandments and revelations, made either by the ~~scribe~~ translation in consequence of the slow way of the scribe at the time of receiving or by the scribes themselves.

Resolved by this conference that Br Joseph Smith Jr correct those errors or mistakes which he may discover by the holy Spirit[1] while ~~receiving the revelations~~ reviewing the revelations & commandments & also the fulness of the scriptures. Resolved by this conference that br Oliver Cowdery shall copy correct and select[2] all the writings which go forth to the world ~~which go~~ through the Printing press (except) the revelations and commandments, by the Spirit of the Lord and this according to the commandment given in Missouri July 20, 1831.[3]

Closed in prayer by br Sidney Rigdon

John Whitmer

---

[1]That there were errors in some of the revelations is only to be expected. Errors could occur when (1) a scribe was unable to keep up with the speed of dictation; (2) when the scribe misunderstood a word or sentence; (3) when copies were inaccurately transcribed; (4) when printers made mistakes in the typesetting; or (5) when the language of the revelator did not adequately express the ideas he was receiving. In any of the above cases, making corrections was justified. Subsequent changes could also occur in any written revelation, since the Prophet received knowledge "line upon line," and by virtue of his position had the prerogative to incorporate new insights into earlier revelations, thereby providing greater understanding for the reader. (See *Journal of Discourses* 12:335; 2:314; and T. Edgar Lyon, *Introduction to the Doctrine and Covenants* [Salt Lake City: LDS Department of Education, 1955], page 23.)

[2]The words "copy correct and select" were added by Andrew Jenson. (See Doctrine and Covenants 58.)

[3]See Doctrine and Covenants 57:13. This statement establishes an exact date for section 57.

November 9, 1831

Minutes of a Special Conference held in Hiram Nov 9 1831

Present

Joseph Smith Jr,	Christian Whitmer
Oliver Cowdery	Sidney Rigdon
John Whitmer	~~William E. McLelin~~
Peter Whitmer	Luke Johnson
Lyman Johnson	

Brs. Oliver Cowdery appointed Moderator & John Whitmer Clerk

Opened prayer by br Oliver Cowdery.

Brs. Sylvester Hulett and John Noah expressed desires to preach the word if thought proper by this conference Voted that these two brethren be ordained according to the voice of the Church in which they live.

Closed. Prayer by Peter Whitmer, jr.

John Whitmer Clerk.

November 11, 1831

Minutes of a Special Conference held in Hiram Portage Co. Ohio November 11, 1831.

Present.

Joseph Smith jr.	Reynolds Cahoon
Oliver Cowdery	William E Mclelin
Peter Whitmer jr.	Luke Johnson
Sidney Rigdon	Lyman Johnson

Opened. Prayer by br Reynolds Cahoon, who then said that the question which he wanted settled was whether it was the will of the Lord that he should go to Zion[1] in the spring. Commandments concerning the duties of the Elders, read by br. Oliver Cowdery.

Voted that it is the mind of the conference that our br. Reynolds is not yet commanded to go to Zion in the spring by any thing yet written; Therefore, Voted that our br. Reynolds be not sent up to Zion in the coming spring.[2]

Commandment to br. Thomas B. Marsh read.[3]

Br. Harvey D. Redfield ordained a priest under the hand of br. Sidney Rigdon.

Closed.

Oliver Cowdery, Clerk of Conference

---

[1]Zion here means Jackson County, Missouri.
[2]See Reynolds Cahoon Journal, Church Archives.
[3]See Doctrine and Covenants 31.

November 12-13, 1831

Minutes of a special conference held in Hiram Portage County Ohio. November 12, 1831.[1]

Present.

Joseph Smith jr	Peter Whitmer jr.
Oliver Cowdery	Sidney Rigdon
David Whitmer	Reynolds Cahoon
John Whitmer	Luke Johnson

Wm. E. Mclellin

Br. Wm. E. Mclellin was appointed moderator & Oliver Cowdery Clerk.

Prayer by the moderator.

Br. Joseph Smith jr. said one item he wished acted upon was that our brs. Oliver Cowdery & John Whitmer & the sacred writings which they have entrusted to them to carry to Zion be dedicated to the Lord by the prayer of faith.

Secondly, Br. Oliver has labored with me from the beginning in writing &c Br. Martin has labored with me from the beginning, brs. John and Sidney also for a considerable time, & as these sacred writings are now going to the Church for their benefit, that we may have claim on the Church for recompense, if this conference think these things worth prizing to be had on record to show hereafter I feel that it will be according to the mind of the Spirit for by it these things were put into my heart which I know to be the Spirit of truth, &c.

Voted that Joseph Smith jr. be appointed to dedicate & consecrate these brethren & the sacred writings & all they have entrusted to their care, to the Lord; done accordingly.

After deliberate consideration in consequence of the book of Revelation now to be printed being the foundation of the Church & the salvation of the world & the Keys of the mysteries of the Kingdom & the riches of Eternity to the Church.[2]

Voted that they be prized by this Conference to be worth to the Church the riches of the whole Earth speaking temporally.

Voted that in consequence of the dilligence of our brethren, Joseph Smith jr. Oliver Cowdery John Whitmer & Sidney Rigdon in bringing to light by grace of God these sacred things, be appointed to manage them according to the Laws of the Church & the Commandments of the Lord.[3]

And also that in consequence of the families of Joseph Smith Hiram Smith Peter Whitmer Christian Whitmer Jacob Whitmer Hiram Page & David Whitmer in administering to their wants in temporal things, & also the labors of Samuel H. Smith Peter Whitmer jr. William Smith & Don Carlos Smith. Voted by this Conference that the above named brethren be recommended to the Bishop in Zion as being worthy of inheritances among the people of the Lord according to the laws of said Church.

Closed. prayer by br. John Whitmer.

Oliver Cowdery Clerk.

---

[1]See *History of the Church* 1:235-36. The conference apparently lasted one evening, all the next day, and into that evening. It was held in "Joseph's Translating Room" (upstairs in John Johnson's home). (See "William E. McLellin Correspondence," *Saints Herald,* July 15, 1872, pages 435-36.)

[2]This statement underscores the significance of the Book of Commandments, later known as the Doctrine and Covenants, when it refers to the revelations as "the foundation of the Church and the salvation of the world."

[3]See Doctrine and Covenants 70. Those appointed to manage the sacred writings were organized as the Literary Firm. (See Lyndon W. Cook, *The Revelations of The Prophet Joseph Smith: A Historical and Biographical Commentary of the Doctrine and Covenants* [Provo: Seventy's Mission Bookstore, 1981].)

November 29, 1831

Minutes of a conference held in Winchester Randolph Co Nov 29 1831.[1]

(Present)

Oliver Cowdery[2]	Seymour Brunson
John Whitmer	Oliver Walker (license taken)
Thomas B Marsh	George Burkett (license taken in 1832 & 1833.)

Conference opened in prayer by br. Oliver Cowdery.

And also the business & duties of conference explained &c.

Br. Seymour Brunson then arose & stated the reason why he called this conference is to have some difficulty settled existing between the Elders residing in this place, &c.

Br. Henry Jackson arose and stated that the origin of the difficulty had arisen between him and the Church in consequence of himself and br. Isaac[3] reading certain passages in the Acts, & also in the book of Mormon for they thought that they found therein recorded that the disciples had ought or was privileged to live in common stock.[4]

Adjourned until to morrow 9 O'clock A.M. Prayer by br. T.B. Marsh.

John Whitmer.

---

[1]Winchester, Randolph County, Indiana, situated near the Indiana-Ohio border, is located approximately 75 miles east of Indianapolis, and about 225 miles southwest of Kirtland, Ohio. The branch of the Church in Winchester, initially built up by Levi Hancock and Zebedee Coltrin during the months of June-September 1831, has been overlooked by nearly all historians. Several of the converts to Mormonism in Winchester gathered with the Saints in Missouri. (See Levi Hancock Journal, Special Collections, Harold B. Lee Library, Brigham Young University.)

[2]Oliver Cowdery and John Whitmer left Ohio for Missouri on November 20, 1831, and arrived in Jackson County, Missouri, January 5, 1832. (See Book of John Whitmer, chapter 10.) They were to carry the revelations to Missouri for printing as per the Hiram, Ohio, Conference in November 1831. While en route to Missouri, the two brethren stopped in Winchester, Indiana, to regulate the affairs of the Church there. See Levi Hancock Journal, Special Collections, Harold B. Lee Library, Brigham Young University.

[3]Isaac Follis.

[4]Here is evidence of confusion on the matter of common ownership of property among new converts in eastern Indiana. Early members of the Church in Kirtland, Ohio (including Levi W. Hancock, whose letter seems to have been the source of the problems being addressed in the text) had practiced a system of consecration known as "common stock" (communal ownership of real and personal property). After the arrival of the Prophet to the area in February 1831, official guidelines clarified that each member should be allocated his own portion. However, the 1831-33 phase of the Church's law of consecration did not secure private ownership of property. Early contracts used by Bishop Partridge in Jackson County, Missouri, stipulated that real estate was "leased" to the individual member, that personal property was "loaned," and that in cases of transgression or unworthiness, members forfeited any or all of their stewardship properties. These early arrangements were defective for obvious reasons, and, when challenged by some dissenters, were not upheld by the courts. These procedures were subsequently modified so as to "give a deed, securing to him who receives ... his inheritance ... to be his individual property, his private stewardship." (See letter from Joseph Smith to Edward Partridge, 2 May 1833, Joseph Smith Collection, Church Archives. For references to the challenging of the legality of these proceedings, see *History of the Church* 1:380, cited from *Evening and Morning Star* 2[July 1833]:110 and the *Painesville Telegraph* [Painesville, Ohio], April 26, 1833.)

November 30, 1831

Conference convened according to appointment.[1] Opened in prayer by Thomas B. Marsh. Observations made by all the Elders present & they unanimously agreed that all this difficulty has arisen in consequence of misrepresentations of a writing which was represented to have been written by br. Henry Jackson & a letter written by br. Levi Hancock & Zebbedee Coultrin to br Henry Jackson in consequence of misrepresentations thereof all these difficulties have arisen.

Br. Oliver Cowdery then arose & made a proposition that br. Henry Jackson be restored to his former standing providing he make a statement to the branch that he had done & said things that were wrong for which he was sorry in all humility.[2]

Resolved that this Conference be adjourned until the Church is notified and assembled & this subject laid before them.

Conference adjourned until to-morrow P.M. early candle lighting[3]

Prayer by br. Oliver Cowdery

John Whitmer Clerk.

---

[1]November 30, 1831.

[2]Note that Henry Jackson publicly acknowledged his error and was officially forgiven by the Church.

[3]An expression used to indicate the evening hours.

December 1, 1831

Conference convened according to adjournment.[1] Opened. prayer by Seymour Brunson. Minutes read by John Whitmer. Observations by Oliver Cowdery by way of exhortation to the Church.

All the brethren forgave br. Henry Jackson and he the brethren and thus this difficulty is settled.

Br. Seymour Brunson was ordained to the High Priesthood and br. Henry Jackson again ordained an Elder under the hand of Oliver Cowdery. Conference closed in prayer by br. Oliver Cowdery.

John Whitmer Clerk.

---

[1]December 1, 1831.

December 6, 1831

Minutes of a Conference held in Randolph County Indiana December 6. 1831.

Present.

Oliver Cowdery	Isaac Follice
John Whitmer	George Heartly
Thomas B. Marsh	George Burkett
Seymour Brunson	Oliver Walker
Henry Jackson,	(These two lost both licenses or taken at present.)[1]

Br. Oliver Cowdery appointed Moderator & John Whitmer Clerk.

Prayer by br. Seymour Brunson.

Br Oliver Cowdery then arose and addressed the Elders, showing them the necessity of having their hearts drawn out in prayer to God & also realize that they are in the immediate presence of God & also explained the order of the HighPriesthood &c The Church then proceeded to settle some difficulty that existed between them in the presence of the conference.

Firstly the case of Sister George Burkett & Sister Eunice. Statement of both parties, Sister Burkett manifested a spirit of humility and contrition Sister Eunice a Spirit of hardness and self justification

Resolved that Brs. Seymour Brunson & Isaac Fallace, go and visit Sister Eunice as soon as possible

Secondly the case of br George Burkett br Eunice br Burkett made the same acknowledgement that his wife did the afore mentioned Elders also laboured with br Eunice

Br Oliver then arose & chastised br Burkett in the name of the conference for his previous neglect of duty, &c.

Thirdly. The case of br James More was then called in question misconduct in his family. the letter which he had previously writen to the Church was then read in the conference. Some further remarks were then made by br Lee stating that br More was guilty of bad conduct since the letter was written James More acknowledged that he was guilty of whipping his wife.[2] After that he was questioned by br Thomas B. Marsh Whether he thought that he was worthy to retain his license in the Church as a Teacher he answered in the negative & desired that this conference would receive his license which was done accordingly.

Fourthly the case of brs George Heartly & Oliver Walker called in. Conference adjourned until tomorrow morning at 9 P.M.

Prayer by br Seymour Brunson

John Whitmer

---

[1]George Burkett and Oliver Walker.

[2]Here we see that the Church did not approve of wife-whipping; on the other hand, James More was not severely punished.

December 7, 1831

Conference Convened according to adjournment[1] opened by singing, "Go On Ye Pilgrims, &c" & Prayer by br. Thomas B. Marsh.

Brother Oliver Cowdery then read the 15 Psalm & 24 Ps.[2] & 33 chapter & 13 verse of Isaiah's Prophecy. Brs. George Heartley & Oliver Walker then withdrew to settle the difficulty between themselves but could not agree Therefore decided that two should be appointed by the Moderator. Brs. John Whitmer & Thomas B. Marsh to go.[3] Conference suspended. After some conversation with the parties they agreed to abide the decision of John & Thomas who concluded that Oliver Walker pay George Heartly which was his just due. After which it was laid before the Conference but it was with much cavilling on the part of Walker to stand or hold fast to his agreement. Finally Walker did agree & truly humbled himself & they came together as brothers and disciples & all matters were settled & buried.[4]

Conference closed by singing "My Loving Fellow Travelers," & prayer by br Oliver Cowdery

John Whitmer Clerk of Con. Dec. 7. 1831.

---

[1]December 7, 1831.

[2]Note the reading of scriptures in Church meetings.

[3]Going two by two was customary not only in missionary work, but in laboring with recalcitrant Saints.

[4]Although the problem was considered "buried" at this conference, it surfaced again and was a matter of business in Kirtland in December 1834. See Kirtland Council Minute Book, page 81.

1832

January 23, 1832

Minutes of a general Conference held in the land of Zion. (Kaw Township Jackson County Missouri) at the dwelling house of Newel Knight. January 23. 1832.[1]

Present

Edward Partridge John Corrill Isaac Morley John Whitmer John Murdock William W. Phelps Lyman Wight Harvey Whitlock Newel Knight Parley P. Pratt Oliver Cowdery Levi Hancock Zebedee Coultrin Selah J. Griffin Calvin Beebe Joshua Fairchilds (license taken) Peter Dustin (Priest) Hezekiah Peck (Teacher) Isaac Bebee.

Br Edward Partridge appointed moderator & Oliver Cowdery Clerk. Prayer by br John Murdock. Various commandments read.

Resolutions offered by br Lyman Wight to take into consideration the circumstances of two brethren present. Isaac & George Bebee who desired to preach the Gospel Commandment read by the Clerk certain remarks made by him ~~also~~ & br William W Phelps The duty of the Priests Teachers & Deacons read by br John Whitmer from the Articles & Covenants Remarks by br John Corrill, stating that the offices of Priests, Teachers, & Deacons, to be as important as any in the Church

Resolved therefore that there be no person ordained in the Land of Zion to the office of Elder Priest Teacher or Deacon without the united voice of the Churches[2] in which such individual resides Closed. Prayer by John Corrill

Oliver Cowdery Clerk of Conference.[3]

---

[1]See Book of John Whitmer, chapter 10. Whitmer notes that he and Cowdery arrived in Missouri on January 5, 1832, and refers to this conference. The conference was held three different days, January 23, 24, and 27. Only the minutes from January 23 are in the Far West Record. The other minutes are in the Joseph Smith Collection, Church Archives.

[2]This procedure was in keeping with the counsel given in Doctrine and Covenants 20 and 26.

[3]Oliver Cowdery, the clerk of this conference, wrote a letter to Joseph Smith on January 28, 1832, containing the minutes of all three days of the conference. This important letter is in Appendix A. An examination of his letter shows that the minutes in the Far West Record are abbreviated.

March 10, 1832

Minutes of a special Conference in Zion March 10 1832.[1] Br. John Whitmer Moderator and Oliver Cowdery Clerk.

Present.

John Whitmer
Edward Partridge
John Corrill
Isaac Morley
William W. Phelps
Sidney Gilbert
Selah J. Griffin

Resolved. That this conference write to our br. Sidney Rigdon. Wrote as follows. First as to the charges preferred against our br. Edward Partridge in a letter addressed to brs. John Corrill & Isaac Morley dated Hiram, Nov. 14, 1831. We learn by conversing with br. Edward and those personally conversant with the circumstances that the said charges are partially correct But as the most of them transpired previous to a Conference[2] held on this land[3] at which our brs. Edward and

Sidney were present face to face when confessions were made by several brethren & by br. Edward in particular, to our joy and thanksgiving to our God we can truly say his spirit was there also, we cannot consider them[4] justifiable.[5]

Secondly, As three of the charges are prefered after said Conference one of them is respecting the handing over money to brs Joseph Oliver & Sidney for their expense to Ohio, to which br. Edward says he had no disposition to defraud or deceive his brethren in that case & if any damage has accrued to the Church, or the feelings of any of his brethren been aggrieved in consequence of the same he now asks their forgiveness as well as the forgiveness of the Lord.

The other two are not considered by this Conference just accusations; but in relation to the fifth charge which reads: "His having insulted the Lord's prophet in particular & assumed authority over him in open violation of the Laws of God."[6]

Br. Edward says that in relation to the same although the circumstances occurred previous to said conference if Br. Joseph has not forgiven him he hopes he will, as he is & has always been sorry.

Resolved that whereas the duty of a disciple of Christ[7] is to promote ~~peace~~ union harmony & brotherly love & not at any time imprudently prefer charges & demand confession & settlement of the same in the absence of a br. after having had a privilege of doing the same face to face, and more expecially after sitting in Conference in the name of the Lord & communing together at sacrament. We do therefore after deliberately weighing the subject before us earnestly entreat our br. Sidney for the good of the cause in which we labor & for which we suffer persecutions, to candidly reflect upon the subject of the aforementioned letter and ask himself whether he was not actuated by his own hasty feelings rather than the Spirit of Christ when indicting the same.

After having conversed with br. Edward freely upon the subject we can say with assurance that he is willing to make every confession which br. Sidney as a disciple of Christ could require

& forever bury the matter. And we do advise that such may be the resolution and thereby the wound in the Church be healed & they walk together as brothers filling the important stations in the Kingdom of God in honor to themselves & the advancement of our Redeemer's Cause: Amen.

Closed. Prayer by br. Isaac Morley

Oliver Cowdery Clerk of Conference.

---

[1]By this time, John Whitmer notes that there were 402 members of the Church in Jackson County. (See Book of John Whitmer, chapter 10.) The *Evening and Morning Star* (November 1832) lists 465.

[2]See page 9.

[3]Jackson County, Missouri.

[4]The charges.

[5]Edward Partridge and Sidney Rigdon worked out their problems on April 26, 1832. (See *History of the Church* 1:267; see also page 45.)

[6]Apparently the charges against Partridge related to money and apostasy. (See Doctrine and Covenants 60:10 and 64:17.) Much of the business in early Church meetings involved settling disputes.

[7]Note that the brethren were concerned with defining the duty of a disciple of Christ.

October 21, 1831

Minutes of a Conference held at the dwelling house of Newel Knight's October 21. 1831.[1]

Br. Isaac Morley was appointed Moderator & Harvey Whitlock Clerk.

Present

Isaac Morley	Parley P. Pratt	John Murdock
Calvin Bebee	Harvey Whitlock	Selah J. Griffin
Zebedee Coultrin		Lyman Wight
		Edward Partridge

The object of the meeting as explained by Parley P. Pratt was to search out & examine into the nature of grievances as set forth by sister Emily Coburn & Elizabeth Gilbert respecting the teaching & Spirit which had actuated br Newel Knight for a length of time past.

The testimony was all had on both sides & br. Newel said a considerable after which it was agreed that the Elders should descide upon the Spirit which br. Newel was actuated by this evening.

And after having two votes or lots written for each Elder & the Elders not consulting each other upon the subject the vote was taken or lot cast whether good or bad & on looking over the votes or lots they all agreed & came out bad; brs. Sealey J. Griffin & Zebedee Coultrin not voting being excused. br. Newel then spoke until interrupted by the Moderator. the Elders immediately one after another that had not voted or cast lots raised their voices against the spirit manifested by br. Newel.

After which they reproved the two sisters for some things they thought they were out of the way and afterwards at the request of br Newel to know what he should do or what was to be done with him it was thought advisable that he should not officiate as an Elder until he ~~sh~~ could see with the other Elders & be able to discover that he had a bad spirit.

Harvey Whitlock Clerk of Con.

---

[1]These minutes are out of chronological order, appearing in the middle of notes for 1832.

April 26, 1832

Independence[1] April 26. 1832.[2]
Met in Council.

High Priests Present

Joseph Smith, jr	John Corrill
Sidney Rigdon	Isaac Morley
Jesse Gauss	

Elders Present

Newel K. Whitney	Sidney Gilbert
Edward Partridge	Joshua Fairchilds (license taken at present)
William W. Phelps	James Emmett
Oliver Cowdery	Sanford Porter.

First. Joseph Smith Jr. acknowledged by the High Priests in the land of Zion to be President of the High Priesthood, according to commandment and ordination in Ohio, at the Conference held in Amherst January 25 1832.[3] And the right hand of fellowship given him by the Bishop Edward Partridge in the land of Zion in the name of the Church.

Br. Sidney Gilbert was ordained a High Priest under the hand of br. Joseph Smith jr.

Br. Sidney Rigdon then stated the items embraced in a Revelation received in Ohio[4] & the reason why we were commanded to come to this land & sit in council with the Highpriests here, for the particulars of which read the Commandment.

Conference adjourned for one hour.

John Whitmer Clerk.

---

[1]When the Mormons came to Independence it was still a frontier settlement. (See T. Edgar Lyon, "Independence, Missouri, and the Mormons, 1827-1833," *Brigham Young University Studies* 13 [Autumn 1972]: 10-19.)

[2]This conference was held pursuant to a revelation given on March 1, 1832, to Joseph Smith, instructing Joseph, Newel K. Whitney, and Sidney Rigdon to "sit in council with the saints which are in Zion." (See Doctrine and Covenants 78:9.) Joseph left Hiram, Ohio, April 1, 1832 (*History of the Church* 1:265), in company with the above brethren, as well as Jesse Gause, and arrived in Jackson County on April 24, 1832.

[3]Joseph Smith had already been sustained to this position by the Ohio Saints on January 25, 1832, and was now being sustained by the Missouri Saints. Since there was no office of President of the Church at this time, the office of president of the high priesthood was the highest office in the Church. Note that the high priests in Missouri did not sustain Joseph Smith as President of the Church, but as president of the high priesthood. (See page 8, note 5.)

[4]See Doctrine and Covenants 78.

Council convened
Prayer by br. Edward Partridge.
All differences settled & the hearts of all run together in love[1]
A Revelation received through him whom the Church has appointed respecting organization.[2]
Council adjourned until to-morrow 9 o'clock A.M.
Prayer by Jesse Gauss.

John Whitmer.

---

[1]Reference is made here to the Partridge-Rigdon controversy. (See pages 40-42.)

[2]See Doctrine and Covenants 82. Verse 1 of this revelation has direct reference to the Partridge-Rigdon controversy.

April 27, 1832

Council convened. Opened by singing "He dies the friend of sinners dies &c" & prayer by br. Sidney Rigdon

Resolved, that the name of the Firm mentioned in the Commandments yesterday be Gilbert, Whitney & Company in Zion. And Newel K. Whitney & Company in Kirtland Geauga Co. Ohio.[1]

Resolved that brs. William W. Phelps & Sidney Gilbert draft the bond for the above named Firm. As there was not any business of importance before the Council Brothers Sidney, Joseph & William gave desertations on the Gospel, its appendages &c. Council Closed in prayer by br. Joseph Smith jr.
April 27. 1832. John Whitmer, Clerk

---

[1]The firms handling the mercantile interests of the Church were to be divided into two branches—one in Ohio and one in Missouri. These branches were known as the United Firm.

April 30, 1832

Minutes of a Council of the litterary Firm[1] Zion April 30. 1832

Present.

Joseph Smith jr. Prisident.	Oliver Cowdery
Sidney Rigdon	William W. Phelps
John Whitmer	Jesse Gauss, one of the President's councillors.[2]

Ordered by the Council that three thousand copies of the book of Commandments be printed the first edition.[3]

Secondly: Ordered by the Council that the printing of an alminack[4] for Zion this season be left at the option of brs. William Oliver & John.

Thirdly: Ordered by the Council that all Revelations be limited to the parties concerned until printed.

Fourthly: Ordered by the Council that brs. William, Oliver & John be appointed to review the Book of Commandments & select for printing such as shall be deemed by them proper, as dictated by the Spirit & make all necessary verbal corrections.[5]

Fifthly: Ordered by the Council that the Hymns selected by sister Emma be corrected by br. William W. Phelps.[6] Closed

Prayer by br. Sidney Rigdon.

Oliver Cowdery Clerk.

---

[1]This firm, a companion firm to the United Firm, was formed in November 1831. (See Doctrine and Covenants 70; see also *History of the Church* 1:363-66.) This firm concerned itself with the printing of the revelations, the new translation of the Bible, the hymnbook, and other Church publications. The firm was to produce a revenue for the Church. Section 83 was received at this conference.

[2]Here Jesse Gause is referred to as counselor to Joseph Smith. Gause, the recipient of Doctrine and Covenants 81, was called as Joseph's counselor in the

presidency of the high priesthood on March 8, 1832. (See Kirtland Revelation Book, page 11. Also see Robert J. Woodford, "Jesse Gause, Counselor to the Prophet," *Brigham Young University Studies* 15 [Spring 1975]: 362-64.) Note that the presidency of the high priesthood had been organized by March 1832. This presidency evolved into the First Presidency of the Church by March 1835.

[3]*History of the Church* 1:270 notes that this action (to print 3,000 instead of 10,000 copies of the Book of Commandments) occurred on May 1, 1832, not April 30.

[4]This almanac was proposed, but apparently never published.

[5]See page 29 , note 1. "Verbal" here means "grammatical." Joseph Smith warned W.W. Phelps on July 31, 1832, not to alter the language of the revelations. See letter in Joseph Smith Collection, Church Archives.

[6]In July 1830, Emma had been commanded to "make a selection of sacred hymns." (Doctrine and Covenants 25:11.) The hymns selected by Emma were not published until 1835. The Kirtland high council decided in September 1835 that "Sister Emma Smith proceed to make a selection of sacred hymns according to the revelation and that President W.W. Phelps be appointed to revise and arrange them for printing." (See Kirtland Council Minute Book, page 108.)

April 30, 1832[1]

Minutes of a meeting of the United Firm.[2]

Present.

Joseph Smith jr. President of Conference & also of the Highpriesthood
Oliver Cowdery, Clerk of Conference, and printer to the Church
Edward Partridge Bishop
Newel K. Whitney Bishop of Kirtland
Sidney Gilbert Agent in Zion
Sidney Rigdon, Counsillor of President.
John Whitmer, Lord's Clerk.
William W. Phelps, printer to the Church
Jesse Gauss Counsillor to the President (denied the faith).[3]

Resolved that A.S. Gilbert & Newel K. Whitney be appointed agents to act in the name of this Firm.

Resolved that whenever any special business occur it shall be the duty of the United Firm by their branches at Jackson County Missouri & Geauga County Ohio to regulate the same by special agency.

Resolved That the firm loan[4] fifteen thousand dollars for five years or longer at six per cent anually or semi-anually as the agreement can be made, & that N.K. Whitney & Co. be appointed to negotiate the same.

Closed. Prayer by br Sidney Rigdon.

Oliver Cowdery, Clerk of Conference.

---

[1]This date is probably correct, but the meeting could have been held May 1.

[2]The United Firm, also known as the United Order or the Order of Enoch, was a Church-owned firm organized as early as April 1832 for the purpose of generating revenue for the financial operation of the Church.

The foundation of the firm was initially the Gilbert-Whitney store in Kirtland, Ohio. This mercantile establishment was expanded to include two branches in 1832, one in Kirtland and one in Jackson County, Missouri. The original members of the firm were Joseph Smith, Sidney Rigdon, Jesse Gause, Oliver Cowdery, Martin Harris, William W. Phelps, A. Sidney Gilbert, Newel K. Whitney, John Whitmer, and Edward Partridge. Later Frederick G. Williams and John Johnson were added.

The members of this order were consecrated in their respective responsibilities, and while they were to benefit personally from the profits of the firm, the surplus profits were to be used for the operation and blessing of the whole Church.

The two branches of the United Firm became separate entities in April 1834, according to divine direction (see Doctrine and Covenants 104 and an unpublished revelation in the Kirtland Revelation Book, page 111), but due to the hardships of the Missouri Saints during that period and the death of A. Sidney Gilbert in June 1834, the Missouri branch became defunct.

[3]The words in parentheses were added when the minutes were recorded into the Far West Record. Gause would have been in good standing at the time of the conference.

[4]That is, secure a loan.

May 26, 1832

Minutes of a conference held in Zion, May 26 1832 at the house of br. Sidney Gilbert.

High Priests Present.

Edward Partridge	Jesse Gauss
John Corrill	Elders Present
Isaac Morley	
W.W. Phelps	Titus Billings
Sidney Gilbert	Calvin Bebee

To take into consideration a certain transgression of our br. Oliver committed in the fall of 1830 in the Township of Mayfield Cuyahoga County State of Ohio.[1]

Which after some discussion he having frankly confessed the same to the satisfaction of all present; it was resolved that these proceedings be recorded for the benefit & satisfaction of the Church of Christ.

The reason why the above case was not taken into consideration by proper authority in the Church previous this day, is that some of the Elders supposed that the affair had been adjusted last year when brother Oliver made his confession to the individuals injured & received their forgiveness.

---

[1]Oliver's "transgression" consisted of proposing marriage to a young woman in Ohio after having entered into an engagement to marry Elizabeth Ann Whitmer in New York. (See E.D. Howe, *Mormonism Unvailed* [Painesville: E.D. Howe, 1834], pages 208, 217-18. We are indebted to Richard L. Anderson for this reference.)

May 29, 1832

Minutes of a Conference held at the office of the Evening & Morning Star[1] on Tuesday 29th day of May 1832 for the purpose of dedicating to the Lord in conformity to certain Revelations given concerning the Printing Establishment

Present

Edward Partridge	William W. Phelps	Elders Present
Isaac Morley	Harvey Whitlock	Calvin Bebee
John Corrill	Jesse Gauss	Peter Dustin
Oliver Cowdery	Sidney Gilbert	Sealy J. Griffin
John Whitmer		

The conference was opened by prayer by John Whitmer. Several appropriate commandments read by br. John Whitmer, after which some explanatory remarks were made by brs. Phelps Oliver & others in relation to rules & regulations of the office & the important duties devolving upon those whom the Lord has designated to spread his truths & revelations in these last days to the inhabitants of the earth.

After which the Bishop proceeded Solemnly to dedicate the building for Printing & all materials appertaining thereto unto the Lord.

This meeting concluded in prayer by brother William W. Phelps.

Sidney Gilbert, Clerk of Meeting.

---

[1]Phelps's printing office and house were located on lot 76 in Independence, Missouri. This lot had been purchased for fifty dollars by Edward Partridge from James Gray, August 8, 1831, for Church use. It had on it a two-story brick house which Phelps used as his home and printing office. The first issue of the *Evening and Morning Star* appeared in June 1832. (See Max Parkin, "A History of the Latter-day Saints in Clay County, Missouri, from 1833 to 1837," Ph.D. dissertation, Brigham Young University, 1976. See also Doctrine and Covenants 58:37.)

July 3, 1832

Zion July 3, 1832

Minutes of a special council held at the dwelling house of Edward Partridge[1] (Bishop) conference opened in prayer by William W Phelps

High Priests	Elders
Edward Partridge	Calvin Bebee
John Corrill	Peter Dustin
Isaac Morley	Jesse Hichcock
William W Phelps	Stephen Chase
Oliver Cowdery	Thomas Willes
John Whitmer	Selah J Griffin
Newel Knight	Titus Billings
William E McLellin	Christian Whitmer
Major N Ashley	
Harvy Whitlock	

Resolved that the mode and manner of regulating the Church of Christ Take effect from this time, according to a Revelation received in Hiram Portage County Ohio Nov 11, 1831[2]

Adjourned for one hour, Prayer by Elder Calvin Bebee

Convened, Prayer by the Bishop

A letter from Br Patten from Indiana, was exhibited & discussed & advised that he come to this land & also agreed by the conference that an Epistle be written to the church scattered abroad[3]

Prayer by Isaac Morley

John Whitmer Clerk of conference

---

[1]Note that meetings were often held in the homes of members; meeting-houses were generally not built until the Saints arrived in Utah.

[2]Doctrine and Covenants 68. This statement is important because it establishes a date for section 68.

[3]This epistle was printed in the *Evening and Morning Star*, July 1832, page 13.

July 13, 1832

Minutes of a special Conference held in Zion July 13, 1832 at the house of Joseph Knights in Kaw Township for the purpose of dividing the Church on the land of Zion, into branches[1] for the better convenience of holding meetings & organizing the Church &c.

Present.	Elders	Priests
Edward Partridge	Stephen Chase	Hezekiah Peck
Isaac Morley	Selah J. Griffin	
John Corrill	Thomas Wiles	Teacher
Harvey Whitlock	Christian Whitmer,	Isaac Bebee
	Sanford Porter	
	Jonathan Sumner	

Prayer by br. Stephen Chase.

Br. John Corrill appointed Clerk.

After considerable consultation upon the subject it was voted that the branches in each Township be numbered as they are set off.

Voted that for the time being the Disciples in Kaw Township now living & that shall hereafter settle upon Sections No. 25.26.27.28.33.34.35. & 36. be considered in the branch No. first: those on Section No. 29.30.31. & 32.[2] And those on the 24 first no. Sections[3] in Second Township in branch no. 3. & also those in Blue Township be considered a branch.

Closed in prayer by br Jonathan Sumner.

John Corrill Clerk of Con.

---

[1]The conference divided the Church in Missouri into small geographical units to facilitate Church administration. Note the use of the word "branch" in place of "church."

[2]These land survey sections would consitute branch number 2.

[3]Sections 1-24.

August 24, 1832

Minutes of a Conference held in Kaw Township August 24. 1832.

Present

Edward Partridge	Peter Whitmer jr.
Isaac Morley	Harvey Whitlock
John Corrill	Major N. Ashley
Oliver Cowdery	Peter Dustin
Lyman Wight	Elders.
William E. Mc.lellin	Christian Whitmer
Newel Knight	James Emmet
Levi Jackman	Sanford Porter
	Jonathan Sumner

Harvey Whitlock proposed the following questions

1st. Can a man in the Church of Christ walk by faith without law?

2nd. Was the law given to bring men to faith?

3rd. Was the law added because of transgression?

4th. Was the law given because it was asked for?

William E. Mc.lellin Clerk of Conference.

September 15, 1832

Met in Council September 15. 1832 to choose an Elder to be a President over the Elders in Zion[1]

Opened in prayer by br Calvin Bebee. Then proceeded chose & Elected[2] br. Christian Whitmer to be our President

Peter Dustin appointed Clerk pro tem.

Resolved that the Elders meet the first Saturday of December next for the first General Conference according to the Commandments and Covenants.[3] Were present then at this meeting:

Calvin Bebee
Peter Dustin
Christian Whitmer
Jonathan Sumner
Sanford Porter
William Bolton,[4]
Thomas Laplesh
James Emmet

---

[1]This is the first record of an elders' meeting recorded in the Far West Record. Most of the minutes in the Far West Record are of high priests' meetings.

[2]Note that officers were elected.

[3]Doctrine and Covenants 20:61.

[4]Undoubtedly William Batson.

September 27, 1832

At a special conference of Elders held at the Big Blue[1] on Friday the 27th, Sept. Opened. prayer by Christian Whitmer & proceeded to organize by ordaining the President chosen at the last conference.

Present.

Christian Whitmer	David Bennet,
Selah J. Griffin	Isaac Follise
James Emmet	Henry Jackson
	Orson Johnson

Read the laws & Commandments & adjourned until the 2nd Monday in November next to meet at Porter Rockwell's at the Blue.[2] Closed prayer by James Emmet.

Orson Johnson Clerk.

---

[1]The branch in Blue township was located on the Big Blue River in Jackson County, Missouri.
[2]Porter Rockwell operated a ferry here.

October 25, 1832

Concil met according to adjournment Oct 25 1832 endeavoring to obtain wisdom, on certain points, relative, to the Welfare of the Church of Christ

Present

Edward Partridge	Levi Jackman
Isaac Morley	Peter Dustin
John Correll	William E. Mclellin
Oliver Cowdery	Wheeler Baldwin
John Whitmer	

Opened. Prayer by Levi Jackman

William E. Mc.lellin Clerk.

October 2, 1832

Minutes of a Conference held, October 2. 1832.

Present

Edward Partridge	Elders
Isaac Morley	Sanford Porter
John Corrill	Christian Whitmer
William W. Phelps	James Emmet
Oliver Cowdery	Robert Rathburn
John Whitmer	Stephen Chase
Lyman Wight	Isaac Follis
Major N. Ashley	Elisha H. Groves

William E. Mc.lellin	Daniel Cathcart
Peter Dustin	Henry Jackson
Calvin Bebee	James Johnson
	George M. Hinkel

Conference opened. ~~in prayer~~
Prayer by Brother Lyman Wight
Br. Phelps motioned that br. Ziba Peterson's case should be taken in consideration, after some conversation & examination br. John Corrill motioned that he be reordained and Elder;[1] seconded by Christian Whitmer. Voted that he should be reordained to the office of an Elder by br. Lyman Wight.

Motioned by br Oliver Cowdery that this Conference be closed, seconded by M.N. Ashley and was dissmissed in prayer by Ziba Peterson

William E. Mc.lellin Clerk.

---

[1]See page 9 and Doctrine and Covenants 58:60. After a period of probation he was reordained, that is, again given his priesthood privileges.

October 5, 1832

Council of High Priests met in Independence, October 5. 1832. for the purpose of counselling upon certain points relative to Zion.

Present

Edward Partridge	Lyman Wight
Isaac Morley	Wheeler Baldwin
John Corrill	Levi Jackman
Oliver Cowdery	Newel Knight
David Whitmer	Major N. Ashley
John Whitmer	William E. Mc.lellin,
Peter Whitmer	Harvey Whitlock
William W. Phelps	

Br. Edward Partridge President & Wm. E. Mclellin Clerk pro tem.

Opened in prayer by William W. Phelps

Moved by br. Phelps that a revelation given 11th November be read.[1]

Query, What is the duty of the High Priests.

Are the High priests in the land of Zion required to meet as Elders in the three month Conference according to the Articles & Covenants to do Church business.[2]

Is the council of Elders where the president of the Elders resides to teach them their duty the same as the three month conference mentioned in the Covenants.

Moved by br. Wm. E. Mc.lellin that certain Elders present should express their minds concerning ordination to the High Priesthood. brs. Calvin Bebee & Peter Dustin desired the office & were ordained under the hand of br. Oliver Cowdery[3]

William E. Mclellin Clerk.

---

[1]Doctrine and Covenants 68.

[2]Having read the revelations (Doctrine and Covenants 20 and 68), the high priests were trying to determine the frequency of their meetings as opposed to the elders' meetings.

[3]Note that it was not inappropriate to request ordination to a given priesthood office.

December 3, 1832

A Council of High Priests assembled at Sidney Gilbert's December 3. 1832

Present

Edward Partridge Bishop	Parley P. Pratt
John Corrill	Thomas B. Marsh
Isaac Morley	Peter Whitmer
William W. Phelps	William E. Mc.lellin

Oliver Cowdery
John Whitmer
Sidney Gilbert
Wheeler Baldwin
Newel Knight
Lyman Wight

Opened. Prayer by William W. Phelps

Resolved that the Highpriests meet alone except when the Elders, Priests Teachers or members shall have business at conference & this according to Revelation.[1]

Resolved that Brs John Corrill & Isaac Morley be appointed to go forth and set in order the different Branches of the Church of Christ in the land of Zion & see that there are High Priests or Elders set apart to see that meetings are held & the officers & members do their duties according to Revelations & Commandments[2]

Resolved that the following person Viz Edward Partridge Isaac Morley John Correll Sidney Gilbert William W Phelps Oliver Cowdery & John Whitmer be a committee to examine into the qualifications of High Priests Elders & Priests as shall be reported to them by brs Corrill Morley or stationed high Priests or Elders over the various branches of the Church of Christ in Zion, as to the propriety of their going forth a broad into the world to preach the gospel of peace. Closed. prayer by Lyman Wight

John Whitmer

---

[1]The question at the last conference was whether the high priests should meet together with the elders to receive instruction. The decision settled the matter. A letter from the Presidency of the High Priesthood to W.W. Phelps and others on July 25, 1833, noted: "We commend highly of your choosing a teacher to instruct the High Priests, that you may be able to silence gainsayers." (See *History of the Church* 1:363.)

[2]Prior to the organization of the first high council, high priests and elders were called upon to perform functions later assigned to the high council.

December 15, 1832

Zion, December 15, 1832 Convened in council Edward Partridge Isaac Morley, John Corrill, Sidney Gilbert, William W

Phelps, Oliver Cowdery, & John Whitmer to take into consideration the case of Thomas Mils[1] who was going about preaching much.

By due examination we found that he taught contrary doctrine to the revelations & prophesied things contrary to scripture. We therefore received his license & silenced him & advised him, if he would still persist in his foolish doctrine to withdraw from the Church & save us the trouble of excommunicating him from the same, which he did[2]

John Whitmer Clerk.

---

[1]Mils or Meis, almost indecipherable.

[2]Here one observes the great concern with teaching false doctrine. A person who taught false doctrine could lose his license to preach, as in this case. Note also that one could leave the Church without being officially excommunicated.

1833

February 26, 1833

Zion February 26 1833 A special council of High Priests[1] met to transact such business as by them shall seem proper

Present

Edward Partridge	Oliver Cowdery
Isaac Morley	John Whitmer
John Corrill	Sidney Gilbert
William W. Phelps	David Whitmer
Thomas B. Marsh	Peter Whitmer
Lyman Wight	Harvey Whitlock
Wheeler Baldwin	Simeon Carter
Newel Knight	Daniel Stanton
Peter Dustin	Solomon Hancock
Levi Jackman	Calvin Beebee.

First. The Bishop laid before the council the effect of the proceedings of the Solemn Assemblies[2] as held throughout Zion attended by brs Edward Partridge John Corrill Isaac Morley Oliver Cowdery & John Whitmer.

Resolved that a committee be appointed to write an epistle to our brethren in Kirtland: Voted that Oliver Cowdery William W. Phelps & John Corrill be the Committee to write the epistle.

Conference adjourned until six O'clock in the evening, in the meantime the epistle to be written. Prayer by Simeon Carter.

Convened according to adjournment, the epistle accepted by the conference. We then all kneeled before the Lord & asked him to effect a perfect harmony between us & our brethren in Kirtland which was the desire of our hearts.

Conference adjourned until four weeks from to-morrow

Prayer by br. Solomon Hancock.

John Whitmer Clerk.

---

[1]See *History of the Church* 1:327: "A special council of High Priests assembled in Zion, to take into consideration my letter to Brother Phelps, of the 11th of January, and the revelation called the Olive Leaf, referred to in my letter, and the epistle of Orson Hyde and Hyrum Smith of the 14th of January, in behalf of the conference of High Priests: and Oliver Cowdery, William W. Phelps, and John Corrill were appointed a committee to write an epistle from the conference to the brethren in Kirtland; which was written and sanctioned by the conference."

[2]Direction to hold a solemn assembly was first given in the Olive Leaf. (See Doctrine and Covenants 88:70.)

Concerning these solemn assemblies held in Zion, David Pettigrew said: "Soon after this [Dec. 1832], Bishop Partridge appointed a Solemn Assembly in all the branches, which was to be held as a day of confession and repentance. He went from branch to branch exhorting, until he had gone through them all, and in a few months we were informed that we had repented and the angels were rejoicing over us, but there yet remained a "Scourge and a judgment to be poured out upon the children of Zion." (See David Pettigrew Journal, Special Collections, Harold B. Lee Library, Brigham Young University, page 15.)

March 26, 1833

Independence, March 26. 1833.[1] A Council of Highpriests met according to adjournment 21[2] in number resident in Zion at this time.

Opened in Prayer by Br. Thomas B. Marsh.

The order that was taught at the solemn assemblies was accepted after much discussion.[3]

Resolved that the Churches meet according to the appointments of the several highpriests stationed over their respective branches.

Closed in prayer by A.S. Gilbert.

John Whitmer Clerk.

[1]See *History of the Church* 1:335.

[2]These high priests are those men listed on page 60. This council of high priests constituted the governing body of the Church there.

[3]The order was this: "That the seven High Priests who were sent from Kirtland to build up Zion, viz.—Oliver Cowdery, W.W. Phelps, John Whitmer, Algernon Sidney Gilbert, Bishop Partridge, and his two counselors [John Corrill and Isaac Morley]—should stand at the affairs relating to the Church, in that section of the Lord's vineyard; and these seven men, with the common consent of the branches comprising the Church were to appoint presiding Elders, to take the watchcare of the several branches....After a long discussion, it was decided from the revelations, that the order taught in the solemn assembly was correct; and that the Elders, when they arrived in Zion, were bound by the authorities set in the Church, to be submissive to the powers that be." (See *History of the Church* 1:336.)

August 21, 1833

Zion, August 21. 1833.[1]
Met in Council.

Present

Edward Partridge	William W. Phelps
Isaac Morley	John Whitmer
John Corrill	David Whitmer
Peter Whitmer	Thomas B. Marsh
Parley P Pratt	Alpheus Gifford
Lyman Wight	Algernon S. Gilbert
Harvy Whitlock	Calvin Bebee
Simeon Carter	Peter Dustin
Wheeler Baldwin	Daniel Stanton
Levi Jackman	Newel Knight
William E. Mc.lellin	

First: Br. Harvey Whitlock laid before the council the case of Br. Christian Whitmer the President of the Elders who desired the office of the Highpriesthood, he also stated it himself by request of & others. Simeon Carter also said he had a testimony of the Lord that it was his will &c.

Ordained under the hand of Simeon Carter & sit in council with us.

Much consultation concerning the gift of tongues &c.[2] And a rebuke of the Lord for reasoning in our own wisdom, & c.

Conference adjourned until Wednesday next at 9. O'clock A.M.

Prayer by the Bishop.

John Whitmer, Clerk.

---

[1]See *History of the Church* 1:407. Note that Oliver Cowdery did not meet with the council. He had been sent to Kirtland to discuss the Jackson County difficulties.

[2]Many of the Saints in Missouri were experiencing a great manifestation of the gift of tongues at this time. John Whitmer in a letter to Oliver Cowdery said: "The gifts are breaking forth in a marvelous manner. . . . God is pouring out his Spirit upon his people." W. W. Phelps added: "Everyone that is a Saint or nearly so . . . speaks in tongues. Br. David says he can speak in all the tongues on earth, we shall probably begin to worship here in tongues tomorrow." (See John Whitmer to Oliver Cowdery and Joseph Smith July 29, 1833, Joseph Smith Collection, Church Archives.)

In the early days of the Restoration, the gift of tongues was restored and became manifest in a number of ways. Many of the early Church leaders spoke in tongues and were anxious to make others aware of the use of the gift. Brigham Young, for example, in his history, wrote: "I spoke in tongues. He called upon me to pray; in my prayer I spoke in tongues." (*History of the Church* 1:297.)

Not only the leaders, but also the Church members experienced the gift of tongues. Describing a baptismal service, Margrette Young wrote: "Elder Babbit then stepped upon a large stone that was near and spoke in tongues . . . .when he had ceased speaking he then gave them the meaning thereof, which was so beautiful, and so filled with the Spirit of God, that every eye was wet with tears" (Autobiography of Margrette W. Pierce Whitesides Young, Church Archives.)

As the use of the gift of tongues became more frequent and some problems and excesses were observed, the leaders of the Church began to issue warnings and cautionary statements. The Prophet Joseph Smith frequently warned the Saints concerning the gift of tongues. Writing to the brethren in Zion in 1833, he said: "We wish you, however, to be careful, lest in this you be deceived . . . . Satan will no doubt trouble you about the gift of tongues, unless you are careful." Later, he noted: "Do not indulge too much in the exercise of the gift of tongues, or the devil will take advantage of the innocent and unwary." (Joseph Fielding Smith, comp., *Teachings of the Prophet Joseph Smith* [Salt Lake City: Deseret Book Co., 1938], pages 25 and 229.)

Church leaders from Joseph Smith on were concerned about possible misuse of the gift of tongues. They were wary of Satan's power and desire to counterfeit the works of God. For these reasons they chose to caution the Saints in the exercise of that gift.

August 28, 1833

Zion, August 28. 1833.[1]
Convened according to adjournment. Present.

Edward Partridge	Newel Knight
John Corrill	Calvin Bebee
David Whitmer	William E. Mclellin
Peter Whitmer	Alpheus Gifford
John Whitmer	Peter Dustin
Christian Whitmer	Thomas B. Marsh
William W. Phelps	Simeon Carter
Harvey Whitlock	Sidney Gilbert
Lyman Wight	Levi Jackman
Parley P. Pratt	Roberts

Bishop Moderator. Opened in prayer by the same.

Resolved that no High priest Elder or Priest shall ordain any priest Elder or High priest in the land of Zion without the consent of a Conference of Highpriests.[2]

Adjourned until the 11 of Sept, next, at br Lyman's house. Prayer by the Bishop.

John Whitmer Clerk

---

[1]See *History of the Church* 1:407.

[2]No high priest was to be ordained without the consent of the council of high priests. Here a procedure for approving names was beginning to develop. This approval is now a function of the stake high council.

September 11, 1833

Zion September 11. 1833.[1]
Met in Council according to adjournment

Present.

Edward Partridge	Harvey Whitlock
Isaac Morley	Levi Jackman
John Corrill	Daniel Stanton
William W. Phelps	Parley P. Pratt
David Whitmer	Newel Knight
John Whitmer	Wheeler Baldwin
Christian Whitmer	Solomon Hancock
Sidney Gilbert	Simeon Carter
Calvin Bebee	Thomas B. Marsh
William E. Mc.lellin	Lyman Wight
Alpheus Gifford	Peter Dustin

The Bishop Edward Partridge was acknowledged to be at the head of the Church of Zion at present consequently will be our Moderator in councils or conferences by virtue of his office[2]

Proceeded to business as follows

First Appointed High Priests to wach over the several ~~Churches~~ Branches as follows[3]

	Branches	
Newel Knight	No.	1
Daniel Stanton	"	2
David Whitmer	"	3
John Corrill	"	4
Thomas B Marsh	"	5
Peter Dustin	"	6
Lyman Wight	"	7
Parley P Pratt	"	8
Simeon Carter	"	9
Calvin Bebee	"	10

Adjourned half an hour for noon

Commenced again according to adjournment

A Hymn sung by Br W W Phelps in tongues and interpreted by Lyman[4] Ideas &c. concerning the travelling of the Nephites their toils troubles & tribulations &c.

Prayer by the Bishop

Some points of the law discussed & also concerning tything &c

Adjourned untill two weeks from to day or September 25, 1833

Prayer by the Bishop

John Whitmer Clerk

---

[1]See *History of the Church* 1:409.

[2]Edward Partridge was the first man to be appointed as the presiding officer of the Church in Missouri.

[3]This action was pursuant to a decision made on March 26, 1833. (See page 61.) This appointment to watch over the branches is similar to the assignment of high councilors to wards and branches today.

[4]Hymns were occasionally sung in tongues in the early Church.

September 26, 1833

September 26, 1833[1]

Met according to adjournment

Opened in prayer by Edward Partridge the Bishop

Proceeded to business Agreed that Jesse Hitchcock Elias & Isaac Higbee be ordained to the High Priesthood[2] Adjourned ¾ of an hour

Sung a hymn

Opened in prayer by Edward Partridge (the Bishop) for the evening Proceeded to business

Br. Tanner desired to be ordained. But the Conference declined at present to give him their voices.

Br. Hinkle presented the situation of the Salt River Church[3] desiring to know whether they had better move to this place this fall or not no definite answer given by this Conference at present.

This day four weeks the Conference meets again.

Prayer by Levi Jackman

Calvin Bebee Clerk of Conference.
John Whitmer Recorder.

---

[1]*History of the Church* 1:409-10.

[2]The *History of the Church* indicates that these three brethren were ordained high priests on September 26, 1833. They were not ordained, however, until August 7, 1834. (See page 95.)

[3]The Salt River Branch, also called the Allred Settlement, was located in Monroe County, Missouri. Edward Partridge notes that there were forty members of this branch in February, 1835. (See Edward Partridge Journal, Church Archives.)

1834

June 23, 1834

Clay County June 23, 1834[1]

A Council of High Priests met according to revelation[2] in order to choose some of the first Elders to receive their endowments[3] being appointed by the voice of the Spirit through Br. Joseph Smith, jr. President of the Church of Christ.

Proceeded First:

Edward Partridge—Is called & chosen and is to go to Kirtland to receive his endowment with power from on high—And also stand in his office as Bishop to purchase lands in the land of Missouri.

William W. Phelps—Is called and chosen and it is appointed unto him to receive his endowment with power from on high & help carry on the printing establishment in Kirtland till Zion is redeemed.

Isaac Morley is called & chosen and is appointed unto him to receive his endowment with power from on high in Kirtland and assist in gathering up the strength of the Lord's house and preach the Gospel.

John Corrill The same as Isaac Morley

John Whitmer Is called and chosen And it is appointed unto him to receive his endowment ~~with power~~ in Kirtland with power from on high—And to continue in his office

David Whitmer Is called and chosen and it is appointed unto him to receive an endowment from on high in Kirtland—And to stand in the office that is appointed unto him.

A.S. Gilbert—Is called and chosen and it is appointed unto

him to receive his endowment from on high in Kirtland—And to assist in gathering up the strength of the Lord's house and to proclaim the everlasting gospel until Zion is redeemed—But he said he could not do it—And truly he departed his life a few days after this was given[4]—And we are left to lament his loss.

Peter Whitmer, jr. is called and chosen and it is appointed unto him to receive his endowment, in Kirtland with power from on high and assist in gathering up the strength of the Lord's house and proclaim the Gospel.

Simeon Carter is called and chosen and it is appointed unto him to receive his endowment in Kirtland with power from on high, and to assist in gathering up the strength of the Lord's house, and proclaim the everlasting Gospel.

Newel Knight is called and chosen and it is appointed unto him to receive his endowment in Kirtland with power from on high and to assist in gathering up the strength of the Lord's house, and to preach the Gospel.

Thomas B. Marsh is called and chosen and it is appointed unto him to receive his endowment in Kirtland with power from on high, and his office made known hereafter.

Lyman Wight is called and chosen, and it is appointed unto him to receive his endowment in Kirtland with power from on high—And return to Zion and have his office appointed unto him hereafter.

Parley P. Pratt is called and chosen and it is appointed unto him to receive his endowment in Kirtland with power from on high and assist in gathering up the strength of the Lord's house and proclaim the gospel.

Christian Whitmer is called and chosen and it is appointed unto him to receive his endowment in Kirtland with power from on high and to assist in gathering up the strength of the Lord's house, and preach the gospel.

Solomon Hancock is called and chosen and it is appointed unto him to receive his endowment in Kirtland with power from on high and proclaim the everlasting Gospel and assist in gathering up the strength of the Lords house.

F.G. Williams Clerk.

[1]See *History of the Church* 2:112-13. Note that there are no minutes in the Far West Record for the period September 1833 to June 1834. In the interim the Saints had been expelled from Jackson County and were relocating, primarily in Clay County. The year "1834" was entered by Andrew Jenson.

[2]Doctrine and Covenants 105. This revelation was received the previous day, June 22, 1834. The meeting apparently convened in George Burkett's field. See *History of the Church* 2:112.

[3]Only a chosen few of the Missouri Saints were given the privilege of receiving this endowment. At this meeting Joseph Smith appointed fifteen high priests to travel to Kirtland to receive this blessing. Others were subsequently appointed to receive the endowment (see *History of the Church* 2:144). The "endowment of power from on high" to be received in Kirtland was to consist of a significant outpouring of spiritual power upon the participants at a solemn assembly (held March 30, 1836). Preparations for the Kirtland endowment included confession of sins, washings, anointings, covenant-making, and sealings. (See *History of the Church* 2:373-428 and "A Record of the First Quorum of Elders Belonging to the Church of Christ in Kirtland, Geauga Co., Ohio," pp. 2-19, RLDS Library-Archives, Independence, Missouri.)

[4]Gilbert died June 29, 1834. (See *History of the Church* 2:118.)

July 3, 1834

Clay County, July 3. 1834.[1]

The High Priests of Zion assembled for the purpose of organizing a general Council [2] of High Priests, agreeable to the revelation[3] for the purpose of settling important business that might come before them which could not be settled by the Bishop and his council.

Proceeded to make choice of the President. It was agreed that David Whitmer should be the first President and to be assisted by William W. Phelps and John Whitmer.[4]— and the following High Priests as Councillors:

Christian Whitmer	Thomas B. Marsh.
Newel Knight	Simeon Carter.
Lyman Wight	Parley P. Pratt.
Calvin Bebee	Orson Pratt.
William E. Mc.lellin	John Murdock.
Solomon Hancock.	Levi Jackman.

After which the meeting adjourned to meet on monday, the ~~8th~~ inst.[5]

Frederick G. Williams (Clerk

---

[1]See *History of the Church* 2:122. This meeting convened in the yard of Col. Michael Arthur. Arthur, who employed Lyman Wight and others, was sympathetic to the Church.

[2]The high council, as it was organized in 1834, both in Kirtland and Missouri, consisted of three presidents and twelve councilors, all high priests. The fifteen high priests constituted the high council, not merely the twelve councilors. This arrangement began to change almost immediately, however, and soon only twelve councilors were recognized as the high council. Unlike today, neither the three presidents nor the twelve councilors were to meet alone to transact business for the Church.

[3]Doctrine and Covenants 102.

[4]At this meeting nominations were made for a presidency and twelve councilors, but no ordinations took place until July 7, 1834.

[5]Andrew Jenson changed the date to read "7th inst."

July 7, 1834

Clay County July 7th 1834.[1]

Agreeable to adjournment the council of High Priests assembled at the house of Lyman Wights—and opened the meeting by singing—age after age has rowled away, &c. and prayer by Joseph Smith, Jun. Present fifteen High Priests, eight Elders, four Priests, eight Teachers, three Deacons,—together with a number of Members

After which br. Joseph Smith, Jun. proceeded to give the council such instruction (relative to their high calling) as would enable them to proceed and minister in their office—agreeable to the pattern given heretofore—also read to them the Revelation speaking on the subject—[2]He also informed them if he should now be taken[3] away that he had accomplished the great work which the Lord had laid before him,[4] and that which he had desired of the Lord, and that he now had done his duty in organizing the High Council, through which Council the will of the Lord might be known on all important occasions in the building up of Zion, and establishing truth in the earth.

A vote was then taken whether the brethren that were appointed on the 3rd of July should stand according to appointment. The vote was clear in their behalf.

Br. Joseph Smith, jr. then proceeded and ordained the three Presidents, David Whitmer as President and William W. Phelps & John Whitmer assistants and their twelve Counsillors.[5]

The twelve Counsillors then proceeded to cast lots to know who should speak first,[6] and the order in which they should speak which is as follows:

Simeon Carter	No. 1.	Parley P. Pratt	" 2.
William E. Mc.lellin	" 3.	Calvin Bebee	" 4.
Levi Jackman	" 5.	Solomon Hancock	" 6.
Christian Whitmer	" 7.	Newel Knight	" 8.
Orson Pratt	" 9.	Lyman Wight	" 10.
Thomas B. Marsh	" 11.	John Murdock	" 12.

After which Father Whitmer came forward and blessed three of his sons in the name of the Lord Viz: David, John & Christian Whitmer, & also Father Knight blessed his son Newel Knight in the name of the Lord.

After the council of High Priests were organized the Bishop, Edward Partridge came forward and stated to the Council that a greater responsibility devolved upon him that before as he had not the privilege of counselling with any of the high council save one of the Presidents and his own Counsillors, and desired to have the prayers of all the Church that he might be able to act in his station in righteousness.[7]

After which br. Joseph Smith, jr. laid the case of William W. Phelps before the Council to have their decision whether he should take his family to Kirtland and when it shall be wisdom for him to go. As it has been deemed necessary for him to go and assist in the printing establishment.[8]

Nominated Voted and Carried that four of the Counsillors

shall speak on the subject, two on each side, Viz: Simeon Carter & William E. Mc.lellin on the side of the plaintiff, and Parley P. Pratt & Calvin Bebee in behalf of the Church. After they had said on this subject all they had to say, the President decided that it is the duty of Br. W.W. Phelps to go to Kirtland to assist in the printing business and that his family remain in this region of country and that he have an honorable discharge of his station in this place for a season (as soon as he can accomplish his business in this place) signed by the President & Clerk.

Proposed by br. W.W. Phelps that br. David Whitmer the President of the Church in Zion should go to Kirtland as being one of the three witnesses and assist in promoting the cause of Christ.

The case was argued by br. Levi Jackman & Christian Whitmer in behalf of the plaintiff, and Solomon Hancock & Newel Knight for the church. And after their pleadings it was descided that br. David Whitmer go to the East[9] and assist in the great work of the gathering and be his own Judge, as to leaving his family or taking them with him. And also that John Whitmer[10] and William E. Mc.lellin go to the East. All the above named brethren to prepare and go as soon as convenient.

After all this was done the afore mentioned High Priests, Elders, Priests, Teachers, Deacons & members convenanted with uplifted hands to heaven that they would uphold Brother David Whitmer as President, head and leader in Zion (in the absence of br. Joseph Smith jr.)[11] & John Whitmer & W.W. Phelps as assistant Presidents and Counsillors also convenanted to uphold him and one another at the throne of grace.[12]

Council closed.[13] Prayer by David Whitmer President.

Frederick G. Williams Clerk

---

[1]*History of the Church* 1:124-26. Zion's Camp was disbanded on this day.

[2]Doctrine and Covenants 102.

[3]Doctrine and Covenants 43:3-4.

[4]That is, the appointment of a successor and a governing body in the Church.

[5]This action by Joseph Smith established a second high council for the Church. An earlier appointment created the Kirtland high council in February 1834. Both bodies functioned simultaneously.

[6]Note that the high councilors cast lots to determine the order of speaking as is done in Church court cases today. This procedure was used here for administrative as well as judicial cases.

[7]With the reorganization of the Church in Missouri, Partridge was no longer the presiding officer of the Church there. Whereas before he met with all the high priests in Missouri to direct the affairs of the Church, now his responsibilities were changed.

[8]See *History of the Church* 1:417.

[9]David Whitmer left Missouri the first of September 1834, and arrived in Kirtland before October 16. While in Ohio, Whitmer helped choose the Twelve Apostles, helped administer the affairs of the Church, and participated in the Kirtland Temple dedication. During the winter of 1836-37, Whitmer united with others in opposing Joseph Smith's presidency, but apparently made restitution before returning to Missouri in the summer of 1837.

[10]John Whitmer, who arrived in Kirtland on May 17, 1835, edited the *Messenger and Advocate* from June 1835 to March 1836. (See the Book of John Whitmer, chapter 14.)

[11]That David Whitmer was ordained Joseph Smith's successor at this conference is substantiated by several documents, including a statement by the Prophet himself. (See page 151.) Exactly what this means in relation to other possible successors is unclear. That even Whitmer himself failed to understand his position is evident in subsequent statements made by him at his excommunication trial. (For a treatise on this problem see D. Michael Quinn, "The Mormon Succession Crisis of 1844," *Brigham Young University Studies* 16 [Winter, 1976]: 187-233.)

[12]As these minutes were included in the *History of the Church,* changes were made concerning the presidency of David Whitmer vis-a-vis the presidency of Joseph Smith. (See *History of the Church* 2:126.) Editors have taken liberty to more clearly define the function of the two presidencies.

[13]*History of the Church* notes that an appeal was written and sanctioned by the high council. This was according to Doctrine and Covenants 105:38-39. The appeal is found in *History of the Church* 2:126, and was signed by members of the presidency, bishopric, and high council in Zion. It was first published in the *Evening and Morning Star* 2 (August 1834): 183-84.

July 12, 1834

Clay County July 12, 1834.[1]

Council convened according to appointment. Opened in prayer by br. David Whitmer.

Voted & carried that Peter Dustin fill William E. Mc.lellin's place pro tem.[2]

Remarks by the President respecting the responsibility of the Counsillors in their high and holy callings, &c.

Constitution read by John Whitmer and also the minutes of the proceedings of our last Council.[3]

The President then arose and addressed the Counsillors—saying that it was necessary to take into consideration the situation of the scattered Saints of Zion—stating that it was necessary to do something and this is wisdom and appoint some one or ones to labor with the scattered disciples in this region.

First: Shall we appoint two four or six to visit our scattered and afflicted brethren in this region, ~~of country~~ and lay before them their duty &c. or shall we appoint more or how many shall we appoint. And also shall Lyman Wight fill his mission appointed him by the seer,[4] and shall he have any assistance in his temporal business to ascertain the strength of the Lord's house, &c.

Resolved that six speak upon this case. Viz:

Orson Pratt—	Lyman Wight
Thomas B. Marsh—	John Murdock.
Simeon Carter—	Parley P. Pratt.

After these six had spoken on the case, it was deemed necessary that four should be appointed to go and visit the scattered brethren and teach them in the ways of truth and holiness, &c. And also that one be appointed to go with Lyman Wight and assist him in his business.

Recommended that Edward Partridge Orson Pratt Isaac Morley & Zebedee Coultrin be appointed for to see to these things, and that Amasa Lyman assist Lyman Wight in his mission.[5]

Voted and carried that the above named six attend to their several missions as above mentioned

After which the cases of Zebedee Coultrin David W. Patten Warren Parrish George M. Hinkle & Samuel Brown, who desired to promulgate the everlasting Gospel.

Voted that two speak upon the above cases, Viz: Peter Dustin & Calvin Bebee.

Descided by the president that none of the above named brethren go to preach at present except George M. Hinkle, and this because of his over much wearying the Lord[6] and if he can get a faithful br. to go with him he will be blessed if he is faithful. And also Zebedee Coultrin is at liberty to go to the east after he has attended to his mission in company with Isaac Morley

The above decision sanctioned by the counsillors.

W.W. Phelps proposes to the councilors to take into consideration the propriety of holding meetings among our brethren breaking bread &c. while we are in captivity[7] desiring that they would consider these things

Voted that four speak on this occasion Viz Levi Jackman, Solonon Hancock, Christian Whitmer & Newel Knight. After these four had discussed the matter the President Decided that it was not our privilege at present to hold publick meetings,[8] but the four, viz E Partridg, O Pratt I Morley & Z Coultrin should go and set the disciples in order according as the Lord shall direct and he will bless their labours. This decision sanctioned by the councillors.

After which Parley P. Pratt gave a few leading principles respecting the conducting these Councils, by saying that it was necessary that all these things be conducted with the strictest order and attention by all as well the standers by as the Council &c.

Closed in prayer by David Whitmer President

John Whitmer Clerk.

---

[1]*History of the Church* 2:136. Joseph and his party left Missouri for Ohio on July 9, 1834.

[2]A precedent for providing subsitutes for high councilors who were absent was established here.

[3]The constitution, Doctrine and Covenants 102, was read. Also the precedent of reading the minutes of the previous meeting was established.

[4]Doctrine and Covenants 103:30, 34.

[5]See *History of the Church* 2:136. On Wight's call, Amasa Lyman noted: "In council held on the 12th [of July] I received a mission to go with brother Lyman

Wight to visit the brethren who were driven out from their inheritances and learn the strength of the Lords house in this land on monday the 14th [of July 1834 until]... the 3d of August attended to the business of my mission agreeable to appointment in numbering the saints." (Amasa Lyman Journal, Church Archives.) To learn the strength of the Lord's house must have meant to number the Saints in Missouri.

Orson Pratt records: "Bishop Partridge and myself having been appointed by the High Council to visit the scattered saints throughout Clay Co., and set the churches in order, commenced our mission. We held eight meetings in different parts of the country." (*The Orson Pratt Journals*, Elden J. Watson, comp. [Salt Lake City: Elden J. Watson, 1975], pages 42-43.)

[6]Apparently even the Lord's patience could be tried by some of the early Saints.

[7]In other words, exiled from Zion (Jackson County, Missouri).

[8]See *History of the Church* 2:136.

July 31, 1834

July 31. 1834.[1]

Council met according to appointment.

Opened in prayer by David Whitmer President.

Resolved that Peter Dustin be appointed in William E. Mc.lellin's place Pro Tem. and that

Zebedee Coultrin fill Thomas B. Marsh's place pro. tem.

Amasa Lyman " John Murdock's place "

Constitution read by John Whitmer;

After which the report of Edward Partridge & Orson Pratt was read and laid on the table.[2] And also Zebedee Coultrin's and Isaac Morleys which were appointed them in the Council previous to this and were received.

After which the President arose and addressed the Counsillors, saying that ~~I hope~~ it is the duty of us to transact all business in order. Saying that I hope when there shall be any case brought forward all should be patient and attention to what is passing for I know that it is your duty to do so in all cases, and avoid confusion & contention, which is offensive in the sight of the Lord.[3] And also addressed himself to the Elders: saying that it is not pleasing unto the Lord for any man to go forth to preach the gospel of peace unless he is qualified to set forth its principles in plainness to the understanding of those whom he endeavors to instruct: and also the rules and regulations of the Church of Latter Day Saints[4]—For just as a man is and as he teaches and acts so will his followers be let them be ever so full of notions & whims.

And also spake to the congregation as well as to councillors, that it was not the will of the Lord that our brethren should vote at this approaching Election.[5] Br. W.W. Phelps spake on the same subject & John Whitmer also, who acquiesced with David Whitmer. The counsillors then sanctioned the above remarks.

After which the minutes of our last council read by J. Whitmer.

After which a case was proposed by W.W. Phelps, as follows, desiring the Counsillors to take into consideration the propriety of appointing a certain number of brethren to be stationed to preach to the brethren in this section of country from time to time as often as shall be deemed necessary as proposed by Edward Partridge & Orson Pratt. These meetings to be held in public.[6]

Nominated, Voted & Carried, that two speak on this subject, viz: Orson Pratt & Lyman Wight.

After which the President arose and said, That I feel brethren, that according to the spirit which is in me to say that I deem it necessary that there are four appointed to the above named mission to teach the Disciples how to escape the indignation of our enemies and to keep in favor with those who feel well disposed towards us. And live as disciples in all lowliness of heart &c. These four to hold meetings in public and teach as they shall be directed by the Holy Spirit.[7] And nominated for these four Simeon Carter, John Corrill, Parley P. Pratt & Orson Pratt, to fill the above named mission.[8]

This decision carried by a unanimous voice of counsillors and whole congregation present which was large.

Adjourned for one hour.

Convened[9]

Opened in prayer by D. Whitmer President.

After which charge made by Nathan West read by John Whitmer, as follows

To the high Council of the Church of Christ organized by the will of God on the 7th of July, 1834.

Know ye that, where as, Br. Brown[10] an high priest of this Church of Christ did on the last week come into this Branch[11] and taught certain of the brethren & sisters things much the reverse of what we had by encouraging them in practising gifts. And where as said Brown did in an underhanded, (and as we conceive) clandestine manner ordain Sylvester Hulett to the office of high priest; insisting that he had obtained a witness from the Lord for the same, which witness he said was the promise of performing the ordination on receiving the gift of tongues: which gift he said he had never received before but afterwards said that he had been in possession of the same gift for the space of a year.

And whereas, said Brown seemed to undervalue the authority or at least the righteousness of the high Council by charging me not to say any thing that would tend to prejudice their minds that they might not judge righteously.

I therefore, as an Elder of the Church of Christ do earnestly solicit the attention of the council in considering the same

Yours in bonds of Love

July 30, 1834 Nathan West

After the foregoing charge was read the President D. Whitmer asked Brown whether he acknowledged these charges or not; answered that he acknowledged some of them, but not all.

After which the counsillors considered that it was a difficult case, and motioned seconded & carried that four speak on this case, Viz:

Zebedee Coultrin & Amasa Lyman
Simeon Carter " Parley P. Pratt

After which br. Zebedee called for testimony in behalf of the Church.

First. Leonard Rich Testifies that one day last week br. Nathan West came to David Whitmer's and requested me and David to go to the Colesville branch to see br. Cole.[12] While on the way thither Nathan remarked that it was his impression that there was something taught in that branch[13] by Brown contrary to what he[14] and Hiram Page had taught them in the Hulet branch being sent by David Whitmer. In a few days after which we learned that it was the case. After which David requested me to go and learn of S. Brown whether he had done as we were informed. I[15] soon found him and asked him to walk out for I desired to converse with him. I then asked Br. Brown if he had visited the brethren in the regions round about, he said he had. I asked him how he generally found them? He replied that he did not find them in a high sanctified state, not enjoying as much of the spirit as they might; but found the brethren in this branch, (viz: The Hulett branch.) enjoying more of the Spirit than elsewhere. I then asked him if he had been with them on yesterday in improving the gifts (that is in speaking with tongues and interpreting) to this Brown replies that he was not willing to say any thing behind his brethren's backs. I then mentioned to him that the Elders had been requested to visit that branch & teach them not to use their gifts, (that is, to speak in tongues, the gift of seeing & interpretations &c.) but lay them aside at present[16] (that is in our state of captivity &c.)[17] I want to know whether they had been improving on their gifts since they have been visited by these Elders, Viz: Hiram Page & Nathan West, he stated that he believed that they were willing to receive their teachings and abide by them. I asked him again whether they had been speaking in tongues. He then said that he heard Sister Crandle[18] speak a few words in tongues. I then asked him whether he requested her to speak he said that another brother that was with him asked her: and he then said that he would like to hear her speak himself. I then asked him whether they did not get together the day before to improve upon the gifts. He did not appear to be willing to answer the question. I then asked him if he did not speak in the gift of tongues, he said he did, I asked whether Sylvester Hulet did not speak and Sister Crandle interpret. He was not willing to answer the question, he said he did not like to talk behind their backs. I asked him if he had not encouraged them in using the gifts, he then said, that there must be some misunderstanding concerning the Council by those who had taught them respecting the gifts. he stated that he did not suppose that they were to lay aside the gift entirely but use them when it would be wisdom. I then said that Silvester Hulet was an Elder and that he had agreed with Nathan West & Hiram Page to abide the decision of the Council. I told him then that we wanted to know whether Silvester Hulet had spoken in tongues since the Elders had visited the branch or not. He then stated that he should not answer the question he said he would go with me to see Silvester Hulet. I told him that I felt that it was his duty to answer the question without going to Silvester, ~~I told him~~ said that I thought that it would be saving much time and trouble if he would answer the question as Silvester might evade the question, as he had done and leave room for the workings of Satan among them. I then said to him that I believed that it was necessary for him and that God required of him to answer that question yea, or nay. After this he made a few remarks and said he would answer the question. He was then sitting in father Brace's[19] Camp, and Silvester came there a spake a few words in tongues, and Sister Crandal interpreted what he spoke. I asked if she spake and he interpreted, he said he did. I then asked him if he encouraged them in using the gift he said he did not.

Charles English called on testifies that br. Brown met br. Hulet at my fence and says to Nathan West that I am as busy to-day as you was yesterday: Nathan said that he was glad if he was doing good. He said yes and I suppose you thought you was. He charged Nathan not to say any thing to the Council lest their minds should be prejudiced. Nathan says to Brown, if the Lord has given us a Council that will be swayed by this ones say so or that ones say so, we may as well have none.

Br. Brace, testifies that my wife says that Brown says that he had an impression of the Spirit to ordain Silvester to the high priesthood. Then proceeded and ordained him in the presence of my family. he told Silvester that it was not necessary to say any thing about his ordination at present. Brown said that he[20] had better tell the Bishop, Partridge or David the President concerning the matter or he himself would, as there was some considerable excitement at present.[21]

Edward Partridge testifies that some few days after the arrival of Samuel Brown he came to my house in the morning and in the course of conversation he stated some things about the Methodists that gave me to understand that Brown was much tinctured with sectarianism.[22] The conversation above alluded to is not distinctly remembered.

Next Tuesday after br. Brown ordained br. Silvester, Brown met me at or near br. Tub's[23] camp not far from br. Englishe's. He began to talk with me concerning br. Lymans Wight's preaching a few days before Brown's observations to me respecting it was calculated to prejudice my mind against br. Lyman—He then stated that he had obtained the gift of tongues—in coming up there the Sunday before. he states that he visited Sister Crandle, that a brother that was with him asked her to speak in tongues she rather refused at first but Brown said to her he would like to hear her speak, she did speak some and told him he could speak, he spoke and she interpreted it. In the course of this conversation he told me that they had been having a fuss or difficulty that morning over at br. Englishes in consequence of his visiting Sister Crandle and others and getting them to speak in tongues contrary from what they had been taught, he said he thought the difficulty settled or nearly so. I soon saw br Rich[24] Br. Orson[25] & Br. West. Br. Rich & Br. West told me considerable about the difficulty insomuch that I thought that it might be well for Br. Brown to state to the brethren & sisters before sacrament what had transpired between him and the brethren and shew that he was satisfied that they had been taught correct and that he had ignorantly done or said some things that were not wisdom. I saw Br. Brown again before meeting, and stated to him my views and got the impression from what he said that he would state in substance what I wanted. In the meeting at the proper time he arose and observed that he had visited a number of the brethren and Sisters about there—that he found them endeavoring to be faithful that they were willing to hear to the teachings of their brethren. He then went on and justified himself for all he had done since he joined the Camp of Israel.[26] I was much surprised when he sat down for I was very much disappointed for I considered that he had better said nothing,—however I let it pass & dismissed the meeting. In all that passed up to this time I heard not a lisp of the ordination of Sylvester Hulet—just before night I went up to David Whitmers. I found Brown there after a little Br. Rich whispered in my ear & said that Br. Brown had ordained Br. Sylvester Hulet a Highpriest. I was greatly surprised—a few minutes after, Br. D. Whitmer asked Brown about the ordination which introduced the subject. Br. David, Br. Rich, Br. Orson Pratt and myself then asked many questions & got in answer that he had ordained Sylvester. That Br. Cole had recommended Sylvester to him as a man of great faith and thought that he might do much good were he a Highpriest. In going from Br. Coles to Br Englishes he obtained a witness that Sylvester ought to be ordained. He to be sure about it asked the Lord to give him the gift of tongues and should be a sign unto him, and he would ordain him,—he obtained the gift of tongus on the way up—he had not yet seen Br. Sylvester—he was ignorant of any rules here different from those in the world.

I told him that Sylvester had applied to a Council of Highpriests not a great while since to be ordained but was rejected,—and that one of three things must be true,—either the Spirit the Council had or the Spirit Brown had was not of God—or Br. Sylvester stood different in the eyes of the Lord now from what he did at the time the Council rejected him.—

Br. Brown thought probably he was different in the eyes of the Lord.

Considerable was said by most of us. I blamed Br. Brown for what he had done and told him such conduct would have been investigated. He said that if he had known beforehand what he then knew he should not have ordained Sylvester. I have no more to add only to state that the above is but a small part of the conversation I had with Br. Brown—and possibly some things are not stated as they ought to be,—but according to my best recollection I have given the same as I understood it.

Edward Partridge.

Hiram Page testifies that—In obedience to the order of David Whitmer was endeavoring to search out a prophecy which was given in the Hulet Branch; and while I was conversing with Br Nathan West about it—when Br. Brown spoke and said,—that we had better let those brethren alone, if we did not—there would a matter arise out of it that would be serious—that we would be sorry for here after.

Hiram Page

Adjourned until 10 O'clock next morning
Prayer by David Whitmer Moderator
John Whitmer Clerk

---

[1]See *History of the Church* 2:136 and Amasa Lyman Journal, Church Archives.

[2]See *The Orson Pratt Journals,* Elden J. Watson, comp. (Salt Lake City: Elden J. Watson, 1975), page 43.

[3]Note again the concern to proceed in an orderly manner and to avoid strife.

[4]Note the name change, "Church of Latter Day Saints," according to a decision made in Kirtland on May 3, 1834. (See *History of the Church* 2:63.) This decision was first published in the *Evening and Morning Star* 2 (May 1834):160.

[5]With congressional districting under consideration, the general assembly postponed the regularly scheduled 1834 election for representatives until 1835. Politics in Missouri during the Mormon experience in the 1830s was controlled by the Jacksonian Democrats.

[6]See Amasa Lyman Journal, Church Archives.

[7]Note that the policy of not holding public meetings (see page 76) was modified. These decisions reflect the serious problem concerning Mormon-non-Mormon relations in Clay County. (See Max Parkin, "A History of The Church of Jesus Christ of Latter-day Saints in Clay County, Missouri, 1833-36," Ph.D. dissertation, Brigham Young University, 1976.)

[8]See *The Orson Pratt Journals,* Elden J. Watson, comp. (Salt Lake City: Elden J. Watson, 1975), page 43.

[9]See *History of the Church* 2:137.

[10]Samuel Brown.

[11]Colesville Branch.

[12]Either Zerah or Barnet.

[13]Colesville Branch.

[14]Nathan West.

[15]Leonard Rich.

[16]See page 63, note 2.

[17]See page 77, note 7.

[18]Sally Crandall.

[19]Truman Brace.

[20]Sylvester Hulet.

[21]On August 28, 1833, it was decided that no ordination would take place without the consent of a conference of high priests. (See page 64.)

[22]Many of the early Saints had difficulty in breaking with their previous church beliefs and practices.

[23]Probably Nelson Tubs.

[24]Leonard Rich.

[25]Orson Pratt.

[26]The Church in Zion or Missouri.

August 1, 1834

Convened again according to adjournment. Proceeded to business.

Roxa Slade testifies that two or three weeks ago as I was in at Alanson Clevelands, Br. Brown was there, and was talking about sanctification and that there were many sanctified among the sects especially among the Methodists; but this being a greater light, if they did not give heed to it they would fall under condemnation; I then said if there was any person sanctified I should like to see one. He said supposing I should bring myself as a sample.—Have you ever seen anything in me out of the way.—I said no. I said I had belonged to the Methodists once & that I never received but a small spark of the Spirit among them. He said he believed it,—and said I dont think you have as yet received but a very little of the Spirit.—but I have received three or four great sparks among the Methodists.[1] And you are teaching the same doctrine that the heads of this Church do.—and one great reason that we are so chastened, is, that the heads have so little charity for the Methodists.—And unless they repent the scourge will remain upon them. And if you continue in the way you are now in, very soon you will loose all the spirit or it will withdraw from you,—and you shall be buffeted by satan, and you may go and ponder on these things and see if I have not authority to say these things

Roxa Slade

I can testify that the above statement of our sister is true for I was present and heard the conversation.—Alanson Cleveland.

Caleb Baldwin testifies that—Br. Brown said it would not do to go into the world and prech that they are in darkness,—for they were not—He said that he could not preach against the Methodists for he should preach against his own will in so doing—He said many more things which I do not remember,

Caleb Baldwin.

We witness the above to be true— Caleb Baldwin, jr.
Nancy Baldwin.

Silvester Hulet testifies that He and br. Brown ~~met~~ went together to br. Tub's—and on the way there, Br. Brown took his lisence out of his pocket and showed it to me and asked me how I would like to have such paper—to which I answered that I had made application to the Council for an ordination some time since and was rejected.—He seemed to talk to me in such a manner that understood him to sensure the heads of this Church in some things.

Silvester Hulet.

After which the president said that the case was now ready for investigation. Zebidee Coultrin & Simeon Carter spoke in behalf of the Church and Amasa Lyman & Parley P. Pratt for br. Brown.

After the above counsillors and the accused had spoken we adjourned half an hour.

Convened according to adjournment.

Opened in prayer by David Whitmer President

Proceeded to business decided br. Brown's case as follows,

According to testimony and the voice of the Holy Spirit which is in us, we say unto you, that God in his infinite mercy doth yet grant you a space of repentance: Therefore if you confess all the charges which have been alleged against you, to be just—& this in a spirit that we can receive it then you can stand as a private member in this Church—otherwise we have no fellowship for you. And also, that the ordination of Silvester Hulet performed by Samuel Brown is illegal therefore not acknowledged by us to be of God—Therefore is void and good for nothing.

The foregoing decision sanctioned by the unanimous Aye of the counsillors.

Br. Samuel Brown came forward and confessed the charges. Also gave up his licenses of Elder and High Priest[2] Elder's license dated at Pittsburgh Pensylvania February 21. 1833. and by the hand of Phineas Young. And his license for high priest dated at Cincinnatti Hamilton Co. Ohio, June 15. 1833. Given by Luke Johnson. Therefore Br. Brown stands as a ~~high~~ private member in this Church;—all this by the voice of the Counsillors.[3]

David Whitmer)
) Moderators.
W.W. Phelps)

John Whitmer Clerk.

After this was done it was necessary for P.P. Pratt to be absent therefore Leonard Rich was appointed in his place.

After which proceeded and nominated Orson Pratt for a Clerk.[4] Voted and carried unanimous by uplifted hands.

After which a charge against the Hulet branch concerning gifts handed in for consideration by Nathan West. Considered and laid over for next sitting. And also a request by Peter Whitmer jr. & Elisha H. Groves, all of which laid over for our next.

Adjourned until next Wednesday at 10. O'clock at this place.

David Whitmer)
) Moderators.
W.W. Phelps)

John Whitmer Clerk.

---

[1]Many of the Saints were converts from Methodism, and had difficulty making a complete break.

[2]See page 2, note 6.

[3]See Amasa Lyman Journal, Church Archives.

[4]Orson Pratt only served as clerk until August 21, 1834, when he left on a mission to the east.

August 6, 1834

Clay County August 6. 1834[1]

Convened according to adjournment.

Opened in prayer as usual.

Resolved that Leonard Rich act in the place of Parley P. Pratt & Amasa Lyman in the place of William E. Mc.lellin Pro. tem.

After which William W. Phelps read a letter of recommend which was to be given to the four brethren appointed at our last Council.[2]

Br. David Whitmer then arose and addressed the four brethren to visit the Churches, as follows: saying, you are not sent to preach the gospel to the world for the world will not hear it in this place But to instruct the disciples in things pertaining to their everlasting happiness as well as temporal peace & prosperity &c.

After which a charge was read, preferred by Nathan West

against a Branch of the Church known by the name of the Hulet branch which reads as follows

This may certify that whereas the, brethren & Sisters, composing a part in the Church known by the name of the Hulet branch, have imbibed certain principles concerning the gifts that are thought not to be correct by the greater part of the rest of the Church, which principles seem to have a tendency to cause a split and disunion in the Church.

I therefore as a wellwisher to the cause of Christ, and for the peace and love and upbilding of the great cause of God. Do hereby pray that the High Council will take into consideration the above report that we all may come to understanding and grow up as calves of the stall until we arise unto the perfect stature of men and women in Christ Jesus.

Nathan West

Resolved that four should speak upon this case, Viz:

Amasa Lyman	and	Calvin Bebee
Levi Jackman	"	Solomon Hancock.

Called on witnesses

Charles English testifies that, the Hulet branch believed that they received the word of the Lord by the gift of tongues and would not proceed to their temporal business without receiving the word of the Lord. Silvester[3] would speak and Sally Crandle interpreted. Said that they would not receive the teachings of ordained members even br. Joseph Smith jr. unless it agreed with their gifts. Said they received the word of the Lord while they were in Jackson County; that they were to be persecuted by their brethren in Clay County and now it had come—also said that the heads of the Church would have to come down and receive the gifts as they did—Said that they the said branch had come up to their privileges more than the rest of the Church. They thought they were right but if they ~~were wrong~~ could be convinced that they were wrong, they would retract—Sister Crandle profesed to know and see men's hearts.

Philo Dibble testifies ~~testifies~~ that Sister Crandle saw the heart of King Follet that it was not right—also saw the heart of Hiram Page that it was not right, br. P. Dibble concurs with the testimony of br. C. English, said branch the same things that sister Sally Crandle does. Also saw my heart and said he had a gift of knowledge.

Hiram Page testifies that[4]

Lyman Leonard said if it was necessary to lay aside the gifts for a season they would receive a knowledge of it through the gifts. The Church said that there was a prophecy delivered through the gifts while in Jackson County that they were to come over into Clay Co. and there be persecuted by their brethren & said the prophecy must be fulfilled, and carried the idea as though it was now fulfilling.

Hiram Page.

Nathan West testifies that

The foregoing testimonies are true and that Sister Sally Crandle saw his heart and that it was full of eyes, also saw eyes in others hearts some had few and ~~others~~ some many.

Nathan West.

Daniel Stanton testifies that

Sally Crandle said that she saw his heart and saw two books in it, and that there was a Nephite standing behind him to push him into his duty. And says that Silvester Hulet spake in tongues in meeting and and Sally Crandle interpreted thus: Verily, verily, thus saith the Lord unto you little band ye must beware for there are many who are seeking to pry into your privileges.

Daniel Stanton.

Absalom Scritchfield testifies that:

Last spring one time that he was over in Jackson County the Hulet branch said in tongues that they would be safe during the night from any interruption by the <u>mob</u>, but before morning some of them were whiped, Viz: Lyman Leonard and Josiah Sumner, and also testified that they saw my heart and saw three young women in it.

Absalom Scritchfield.

Br. Badson[5] acknowledges that he was present and said with Sally Crandle that he saw three young women in his heart; also testifies that he got sister Sally Crandle to look and see whether his wife was in the faith, she said that she saw her afar off: also testifies that he knew that Sally Crandle's gift of seeing was not of the Lord but it was of the Devil.

Br. Batson

Alpheus Gifford testifies, to many things which had been given in by other witnesses.

Alpheus Gifford.

Council adjourned ¾ hour.

Convened according to adjournment.

Opened prayer as usual.

The President[6] then arose and addressed the Counsillors, saying: that they in speaking ought not to seek to excell but ought to speak according to truth and equity: saying that they should chase away darkness and have their minds exercised upon the subject upon which they are to speak in order that they might touch upon points and bring hidden things to light and make dark things clear &c. &c.[7]

After which John Whitmer arose and said that the Lord had said to him and David Whitmer while pondering upon these things that the High priests and Elders were enveloped in a great degree with that darkness which is spread over all the inhabitants of the earth and that you have lost in part that light which you have once had, and it becomes necessary that your brethren arise and shake themselves from this lethargy for God is not well pleased with this negligence and slothfulness, while in Council.

The Counsillors then proceeded on their part according to constitution.[8]

After which W. W. Phelps made a few remarks upon the pattern given respecting spirits in all cases under the whole heavens.[9]

After this the President said as for the gift of tongues in the manner that they used it in the Hulet branch the Devil decieved them and that they obtained not the word of the Lord as they supposed they did, but were deceived; and as for the gift of seeing as held by the Hulet branch, it is of the devil saith the Lord God.

The above decision sanctioned by the unanimous voice of the Council.

After which the President nominated, Amasa Lyman & Simeon Carter to go & labor with Sister Sally Crandal & ~~Sister~~ Sylvester Hulet and others of like faith & set forth these things in their proper light to them[10]

This also sanctioned by the unanimous voice of the Council,

(Orson Pratt Clerk)
David Whitmer Moderator

After which Br Wm W Phelps read a petition handed in to the Council desiring a recommend from this Council to go to ~~K~~ Kirtland ~~Saying it was never~~

After which Br. Wm W Phelps made some few remarks saying it was necessary for any one that desired to be ordained to obtain a recomend from that part of the brethren where he resides

Voted & carried that Peter Whitmer Jr. receive a recomend from this Council according to appointment to go when convenient.

After which the President called for voluntiers to go and the gospel of peace.[11]

The following presented themselves

High Priests	Elders
Daniel Stanton	Elias Eams
Zebedee Coltrin	L. Barns
Amasa Lyman	Morris Phelps
George M. Hinckle	Solomon Umphrey
Alpheus Gifford	Jesse Hitchcock
Hazen Aldrich	L Robinson
	Nathan West

Elisha H Groves
Solomon Wixon
Isaac Fallis
Willard Snow
Isaac Higbee
Henry Shibly
John Killian & William
Botson

Adjourned until 10 O'Clock A.M. morrow morning

---

[1]See *History of the Church* 2:138.

[2]Previous to the high council's adjournment on August 1, 1834, a letter of recommendation was written for Simeon Carter, John Corrill, Parley P. Pratt, and Orson Pratt authorizing them to meet with and instruct the Saints in Clay County. These four brethren were appointed to this mission on July 31, 1834. (See *History of the Church* 2:138-39.)

[3]Sylvester Hulet.

[4]The notes here are in abbreviated form and unclear.

[5]William Batson.

[6]David Whitmer.

[7]Here David Whitmer elaborates on the instructions received in Doctrine and Covenants 102. As the brethren held Church courts, they were establishing precedents still being used in the Church today. (See Appendix B.)

[8]Some councilors were to speak for the accused and some for the Church, as in Doctrine and Covenants 102.

[9]See Doctrine and Covenants 50.

[10]See Amasa Lyman Journal, Church Archives, concerning this assignment.

[11]Note the voluntary nature of missionary work.

August 7, 1834

Convened according to adjournment[1]

Opened, prayer as usual,

Wm W Phelps then remarked that the ordained members ought to walk so uprightly before God that they might be recommended without any exceptions in his Character

David Whitmer remarked that those who go forth to preach ought to walk before the world in wisdom and in righteousness in all things &c.

John Whitmer said that it was necessary for those who go into the world to preach to be dilligent and faithful in all things so that those who are set as Moderators can license them without scrupulous conciences to be worthy and capable to fill their trust &c, that when they returned their Journals may recommend them to the Bishop, &c

The following are the names of those who are united in the ministry as coupled by this Council:

Daniel Stanton, & Elias Eams,	Hazen Aldrich & Willard Snow
Amasa Lyman & Horace Cowan	Solomon Humphrey " Solomon Wixon
Zebidee Coltrin & Nathan West	Jesse Hitchcock John Killian[2]

Voted and carried that the foregoing receive a recommend signed by the Clerk of Council, if worthy when they apply

Voted and carried that David W Patten, George M Hinkle Elisha H Groves and Charles Patten, Receive a recommend from the Clerk of the Council and chose partners for themselves to journey in the ministry

After this David Whitmer arose and said the William Botson is not capable to fill his office of Eldership in this Church because he has not understanding and discretion sufficient to act wisely in that capacity

Voted and carried unanimously by uplifted hands of this council that his office and License be taken from him to which he consented and gave up his License dated February 17, 1832, Council adjourned half an hour.

Convened, Opened in prayer as usual.

W.W. Phelps then arose and addressed those who had been

appointed to go into the world to preach the Gospel, saying that it is necessary for them to use all wisdom and observe manners among the people, and be virtuous, discreet, meek and lowly of heart, to be cleanly, mannerly & sociable, to be careful about ordaining &c. &c.[3]

After, br Orson Pratt proceeded to ordain Elias & Isaac Higbee & Jesse Hitchcock to the Highpriesthood acording to the voice of a council held in Jackson County, or Zion Sept. 26. 1833. And also ordained William Legg to the office of a priest. All this by the unanimous voice of the council.

Voted and carried that the three presidents receive a recommend from this council to the council in Kirtland.

Adjourned until the 21st inst. at 10 O'clock A.M. at this place.

Closed in prayer by David Whitmer President, or as usual.

Orson Pratt Clerk.

---

[1]Andrew Jenson penciled in the date "August 7, 1834." See *History of the Church* 2:141.

[2]These missionaries were not to preach in Jackson or Clay counties. See *History of the Church* 2:141.

[3]Note the "mission home" type of instruction to the missionaries.

August 21, 1834

Agreeable to adjournment the high Council convened at the house of Lyman Wight's on the 21st of August 1834.[1]

Voted and carried that,

Leonard Rich act in the place of Parley P. Pratt.
Zebedee Coultrin act in the place of William E. Mc.lellin
Peter Dustin " " " Calvin Bebee
Isaac Higbee " " " Newel Knight. and
Elias Higbee " " " Levi Jackman, pro. tem.

Opened in prayer by David Whitmer, President.

After which Brs. Simeon Carter and Amasa Lyman made their returns concerning their mission to the Hulet branch—

stating that they found the brethren and sisters willing to receive the decision of the last council respecting the false spirits with which they had be exercised &c.

Voted and carred that Orson Pratt should be privileged to go into the world to preach, or stay in Zion according as he shall obtain by the manifestation of the Spirit of God through prayer.[2]

Adjourned for one hour.

Convened, opened in prayer, as usual.

Voted and carried that Elders Morris Phelps, Uziel Stevens, Stephen Chase and Harvey Green should go into the world to preach the Gospel in the due time of the Lord

Voted and carried that Alexander Richardson be ordained a Priest, and Philo Dibble a Teacher.

Thomas B. Marsh then proceeded and ordained these two brethren to the offices above named.

After which John Corrill entered complaint against Lyman Wight with teaching this doctrine, saying: "all disease in this Church is of the Devil and that medicine administered to the sick is of the Devil, for the sick in the Church ought to live by faith. And he wished the high council to take it into consideration.

Voted and carried that four speak on the above case, viz:

Christian Whitmer	&	Isaac Higbee,
Orson Pratt	"	Lyman Wight

After which Lyman Wight acknowledged that he had taught this doctrine, or rather believed it to be correct.

After which W.W. Phelps spoke and said this case need no counselling which was agreed to by L. Wight and J. Corrill.

After which the President proceeded and gave the following decision saying: It is not lawful to teach the Church that all disease is of the devil. But if there is any that has this faith let him have it to himself. And if there are any that believe that roots and herbs administered to the sick, and all wholesome vegitables which God has ordained for the use of man and if any say that such things applied to the sick in order that they may receive health, and this applied by any member of the Church, if there are any among you that teach that these things are of Satan, such teaching is not of God.[3]

Council dismissed. Prayer by David Whitmer President.

Orson Pratt Clerk.

---

[1]See *History of the Church* 2:146-47.

[2]See *The Orson Pratt Journals*, Elden J. Watson, comp. (Salt Lake City: Elden J. Watson, 1975), page 44.

[3]Although some individuals have had doubts concerning medicine, the Church has consistently supported the study and practice of medicine.

September 10, 1834

Clay County, September 10. 1834[1]

Convened according to appointment. Opened in prayer by William W. Phelps.[2]

After which proceeded to choose counsellors instead of absent ones.

Zebidee Coultrin instead of Parley P. Pratt.
Hazen Aldrich " " Solomon Hancock
Elias Higbee " " Newel Knight
Isaac Higbee " " William E. Mc.Lellin
Peter Dustin " " Orson Pratt.

Nominated Thomas B. Marsh to be clerk pro. tem. Voted and carried unanimously.

After which W.W. Phelps proceeded and made a few remarks of conducting wisely, more especially the counsellors.

After which Elisha H. Groves desired to be ordained to the highpriesthood, which was considered voted and carried that he be ordained to this office.

Voted and carried that Samuel Musick be ordained a Teacher.

Voted and carried that John Lowry be ordained a Teacher.

Voted and carried that Daniel Stephens and John M. Chitister receive recommends to go forth to preach the Gospel.

After which Simeon Carter was appointed to ordain the above named brethren to their respective offices.

After this a letter written by joseph Smith jr. was read by W.W. Phelps dated August 16. 1834.[3]

A petition written by W.W. Phelps to the Governor of State of Mo. was read and accepted.

Nominated Calvin Bebee and Levi Jackman as first Elders[4] to go forth to the land of Kirtland and preach by the way and if approved of by the Revelator should be accounted worthy and numbered as such.

After this W.W. Phelps proceeded and addressed the Elders on the subject of their teaching, and conduct &c.

Decided by the presidents and sanctioned by the council that the first Elders go forth as soon as they can get ready and preach by the way to Kirtland.

Voted and carried that the first Elders receive a copy of the above resolution.

Application made by James Emmet Elder to be promoted to the highpriesthood.

Voted and carried that Isaac Follis go forth and preach inasmuch as he can situate his family and leave them comfortable

Voted and carried that those Elders that came up in the Camp[5] apply for a dismissal[6] of Lyman Wight, and for a recommend to Edward Partridge Bishop, to go forth to preach the Gospel.

Voted and carried that George Pitkin to be ordained a teacher,

Zebedee Coultrin was appointed to ordain him to that office.

Closed by singing, "Ere Long the Vail Will Rend in Twain &c. and prayer by W.W. Phelps.

Thomas B. Marsh Clerk.

[1]See *History of the Church* 2:164.

[2]Note David Whitmer's absence. He was the president of the Church in Missouri, but had left for Ohio by the time of this meeting.

[3]This letter is in *History of the Church* 2:144-46.

[4]The term "first Elders" had reference to those called to receive Kirtland endowment.

[5]Zion's Camp.

[6]Release or discharge. Wight had been appointed the "General of the Camp," and Joseph authorized him to give a discharge to "every man of the Camp who had proved himself faithful." (See *History of the Church* 2:123.)

November 5, 1834

Council met November 5. 1834.

Opened in prayer by W.W. Phelps. And chose

in the place of Wm. E. McLellin—Elias Higbee
" " Orson Pratt—Daniel Stanton
" " John Murdock—Peter Dustin
" " Parley P. Pratt—Isaac Higbee
Newel Knight—Amasa Lyman

An address was made by W.W. Phelps on the subject of the Meeting.

After which application was made by Wm. Harris, Elder for license to go and proclaim the gospel. Voted and carried that he apply to the Bishop, Edward Partridge for a recommend and if he obtain one he has the voice of the council to obtain one.

Elias F. Wells applied for an ordination. Voted and carried that he be ordained as the spirit direct.

Luman Gibbs applied for ordination. Descided by the President and sanctioned by the council that he stand for a season.

George Burket applied to be reinstated to the office of an Elder. Voted and carried that he receive his former station.[1]

Samuel Brown applied for ordination, decided and sanctioned that he be ordained as the Spirit direct.[2]

George Morey applied for the office of Elder, which he withdrew.

Stephen Winchester teacher Wilford Woodruff teacher and Heman T. Hyde member, applied for ordination, descided and sanctioned that they be ordained as the spirit direct.

Peter Dustin applied for a recommend to go and preach the gospel which was granted him.

James Emmet applied for permission to go and preach the Gospel which was granted, also desired a partner to journey with him. Voted and carried that Peter Dustin journey with him.

After which Simeon Carter was appointed to ordain the foregoing brethren and ordained them as follows:

Elias F. Wells,	an Elder
George Burket	" "
Samuel Brown	" "
Stephen Winchester	a Priest.
Wilford Woodruff	" "
Heman T. Hyde	" "

An address in relation to the duties of Teachers and Priests &c.

Decided and sanctioned that those who have been ordained, and those who are sent forth apply to John Whitmer for licence.

Decided and sanctioned that there be no more slated meetings. The Elders may administer the sacrament if they see a convenient opportunity.[3]

Closed in prayer as usual.

Thomas B. Marsh, Clerk of Con.

---

[1]This request for reinstatement is similar to the practice of requesting priesthood ordination.

[2]Samuel Brown lost his elder's and high priest's license on August 1, 1834. (See page 87.)

[3]This policy underscores the tense situation in Clay County.

1836

January 6, 1836

A Council convened at Kirtland, Ohio, January 6. 1836,[1] for the purpose of filling the vacancies of the High Council of Zion.

Presidents D. Whitmer, J. Whitmer & W.W. Phelps and also a goodly number of high priests and Elders to the No. of 15, and one priest.

Address by Pres. W.W. Phelps, announcing the decease of ~~Christian~~ Counsellor Christian Whitmer who died on the 27th of November 1835.

Four Councilors had been chosen as Apostles and special witnesses, viz: Parley P. Pratt, Orson Pratt, Wm. E. Mc.lellin & Thomas B. Marsh. Proceeded and nominated instead of the above named councilors as follows:

Elisha H. Groves instead of	Parley P. Pratt,
Jesse Hitchcock " "	W.E. Mclellin
George M. Hinkel " "	Orson Pratt,
Elias Higbee " "	T.B. Marsh
Peter Whitmer jr. " "	Christian Whitmer, deceased.

Proceeded and ordained the above named Counsellors and solemnity rested upon the whole congregation, because the Lord was with us, and great blessings were expressed and confirmed upon the heads of the aforementioned Counsellors.

Presidents D. Whitmer, J. Whitmer & W.W. Phelps addressed the congregation in a pathetic manner.

After which, bowed before the Lord with one accord and called upon him to preserve and bless our absent fathers mothers brethren and families until Zion should be redeemed &c. Prayer was made by David Whitmer, sang, Adam on Di Ahman[2] Closed.

Elijah Fordham, Clerk.

---

[1]See *History of the Church* 2:356. Note there are no recorded minutes in the Far West Record for 1835. During 1835 and 1836 most Missouri Church leaders were in Kirtland preparing for the "endowment."

[2]This hymn by W.W. Phelps was first published in the *Messenger and Advocate* 1 (June 1835): 144.

November 15, 1836

November 15, 1836[1]

At a meeting of the presidents, in the City at Shoal Creek: being duly organized proceeded to do business. Selected and appointed Jacob Whitmer, Elisha H. Groves, and George M. Hinkle for a building committee to assist the Presidency to build the house of the Lord[2] in said City.[3]

Meeting closed as usual.

(signed) John Corrill Clerk.

---

[1]This meeting of the presidency (John Whitmer and W.W. Phelps) without the high council was the source of a major conflict in the Church in Missouri. John Murdock, referring to this meeting, said: "The two Presidents did all the business indepen[den]t of [the] Bishopric or High Council and the Church was dissatisfied." (See Murdock Journal, Church Archives, page 17.)

[2]A temple. Elisha H. Groves, speaking of this meeting noted: "Soon after [returning from Kentucky and Tennessee collecting money to purchase lands in Missouri] I was set apart as a building commity to build the Temple in Far West[,] started on that business about the 20 of Dec traveled through the branches [from Missouri] to Kirtland [and] obtained a subscription of $1,500." (See Elisha H. Groves autobiography, Church Archives.)

[3]Far West.

1837

April 7, 1837

At a meeting of the quorums, of the Presidency, and High Council and Bishop and Council convened at the house of Levi Jackman in the City of Far West, on the 7th April, 1837.[1]

Present: John Whitmer & W. W. Phelps, Pres. and John Murdock, Levi Jackman, T. B. Marsh, D. W. Patten, Solomon Hancock, Simeon Carter Lyman Wight, Calvin Bebee and Elias Higbee Counsellors. Also Edward Partridge Bishop, and Isaac Morley and John Corrill his Counsellors.

Meeting opened by prayer and singing, "The Towers of Zion soon shall Rise, &c.

1st Resolved, that John Corrill act as clerk.

2nd Resolved, that the City Platt of Far West remain in its present form or draft.[2] And we unanimously accept of it

3rd. Resolved, that the Alleys be opened by the majority of each square or block when they shall desire it

4th. Resolved, that the price and saile of town lots be left with the Judgment of the wise men, viz W. W. Phelps, John Whitmer, Edward Partridge, Isaac Morley and John Corrill

5th. Resolved thus: These quorums accept of Jacob Whitmer, Elisha H. Groves, and George M Hinkle as building committee of the house of the Lord in this City. Also that Jacob Whitmer be received as a high Counsellor until President David Whitmer arrives at this place.

6th. Resolved, that President David Whitmer, John Whitmer and W. W. Phelps be appointed to superintend the building of the house of the Lord in this City Far West and receive Revelations Visions &c. concerning said house

Closed by singing, and benediction by John Whitmer

(Signed) John Corrill Clerk

---

[1]See *History of the Church* 2:481. Four days previous to this conference, questions were discussed in a conference relative to Whitmer and Phelps platting a city of Zion without the High Council approval. (See pages 107-9.)

[2]This plat, which Phelps and J. Whitmer laid out, was one mile square.

July 25, 1836

Clay County Mo. July 25. 1836[1]

A general assembly met at the house of President Phelps to transact business for the Church.

High Council of Zion organized also the bishop and hid Counsellors.

Opened by singing, "the Spirit of God like a Fire is Burning &c. and prayer by President John Whitmer.

1st. Resolved unanimously that

Whereas this body is informed that about one hundred families of emigrating Saints, being in waggons and tents on Crooked River in the lower part of Ray County and threatened with mobbing and pestilence some being now sick and many of them destitute of means to purchase lands or provisions. And whereas it is allowed or said, that about one hundred families, are on the road between there and the Mississippi River destitute also and will soon be in like condition; and whereas some of both companies, as we are informed, say they have left their money at the East, and we have no doubt, but our brethren there will forward them the money, as soon as they write to them, that they must suffer without it. As land and provisions cannot be had, without means, flour having risen to $3.00 per cwt. and pork to 10 and 12½¢ per lb.

Therefore Resolved, by the High Council, and Bishop and Elders and multitude, to prevent mobbing and confusion, and pestilence and death, if possible, that all the emigrating brethren, who have not means or friends to furnish them, be advised to scatter among the people below where they can find accomodations, and labor for the present. And that two Elders be appointed as a committee to carry them this intelligence and that they be authorized to loan and collect money among the Churches in Mo., Illinois Indiana, Kentucky and Tennessee, and put the same into the hands of the Zion Presidency, for the upbuilding and benefit of "Poor Bleeding Zion."[2]

2nd. Resolved unanimously that, Thomas B. Marsh and Elisha H. Groves be the aforementioned committee.

3rd. Resolved unanimously that, W.W. Phelps, John Whitmer, Edward Partridge, Isaac Morely, and John Corrill be appointed to search out land for the Church to settle upon &c.[3]

Conference closed with appropriate benedictions.

(Signed) Peter Dustin Clerk.

---

[1]These minutes are out of chronological order, appearing in the middle of notes for 1837.

[2]"Poor Bleeding Zion" refers to the distressed Saints in Missouri. Marsh and Groves borrowed $1450 from members of the Church in Kentucky and Tennessee at 10 percent interest for the purpose of purchasing federal land in Caldwell County. (See *Elders Journal* 1(July 1838): 37; see also History of Thomas B. Marsh, Church Archives.)

[3]On March 11, 1836, in Kirtland, Ohio, Joseph Smith appointed Edward Partridge, Isaac Morley, John Corrill, and William W. Phelps as "wise men" to purchase lands in Missouri where the Saints could settle, and they were given money for this purpose. After returning to Clay County, Missouri, in early May 1836, Partridge and Phelps "took a tour" of the northern country where they found a few good mill sites located about thirty-five miles northeast of Liberty. Shortly thereafter several half-quarter and quarter sections were entered in the names of Joseph Smith, Hyrum Smith, and Oliver Cowdery.

While an immediate removal was planned as scores of families were arriving in Missouri, Jackson County suits delayed the move until August. The meeting mentioned in the text appointed the named brethren to locate a settlement where the Saints could gather. But interestingly enough, they did not decide to lay out a city on any of the properties previously purchased, but rather upon a section purchased on August 8, 1836—Far West, Missouri. (See Edward Partridge Journal, The Book of John Whitmer, and John Murdock Journal, Church Archives; and *History of the Church* 2:444-45.)

Date Unknown

At a meeting[1] pursuant to notice by the Presidency the following: quorums met Viz the high council, two of the Apostles and about 10 of the seventies and the Bishop and one of his councilors together with a numerous body of members.

Opened in prayer by President John Whitmer

Appointed John Corrill, clerk of the meeting

1st. Resolved unanimously that we withdraw our fellowship from James Emmet for unwise conduct until he returns and makes satisfaction

2nd. Resolved unanimously that we will not fellowship any ordained member who will or does not observe the Word of Wisdom according to its litteral reading.[2]

3rd. Resolved unanimously that we sanction the Litterary Firm and give them our voice and prayers to manage all the concerns of the same as far as it concerns this place according to revelation in the Book Doctrine and Covenants first Edition published at Kirtland Ohio. Page 152, Section 26, given November, 1831.[3]

4th. Resolved unanimously that John Corrill furnish Bread and Wine[4] for sacrament each Sabbath and receive for his services out of donations for that purpose

5th. Resolved unanimously that John Whitmer, William W. Phelps, Edward Partridge, Isaac Morley and John Corrill be appointed to sell the town plott and manage the affair of the same.

6th. Resolved unanimously that John Whitmer be the receiver of the money resulting from the sale of the lots of the town Far West.

7th. Resolved unanimously that, the heads of the Church or in other words, that those who have been annointed and set apart to regulate the preaching in the County of Caldwell, and the regions roundabout. and all other matters that concerns the management of the said Church.

Meeting closed by singing: "This earth was once a garden place." and Benediction by President John Whitmer

(Signed) John Corrill Clerk.

---

[1]Date unknown. (See *History of the Church* 2:482.) Here, the minutes for 1837 reappear. The exact date of this meeting is unknown, but was sometime in May of 1837. The next three meetings (April 3 and April 5-6) were recorded in incorrect order by the clerk. The correct chronological order resumes with the minutes for April 7, 1837.

[2]This is an example of sporadic attempts to enforce the Word of Wisdom. (See Leonard Arrington, "Have the Saints always given as much emphasis to the Word of Wisdom as they do today?" *Ensign*, April 1977, page 32. See also Paul H. Peterson, "An Historical Analysis of the Word of Wisdom," M.A. thesis, Brigham Young University, 1972.)

[3]Doctrine and Covenants 70.

[4]Although, as Brigham Young said, "The Lord told Joseph that he would accept of water [instead of wine]," pure wine, prepared by the Saints, was acceptable, and was not completely and officially abandoned until July 1906. (See *Journal of Discourses* 10:245 and 19:92, and John Henry Smith Diary, July 1906, Manuscripts Division, J. Willard Marriott Library, University of Utah, Salt Lake City, Utah.)

April 3, 1837

At a meeting of the High Council in Far West, April 3rd 1837.[1] Seven of the standing Counsellors were present. John Murdock was appointed Moderator and Elias Higbee Clerk.

Resolved, That, the Council request that President W. W. Phelps and John Whitmer to give explanation of the following items[2]

1st By what authority was this place pointed out for a city and house of the Lord, and by whom.[3]

2nd By what authority was a committee appointed and ordained to superintend the building of the house of the Lord.

3rd By what authority was Jacob Whitmer ordained to the High Priesthood.

4th Have two Presidents authority to lay out a City, and build a house of God, independently of the Counsel of the High Council and Bishop and his Council.

5th By what authority was one of the High Counsellors disfellowshipped in the name of the H. Council without their knowledge

6th Have any individual or individuals a right to prefer a charge to the Presidency in Kirtland against any High Counsellor, without the knowledge of the Council or individual.

7th Should not the High Council and Bishop of Zion who are appointed to do business for Zion, receive their inheritance in the core of the City in preference to one who is not particularly called to labour for Zion, or an unbeliever.

8th Shall any intelligence relative to the building up of Zion be withheld from the council of Zion.

9th Are the two Presidents entitled to the profits arising from the sale of lands on which the City is to be built in this place, independent of the authorities who have been appointed to labor with them for Zion and have suffered like tribulation with them.

The Council then agreed to invite prests. W. W. Phelps & John Whitmer, also, the Bishop E. Partridge and his counsellors. Also, the two Apostles, viz. T. B. Marsh & D. W. Patten to meet with them on the 5th inst. that the above named Presidents might explain the foregoing questions, and that the subject might be investigated. The Council then adjourned to the 5th at 10 O'clock.

---

[1]See *History of the Church* 2:483. In this meeting the members of the high council were meeting alone without the presidency to decide what to do about the presidency's having met alone without the high council. (See page 102.)

[2]The following questions, directed to Phelps and Whitmer, are in the John Murdock Journal, Church Archives.

[3]When Thomas Marsh and Elisha Groves returned to Missouri from Kentucky and Tennessee, they delivered the $1450 to Phelps and Whitmer, who, instead of using the money to assist the destitute Saints, purchased lands in their own names and for their own benefit.

Referring to this meeting, Thomas B. Marsh wrote: "[W. W. Phelps and J. Whitmer] generally did their business, independently of the aid, or council of either the bishop or High Council. This gave some uneasiness to the two authorities of Zion: not only because they purchased land with Church funds, in their own name, for their own agrandisement, but because they selected the place of the City Far West and appointed the spot for the House of the Lord to be built on, drew the plan of said house, and appointed and ordained a committee to build the same, without asking or seeking council, at the hand of either Bishop, High Council, or first presidency." (See Thomas B. Marsh to Wilford Woodruff, April 30, 1838, Church Archives.)

April 5-6, 1837

Far West April 5. 1837.[1]

The Council convened agreeable to adjournment with the aforementioned Presidents. The Bishop & Counsel; also the 2 Apostles. The Council opened by prayer, but previous to proceeding to business, the said Presidents proposed that the Bishop and his counsel, with the abovenamed Apostles, leave the Council, which was objected to by the Council, the Bishop and Apostles. The Presidents still insisted on having a private Council in the absence of the Bishop & his Counsel & Apostles; when all opposed the two Presidents. The Bishop & two Apostles gave them to understand that they had a right to remain and that they therefore should remain.

Prest. Phelps then said he would disolve the Council, upon which T. B. Marsh declared that if the council should be disolved he would prefer a charge against the two Presidents, before the Bishop & 12 High Priests. The Presidents then said they were willing to let all present remain in the house.[2] The Council then proceeded to the investigation of the above named questions. They were not generally satisfactorily answered, which led the Council & others to strongly rebuke the late improper proceedings of the Presidents. D. W. Patten spoke against them with apparent indignation: stating that these proceedings had been iniquitous & fradulent in the extreme, in the unrighteously appropriating Church funds to their own emolument[3] which had been plainly proven. April 6th was occupied in like discussions.

[1]See *History of the Church* 2:483-84.

[2]Murdock said, "[W. W.] Phelps was for having the Bishopric and two Apostles to withdraw. I being the oldest of the council told him no, or I with the High Council would leave also. And at the snap of a whip the whole church will leave you. So he yielded the point." (See John Murdock Journal, Church Archives, page 17.)

[3]The town plot of Far West, Missouri, as well as four adjacent eighties, was purchased by Phelps and J. Whitmer on August 8, 1836.

April 7, 1837

April 7th Council convened agreeable to adjournment.[1] The Bishop & Counsil present, also the two Apostles. The above named Presidents agreed to give up the Town Plott of Far West with 4 eighties on the Commons[2] to be disposed of by the High Council, the Bishop & his Counsil & the said Apostles. After which, on motion, the Council adjourned. The Council met in Far West to take into consideration the affairs relative to the Town Plott; at which the Council resolved, (it being agreed to by all parties,) to make over, or that W. W. Phelps & John Whitmer make over, or transfer the Town Plott with 4 eighties, which are on the Commons, into the hands of the Bishop of Zion, & that the avails arising from the sale of said lands should be appropriated to the benefit & upbuilding of "POOR BLEEDING ZION." See Pages 69 & 70.[3] In the above resolve, W. W. Phelps & John Whitmer acquiesced. Also, resolved that whereas W. W. Phelps & John Whitmer had subscribed $1,000 each to the House of the Lord to be builded in this place, which they were before intending to pay out of the avails of the Town Plott, be considered exempt from paying that subscription[4]

[1]This meeting apparently is a second session later in the day. See April 7, 1837 minutes, pages 103-4.

[2]Means "adjacent to the commons."

[3]These are manuscript page numbers. (See pages 104-5.)

[4]See *Elders' Journal* 1(July 1838):37.

April 24, 1837

April 24, 1837.[1] A High Council held in the Town of Far West. Presided John Whitmer & W. W. Phelps.

Case Charge preferred against Lyman for teaching erronious doctrine by D W Patten. Counsellors as follows.

Simeon Carter	No 1	John Murdock	No 2
Thomas B Marsh	3	Levi Jackman	4
George M. Hinkle,	5	Elias Higbee	6
Calvin Bebee	7	Solomon Hancock	8
Jacob Whitmer	9	King Follett	10
Charles C. Rich	11	Edmund Fisher	12

Council opened by prayer by W. W. Phelps
Case most difficult

Witnesses

Seymour Brunson testifies that Lyman Wight said that we the Church were under a telestial law, because God does not whip in a Celestial, or under a Celestial law; therefore he took us the Church out doors to whip us—as a parent takes his children out of doors to chastise them. And that the Book of Covinants and Doctrine was a telestial law and the Book of Commandments (a part of the Revelations which were printed in Jackson County,) were a Celestial law.[2]

George P. Dykes witnesses to the same, and George Johnson testifies the same also—

The above is only a sketch of the erroneous doctrine Lyman Wight taught, as proven by the above witnesses—

Descided by the presidency that Lyman has taught erroneous doctrine and that he make acknowledgement to the Council and also that he go and acknowledge to the Churches where he preached such abominable doctrine. The above was unanimously sanctioned by the Councellors. Council closed by singing: "This earth was once a garden place &c." and benediction by John Whitmer.

(Signed) Nathan West, Clerk.

[1]See *History of the Church* 2:481-82. Charles C. Rich recorded that this meeting convened on April 23, 1837. (See Charles C. Rich Journal, Church Archives.)

[2]The leaders of the Church maintained constant vigilance concerning the preaching of false doctrine.

May 22, 1837

High Council convened at the Town of Far West, May 22, 1837.[1]

Present, Presidents W. W. Phelps and John Whitmer.

Presiding Counsillors

John Murdock	No. 1.	Simeon Carter	No. 2.
Elias Higbee	" 3.	D. W. Patten	" 4.
E. H. Groves	" 5.	Lyman Wight	" 6.
Jacob Whitmer	" 7.	Levi Jackman	" 8.
G. M. Hinkle	" 9.	T. B. Marsh	" 10.
Isaac Higbee	" 11.	Thomas Grover	" 12.

Council opened, prayer by President J. Whitmer

After which an appeal was handed to the council from the Bishop's council by John Patten and was rejected because of its illegality

Therefore the former complainants Viz Joshua Fairchilds David Pettigrew Benjamin Johnson and Sheffield Daniels entered the following complaint against the defendant John Patten for not fulfilling his contracts or covenants in consequence of which they were materially injured[2]———

Four of the councillors spoke on the subject. John Murdock, Elias Higbee, Simeon Carter, and D. W. Patten

Testimonies, Lyman Wight, John Killion and Abigail Daniels

The above testimonies plainly manifested that John Patten did break covenant &c

After long investigation by the councillors and parties the Presidency decided that both accuser and accused should be disfellowshiped if they did not settle their difficulty—

Jesse Hitchcock's case was then taken into consideration and was cut off from the high council[3]

James Emmet's case was brought into question who had previously been disfellowshiped.[4] He made satisfaction and was restored to his former fellowship. The Presidency, then nominated John Corrill for an agent to the Church and Keeper of the Lord's Store House Which was seconded and carried unanimously by the High Council and multitude

Council Closed

(Signed) Harvey Green Clerk)
)

---

[1]*History of the Church* 2:482.

[2]The High Council handled difficulties that nowadays would be referred to a civil court. (See Appendix B.)

[3]Hitchcock was appointed as a high councilor in Missouri on January 6, 1836, while in Kirtland. (See page 101.)

[4]See page 106.

May 28, 1837

High Council met at the Committee Store at Far West May 28 1837[1]

Presidents, John Whitmer, and Wm. W. Phelps,

High Councillors

Simeon Carter	1	Elias Higbee	2
G. M. Hinkle	3	T. B. Marsh	4
E. H. Groves	5	Lyman Wight	6
Thomas Grover	7	Calvin Bebee	8
Thomas Gorden	9	Jacob Whitmer	10
Levi Jackman	11	Alva L. Tippets	12

Opened in prayer by W. W. Phelps

Charge again preferred against John Patten for not complying with his agreement &c. by John Corrill. John Killian Lyman Wight, John Corrill, W W. Phelps, Gr M. Hinkle, Abigail Daniels The charge was sustained. And Presidency decided and was sanctioned by the Councillors that John Patten, be disfellowshiped until he makes satisfaction

Closed by benediction by John Whitmer

(Signed) Harvey Green (Clerk)

---

[1]See *History of the Church* 2:482.

June 11, 1837

High Council met at committee Store in Far West[1]
Presidents John Whitmer, and W. W Phelps,

High Councillors

Lyman Wight	1	Levi Jackman	2
Gr M Hinkle[2]	3	Calvin Bebee	4
E H Groves	5	Simeon Carter	6
Jacob Whitmer	7	Elias Higbee	8
Isaac Higbee	9	Harvey Green	10
John Murdock	11	Samuel Thompson	12

John Corrill appointed Clerk.

Council opened in prayer by W. W. Phelps.

Resolved by the Council and all present, that the building Committee be upheld in the mercantile business by our prayers. also that Lyman Wight, Simeon Carter and Elias Higbee, be upheld in a leather Store &c.[3] Also that John Corrill and Isaac Morley, and also that Calvin Bebee, that they engage in the mercantile business if they choose to engage in it. also,

Resolved that the right of no man shall be infringed to do as he choose according to law of God or man. also,

Resolved, that the above named men shall be upheld in purchasing goods as other men.

Resolved, that we will not uphold any man or men to take a partner out of the Church to trade or traffic in this line of business, nor sell for any man or men out of the Church in his name, or on commission.

Resolved that the following request be granted to D. W. Patten:

"I am in debt and want to go away, will the Church pay my debts and take me for the same and let me go and preach the Kingdom of God. D. W. Patten."[4]

Resolved that br. Musick's[5] request concerning dealing in mercantile business, be defered until next Council

Resolved that D. W. Patten & T. B. Marsh receive each of them a lot in the Town of Far West free of pay, and that the Bishop Edward Partridge be hereby authorized to convey a title to them if he concurs with us in this thing.

Adjourned. Sang Adam on di Ahmon &c. And benediction by John Whitmer.

(Signed) John Corrill Clerk—

---

[1]See *History of the Church* 2:491. The *History of the Church* notes that the high council convened on June 11, 1837.

[2]George M. Hinkle.

[3]Note that some members of the high council were operating businesses for the Church.

[4]Unlike missionaries of today, who must be debt free, Patten was able to go on a mission, and the Church assumed responsibility for his debts, which he would later repay.

[5]Samuel Musick.

July 29, 1837

High Council met at the School house in Far West, July 29. 1837.

Presidents David[1] & John Whitmer and W. W. Phelps.

Organized as follows:

John Murdock	No. 1.	E. H. Groves	No. 2.
Elias Higbee	" 3.	Lyman Wight	4.
Simeon Carter	" 5	Jacob Whitmer	6.
Solomon Hancock	7	Thomas Grover	8
G. M. Hinkle	9	Lyman Johnson	10
Luke Johnson	11	Isaac Higbee	12

Opened by John Whitmer as usual.

Application for ordination of Levi Stewart to the office of Elder—and was objected by Bishop, Edward Partridge.

(Signed) Nathan West, Clerk.

---

[1]Note that David Whitmer had returned from Ohio.

August 1, 1837

At a general meeting of the Presidency, High Council, Bishop and Council & multitude, August 1st 1837.[1]

David Whitmer John Whitmer & W. W. Phelps Presidents

Simeon Carter	No. 1.	E. H. Groves	No. 2.
Thomas Grover	" 3.	Calvin Bebee	" 4.
Levi Jackman	" 5.	Solomon Hancock	" 6.
George Morey	" 7.	Newel Knight	" 8.
G. M. Hinckle	" 9.	Lyman Wight	" 10.
Elias Higbee	" 11.	John Murdock	" 12.

Opened by David Whitmer as usual and gave the counsellors charge in an appropriate manner, also all the authorities.

Voted unanimously by the High Council, that Thomas

Grover be a High Counsellor in the place of Jesse Hitchcock—and George Morey in the place of Peter Whitmer jr. deceased.[2]

Voted unanimously that Titus Billings be a Bishop's counsellor instead of John Corrill.[3]

Voted unanimously by the authorities present & the audience—that in the absence of the presidents, Counsillors, Bishop and Counsillors,[4] were at Kirtland the Elders had no authority consequently their acts in that space of time are considered null and void.

Resolved unanimously that every President of High Priests and Elders be ordained by some higher authority, and he the president of any quorum when Counsellors are needed may ordain his Counsellors himself and the Bishop shall take charge of the Lesser Priesthood.

The Presidents appointed the 15th inst. for the High Priests and Elders to meet and choose their respective Presidents.

Council adjourned until 10 O'clock next Saturday.

Council dismissed as usual by D. Whitmer.

(Signed) John Corrill, Clerk.

---

[1]See *History of the Church* 2:504.

[2]Here a precedent is established for having new high councilors approved by the high council. They also approved other officers, such as bishop's counselors.

[3]Corrill had been appointed "Keeper of the Lord's storehouse" on May 22, 1837.

[4]That is, the absence of the Missouri Church leaders who were in Kirtland for the temple dedication. This point has been confused in the *History of the Church* (See *History of the Church* 2:504. See also the Book of John Whitmer, chapter 16, concerning the problems in Missouri during the long absence of the leadership there.)

August 5, 1837

At a meeting of the authorities of the Church at the School house of Far West, August 5. 1837.[1]

David Whitmer John Whitmer & W. W. Phelps, Presidents, and High Counsellors as follows:

Simeon Carter	No. 1	E. H. Groves	No. 2
Thomas Grover	" 3	Calvin Bebee	" 4
Isaac Higbee	" 5	Solomon Hancock	" 6
George Morey	" 7	Samuel Bent	" 8
G. M. Hinkle	" 9	Lyman Wight	" 10
Elias Higbee	" 11	John Murdock	" 12

Edward Partridge, Bishop, Isaac Morley and Titus Billings his Counsellors.

Meeting by D. Whitmer as usual,[2] and also gave an appropriate charge. Also a multitude of Highpriests Elders &c. were present.

Voted unanimously by the authorities present, that we go on moderately and build a house unto the name of the Lord in this place. (Far West), as we have means.

Voted that Edward Partridge be treasurer to receive all the donations and subscriptions for the erection of the house of the Lord.

Voted that Isaac Morley be appointed Secretary for E. Partridge in his business of treasury.

Voted that the Committee stand, viz: Jacob Whitmer E. H. Groves & G. M. Hinkle, until President David Whitmer goes to and returns from Kirtland.

Voted that the building Committee of the house of the Lord have no store connected with the building the house. But that every firm or individual that embarks in that business—have, own and claim such property as their own private individual property and stewardship.

---

[1]See *History of the Church* 2:505.
[2]Prayer by David Whitmer.

August 20, 1837

This certifies that Charles C. Rich was duly elected a president of the Highpriesthood in Zion[1] and was ordained to that office under the hand of John Whitmer and William W. Phelps presidents. Also Harvey Green to the presidency of Elders in Caldwell Co. Mo. at the same time.

August, 20. 1837[2] John Whitmer, Recorder.

---

[1]That is, the high priests quorum in Missouri. The *History of the Church* incorrectly notes that this occurred on August 15.

[2]The Far West Record was used to record priesthood ordinations.

November 6, 1837

Far West Mo. Nov. 6. 1837.[1]

A number of members of the Church of the Latter Day Saints met to take into consideration some of the affairs of said Church; consisting of the Presidency of the Church here,[2] and President J. Smith jr. Sidney Rigdon & Hyrum Smith. With Elders T. B. Marsh, Wm. E. Mclellin, L. E. Johnson, Wm. Smith & Vinson Knight (from Ohio.) The High Counsellors of the Church here, and some other Elders.

Opened by prayer by W. W. Phelps—

Several topics were discussed, when it was unanimously voted, that it be reccommended to the proprietors of the Corporation of Far West, to petition the Trustees of said Corporation, to alter the streets or lessen them so as to make each block contain four acres of ground and each block be divided into four lots.[3]

Secondly: Voted unanimously, that it is the opinion of the Council, that there is sufficient room in this country, for the Churches[4] to continue gathering from abroad.

Third Voted unanimously, that the building of the house of the Lord in this place be postponed till the Lord shall reveal it to be his will to be commenced.[5]

On motion of S. Rigdon the meeting was adjourned until early candlelight.

Council met according to adjournment.

Remarks by John Corrill, Isaac Morley, W. W. Phelps and John Whitmer, and Edward Partridge, Thomas Grover, John Murdock, Wm. Smith, T. B. Marsh, Hyrum Smith, Joseph Smith jr., Sidney Rigdon, upon the previous disposition of the Town Plot and the purchase of land &c. &c.

All difficulties were satisfactorily settled except a matter between J. Smith jr. Oliver Cowdery and T. B. Marsh which was referred to themselves with the agreement that their settlement of the affair should be sufficient for the Council.[6]

W. W. Phelps
President.

Attest.
Oliver Cowdery, Clerk.

---

[1]See *History of the Church* 2:521. Joseph Smith and Sidney Rigdon had been appointed by a conference in Kirtland to go to Missouri and establish stakes and other places of gathering. It was later established by a revelation given January 12, 1838, that only the First Presidency could organize a stake. (See Kirtland Revelation Book. See also *History of the Church* 2:514.)

[2]The presidency of the Church in Missouri.

[3]The public square in the city of Far West contained ten acres. The four main streets were each eight rods wide, the other streets were six rods wide, and each block contained four acres and was designed for four buildings. (See letter of Albert P. Rockwood to his sister, October 6, 1838, Church Archives.)

[4]"Churches" means "branches."

[5]See Doctrine and Covenants 115.

[6]See pages 167-68 for an explanation of this difficulty.

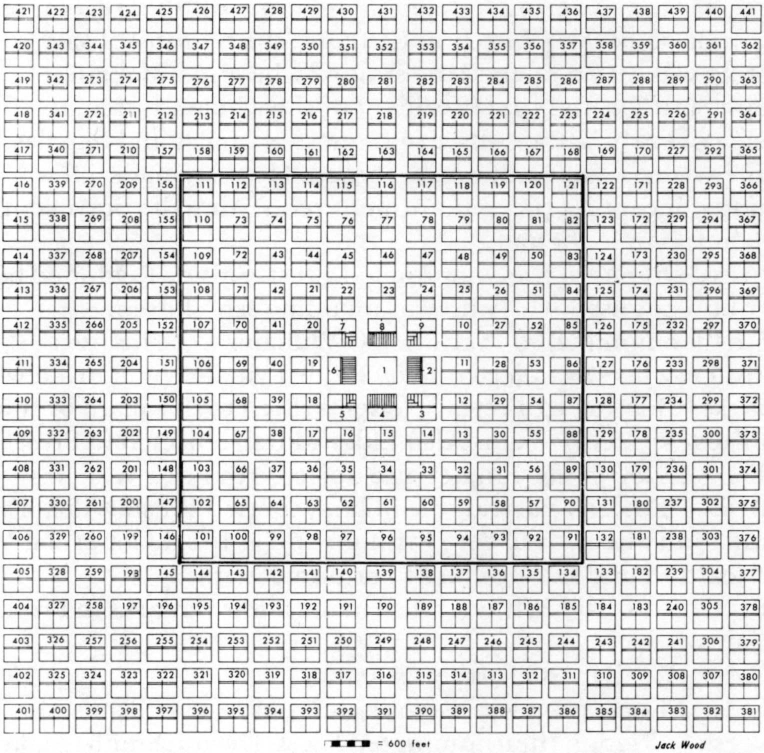

Joseph Smith's proposed two-mile-square revision of the Far West plat, November 1837. W. W. Phelps and John Whitmer's plat of April 1837 (inside the dark line) was one mile square with eight lots per block.

November 7, 1837

Far West. Mo. Tuesday Nov 7 1837[1]

At a general assembly of the Church of Latter Day Saints, assembled at Far West, to take into consideration and transact the business of said Church,

Elder Thomas B. Marsh was chosen Moderator and Oliver Cowdery Clerk.

After singing, the Moderator addressed the Throne of Grace in prayer, after which Prest. Sidney Rigdon explained the object of the meeting, giving a relation of the recent re-organization of the Church in Kirtland; the minutes of said meeting were read by the Moderator,[2] who also nominated Joseph Smith jr. the first President of the whole Church, to preside over the same. All were requested (males and females,) to vote—who was unanimously chosen. He then made a few remarks, accepting the appointment requesting the prayers of the Church in his behalf.

President Smith then nominated Prest. Sidney Rigdon to be one of his counsellors—who was unanimously chosen.

He then nominated Frederick G Williams to be his next counsillor who was objected to by Elder Lyman Wight in a few remarks referring to a certain letter written to this place by the said Frederick G Williams Also Elder Marsh objected to Prest Williams Elder James Emmet also objected to Prest Williams[3]

Bishop Edward Partridge said he seconded Prest. William's nomination and should vote for him; and as to said letter, he had heard it, and saw nothing so criminal in it.

President David Whitmer also made a few remarks in Prest. Williams' favor.

Elder Marsh made further remarks.

Elder Thomas Grover also objected to Prest. Williams.

Prest. S. Rigdon then nominated Prest. Hyrum Smith to take Prest. Williams' place. He then called for a vote in favor of Prest. Williams' who was rejected.[4] He then called for a vote in favor of Prest Hyrum Smith, which was carried unanimously.

Some few remarks were made by Prests. David Whitmer and S. Rigdon.

David Whitmer was then nominated as the first President of this branch of the Church, and was objected to by Elder Marsh. Bishop Partridge said he should vote for prst. Whitmer—also Elder King Follet.

Elder Caleb Baldwin spake against pres't. Whitmer: also Elder Seymour Brunson.

Elder Elisha H. Groves spake in favor of Pres't. Whitmer. Further remarks from Elder Mc.lellin, by request of Pres't.

Whitmer, who made satisfaction for him. Remarks from Pres't. Joseph Smith jr. who called for an expression, which was carried by almost a unanimous vote.[5]

Pres't. Joseph Smith jr. then nominated John Whitmer for an assistant President, who was objected, and Elder Marsh spake in opposition to him, and read a list of charges from a written document against him, and Pres't. Phelps. Pres't. John Whitmer then spake a few words by way of confession, and was followed by Elder Isaac Morley.

The vote was called and carried unanimously.

The meeting adjourned for one hour.

Meeting convened according to adjournment, a hymn was sung and a prayer offered up by the Moderator. Wm W. Phelps was nominated for an assistant President, for this Church, by Pres't Joseph Smith jr. He rose and made certain remarks on the subject of the charges referred to above, by way of confession also, when the vote was put by Pres't. S. Rigdon, and passed unanimous.

Elder John Murdock, Solomon Hancock, Elias Higbee, Calvin Bebee, George Morey, Thomas Grover, and Simeon Carter, were unanimously chosen High Counsellors, and Lyman Wight was objected by John Anderson, who went aside to converse. Newel Knight was unanimously chosen. George M. Hinkle was nominated and was objected by Elder James Emmet because he was to noisy[6]—By King Follet because of his military office, and by James Durfee because he was a merchant—Elder H.[7] made a few remarks, the vote was called and was unanimous. Levi Jackman and Elisha H. Groves were unanimously chosen. John Anderson then took the stand and made his objections to Lyman Wight, after which Elder Wight also spake the vote was called and he unanimously chosen.

The twelve were then called, viz: Thomas B. Marsh, David W Patten, Brigham Young, Heber C. Kimball, Orson Hyde, William E. Mc.Lellin, Parley P. Pratt, William Smith, Luke Johnson, Orson Pratt, John F. Boynton and Lyman E. Johnson, and were unanimously chosen.[8]

Bishop Edward Partridge was then nominated to still act as Bishop, and was unanimously chosen. Who then nominated Isaac Morley and Titus Billings for his Counsellors who were unanimously chosen.

Elder Isaac Morley was then unanimously appointed Patriarch of this Branch of the Church.[9]

Elder John Corrill was chosen to be Keeper of the Lord's Storehouse.

Elder Isaac Morley was then ordained to the office of Patriarch under the hands of Pres'ts. Joseph Smith, jr. Sidney Rigdon and Hyrum Smith.

The congregation then after a few remarks from Pres't. Rigdon, unanimously voted not to support Stores and Shops selling spirituous liquors, Tea, Coffee or Tobacco.

A vote was called on the subject of the Presidents of the Seventies—and those who have been recently appointed to that office, were unanimously received.

The Congregation then united with Pres't. Rigdon who, in the closing prayer, called upon the Lord to dedicate this land for the gathering of the Saints, and their inheritances.

Attest. Thomas B. Marsh, Moderator.
Oliver Cowdery Clerk

---

[1]See *History of the Church* 2:522. These minutes were first published in the *Elders Journal* 1(November 1837):29-30.

[2]Minutes referred to are in *History of the Church* 2:509-11.

[3]The sustaining procedure, which included nominations and statements of objection and support, is indicative of a democratic process.

[4]Frederick G. Williams had imbibed feelings of dissension over the Kirtland Bank prior to his coming to Missouri. Minutes in the Kirtland Council Minute Book affirm that Williams was *unanimously* sustained in his position in Kirtland on September 3, 1837, but Church leaders in Missouri held him more accountable for his actions.

[5]Here is further evidence of the democratic process in the majority rather than unanimous vote for David Whitmer. In Nauvoo Joseph Smith "declared the rule of voting to be a majority in each quorum." (See *Times and Seasons* 1[April 15, 1841]:387.)

[6]Apparently not all objections were over serious matters.
[7]Hinkle.
[8]Whereas John F. Boynton and the Johnson brothers were rejected by the conference in Kirtland, here they were unanimously sustained. See *History of the Church* 2:509.
[9]As Patriarch, Morley continued to serve as counselor to Bishop Partridge.

November 10, 1837

Far West, Tuesday, Nov. 10. 1837.[1]

At a general meeting of the ordained members of the Church of Latter Day Saints in this place, Elder Thomas B. Marsh opened the meeting by prayer, and Pres't. S. Rigdon read the memorial of the Bishop of Kirtland, and his counsellors, to the Churches abroad of Sept. 18th 1837.[2] He then laid before the meeting the subject of laying off cities, of consecrating for public purposes, and for remunerating those who appoint and lay them off, &c. When it was unanimously voted that all city plotts hereafter laid off, after remunerating those for their labors, who may be engaged in appointing and laying off the same, shall be consecrated for the public benefit of the church—for building houses for public worship, or such other purposes as the Church shall say.[3]

President Rigdon then read the prospectus of the "Elder's Journal"—which was unanimously received.[4] It was then also unanimously voted that the persons present use their exertions to support said paper.

It was then voted that the town of Far West be enlarged so that it contain four sections—that is, two miles square.[5]

Voted, that Bishop Edward Partridge and his counsellors be appointed a committee to appraise the land adjacent to the present Town Plott, see that it is enlarged according to the above vote, provided the present holders of the lands will take such price for the same, as the above appraisers shall think worth, and that the same be then disposed of as is voted above.

A call was then made for those whose circumstances were

such as to permit, to go out to preach, to present themselves. There were twenty-three who arose.

Sylvester H. Earl, Henry Jackson, Harrison Sagers and John W. Clark, were ordained Elders, and William J. Lemans was ordained a Priest.

President Rigdon then closed the meeting by prayer.[6]

Oliver Cowdery Clerk.

---

[1]See *History of the Church* 2:524. These minutes were first published in the *Elders Journal* 1(November 1837):30-31.

[2]This memorial, signed by Newel K. Whitney, Reynolds Cahoon, and Vinson Knight, is found in *History of the Church* 2:515-18.

[3]Doctrine and Covenants 42.

[4]The "prospectus" is located in the *Elders Journal* 1(July 1838):34.

[5]The city was initially laid out on a one-mile square.

[6]The minutes of the conferences of November 7 and 10, 1837, were read and approved by a conference of the Church in Kirtland. In effect, they approved the expansion of Far West. (See letter to Thomas B. Marsh, January 10, 1838, author unknown, Thomas B. Marsh Papers, Church Archives.)

December 6, 1837

Far West, Wednesday, Dec. 6, 1837.[1]

The High Council and Bishop and Council met for the purpose of transacting the business of the Church. The Council was organized and opened by prayer of Pres't. David Whitmer.

Several subjects were discussed by the Council when Elias Higbee, Simeon Carter, and Elisha H. Groves were nominated a committee to take into consideration ~~a certain price for services for the Church~~, the propriety of proposing to the Church to pay the Council a certain price for services for the Church when met for that purpose. Elder Marsh made a few remarks on an other Subject and was followed by Pres't. D Whitmer. The above three were appointed said Committee.

~~Bish~~ Bishop Partridge, John Corrill and Isaac Morley were appointed a committee to take into consideration and report upon the subject of raising a revinue to defray the expenses of the Church

David Whitmer was nominated and appointed to Sign Lisences of Elders, as, Chairman, and William W Phelps as Clerk And Frederick G Williams to sign Lisences as Chairman pro Tempore, in the absence of Pres't. D. Whitmer and John Whitmer, as Clerk pro Tempore, in the absence of Pres't Phelps and Oliver Cowdery as Recording Clerk

Oliver Cowdery was then appointed standing Clerk for the Counsil

Council adjourned for two hours

Council met pursuant to adjournment

Philo Dibble requested a hearing in a certain case wherein he had been disfellowshiped before a council of Elders: Charles Hewlet being complainant—dismissed from the council by recommending to the parties to choose two brethren to assist in settling the difficulty. Without troubling the Council.[2] Oliver Cowdery was then nominated and appointed recorder to record the Patriarchal blessing of this branch of the church. The following report was then presented and read by the clerk three times and was accepted—We the undersigned committee chosen by the high council of Zion on this 6th day of December A. D. 1837 to take into consideration the expediency of remunerating the Presidency and high council and also the bishop and his council for their services when employed in doing the business of the church of Latter day-saints having met agreeably to appointment and after taking the aforesaid business into consideration it is out united opinion that the aforesaid officers togegher with the clerk of the council[3] the Patriarch[4] and also the agent of the Church[5] (as also any other person who may be employed in the same or the like business) receive per day each one dollar and fifty cents.[6]

Elias Higby
Simeon Carter
Elisha H. Groves

Bishop E. Partridge then presented the following petition—

To the high council in the land of Zion: Wheras the undersigned has paid six hundred dollars to Lawyers to carry on suits with the Jackson County mob And has also paid three hundred dollars costs in carrying on said suits; For which he has never received any remuneration; In paying the above he has involved himself: having had to borrow it for which, in part, at least, he is now paying ten percent interest, Having a large family to support and no means whereby he can at present extricate himself from these debts He therefore asks the high council whether they are willing that he should pay the said $900. and the interest that has accumulated thereon, out of the property consecrated for the benefit of the church. And charge the Church for the same.

Farwest Dec 6th 1837 E. Partridge

Unanimously voted that said petition be received and and our Bishop Partridge be directed to use the properties of the church for said purposes as requested in said petition.[7]—

Unanimously voted that ~~the~~ the recorder of Licenses and Patriarchal blessings receive for each hundred records $10. for his services.

Council adjourned till tomorrow at 9 O'clock A.M.

Prayer by Prest Phelps.

---

[1]See *History of the Church* 2:527.

[2]The teachers quorum in Far West, Missouri, passed a similar resolution on April 28, 1838: "1st motioned and carryd that we will not hold any member in our quorum in fellowship who will not settle his own difficulties in the Church & show himself approved in all things." (See Teachers' Quorum Minutes, Church Archives.)

[3]Oliver Cowdery.

[4]Isaac Morley.

[5]John Corrill.

[6]See Doctrine and Covenants 42.

[7]It is not known which properties were used to pay these debts. After the expulsion of the Mormons from Missouri, Partridge conveyed 1,080 acres of land to Doniphan and Reese in payment for attorneys' fees. (See Jackson County, Missouri, Land Records, Book F, pages 292, 314, 326.)

December 7, 1837

Thirsday Dec 7th 1837[1]

Council met pursuant to adjournment and was opened by prayer by Prest John Whitmer. Yesterdays proceedings were read by the Clerk.

The committee on Church revinue made the following report which was read by their chairman Bishop E. Partridge and once by the clerk and was then engrossed for a third reading.

Far West Dec. 7th 1837

We the undersigned a committee appointed yesterday by a general council in the Land of Zion for the purpose of adopting a plan wherby the church of Latter Day Saints may voluntarily raise means by tithing[2] themselves to be a fund ready at all times to assist the poor with. and also to compensate the Servents of the Lord for their services in attending to the business of the church. and for other necessary purposes. Having investigated the subject as fully as the time would permit, make the following report.

First. We believe that a voluntary freewill offering from year to year will not only be pleasing in the sight of the Lord but will be in some degree fullfilling the law of consecration.

Secondly. We believe that a per centage on what a man is worth, is a more equal mode of raising funds than the tithing of what a man raises or his income from year to year.

Thirdly. We believe that widows generally and all other families not worth over seventy five dollars each, should not be required to tithe themselves and yet retain an honorable standing in the church[3]

Resolved first, That it is expedient that every man renders an inventory to the Bishop Edward Partridge or his successor in office yearly of what he is worth after deducting his honest debts.

Resolved secondly. That about the commencement of every year the high council together with the Bishop and his Council shall agree upon, and make known to the church the amount of per centage necessary to be raised the following year. And that the same shall be paid over in the course of the following year to the agent of the church John Corrill or his successor in office subject to the order of Bishop Edward Partridge or his successor in office.

Resolved third: That every man in paying the amount of his donation should either deed the same by gift or sign the amount ~~by~~ upon a subscription paper like or similar to the one presented with his report.

This year being nearly spent we have thought that if five mills could be raised upon the dollar which every man is worth it would be sufficient to try the experiment: Therefore we recommend that the Elders holding meetings about among the saints in this region of country read this report to the Churches and instruct them about the necessity of forthwith makeing an estimate of what they are worth and of paying the above named percentage as soon as they conveniently can and let the same be paid in any valuable commodity: We have estimated that two cents upon the dollar for what every man shall be worth when he renders his inventory to the Bishop will raise a sum sufficient for the A. D. 1838. We recommend that the Elders also circulate copies of the subscription paper accompanying this report so that all who are willing to thithe themselves may have an opportunity of manifesting their generosity.

We are of the opinion that if any are not willing to comply with the mode above pointed untill a better one is suggested of raising the means to meet the necessary expenses of the church: they must to say the least of them be considered weak in the faith and also under the influence of covetousness to that degree that their case must be considered hopeless unless they repent: for the scripture informs us that a covetous man who is an idolator hath [not] any part in the kingdom of God.

To close we are of the opinion that this report and subscription paper should not be circulated to obtain funds beyond the bounds of what is attached to this stake of Zion. neither should the funds raised be expended out of the bounds of the same

Isaac Morley
Edward Partridge
John Corril

The Subscription paper

We the undersigned subscribers feeling a deep interest in the prosperity of the Church of Latterday Saints and believing that the prosperity of the Church in some degree depends upon our providing a fund for the purpose of defraying the expenses of the church: In assisting the poor, in remunerating the officers of the church for the time which they are necessarily employed in doing the business of the same: in building houses of publick worship and all such other expenses as shall be deemed necessary by the authorities of the church for the good of the same, And believing that voluntary tithing is better than Forced taxes;[4] We therefore each of us agree to pay ~~to~~ into the hand of the agent of the church John Corril or his successor in office. Subject to the order of Edward Partridge the Bishop or his successor in office: to be expended for any or all of the above named purposes: two cents on the dollar or one fiftieth of what we are worth after deducting what we owe. We further agree that we will furnish the Bishop with ~~furnish~~ a scedule or inventory of our property at or before the time we pay to the agent of the church the above named percentage which we agree shall be done in the course of the year eighteen hundred and thirty eight.

Far West Dec 1837.

The first and second items were read and passed But an amendment was offered to the third by elder Marsh and others which was withdrawn. The Item then passed.

Much discussion was had and the Item of church revinue dismissed till one week from Saturday next and Prest's D.

Whitmer, J. Whitmer, W. W. Phelps and O. Cowdery were added to that committee and were ordered to make a further report ~~on~~ (if time would allow) on said day.[5]

Council adjourned till candle light.

Council met pursuant to adjournment. O. Cowdery and D. W. Patten of the committee sent to explore the north country made a verbal report.[6] Their labours so far as performed were accepted by the council and the subject further laid over till the bills of surveys could be had. F. G. Williams was also aded to said committee now consists of O. Cowdery, D. W. Patten, Lyman Wight and F. G. Williams.

It was the unanimous voice of the council that George Grant be allowed a location for his aged father[7] near the one allotted to himself in consideration of past services rendered the expedition in staying behind to bring in the camp utensils with the teams.

Edward Partridge Isaac Morley and John Corril were appointed a committee to take into consideration the services of the committee previously appointed to obtain subscriptions and build a house for publick worship and to report thereon.

On Motion council adjourned till Saturday. The 16th instant.

Pray by the Clerk.

Oliver Cowdery clerk.

---

[1]*History of the Church* 2:528.

[2]Note the desire to implement a voluntary program of raising revenue for the Church. A revelation concerning tithing was given the following year, July 1838 (Doctrine and Covenants 119).

[3]Note that some would have been exempt from paying tithing.

[4]While member donations were imperative for the operation and function of the Church, the concept of tithing during this period did not include an absolute 10 percent contribution of one's increase.

[5]The voluntary tithing initiative, which was never implemented, is not discussed again in the Far West Record, but may have served as a prelude to the revelation on tithing. (See Doctrine and Covenants 119.)

[6]Oliver Cowdery describes some of the activities of the exploration party in northern Missouri in a letter to Joseph Smith, January 21, 1838, Church Archives.

[7]Joshua Grant, also the father of Jedediah M. Grant.

December 23, 1837

The following is recorded by Hosea Stout[1] Clerk for the High Council of Nauvoo Illinois Dec. 23rd 1837. The High Council met according to adjournment.

Councillors Present.

Simeon Carter	No 1	E. H. Groves	No 2
Dr. McCord[2]	3.	Thos. Grover	4
L. Jackman	5	Benjamin Benson	6
G. Morey	7.	M. C. Allred	8
G. M. Hinkle	9.	John Patten	10
E. Higbee	11.	John Murdock	12

Buisness concerning the committee to build the house of the Lord

Elisha H. Groves presented his bill as follows

To the Presidents and High Council of Zion I have served as one of the committee to build a house to the name of the Lord in the City Far West nine months and have spent one hundred dollars in traveling—sixteen dollars in boarding hands at work in the stone quarry which money I owe and being destitute of means to support my family I ask of them whether they will grant to me orders on the Bishop for the money and one dollar and fifty cents per day for my services. Elisha H Groves

G. M. Hinkle presented his[3] verbally.

Jacob Whitmer presented his as folows—

To the Presidency & High Council of Zion

Will the High Council allow me for my time & expense for serving as a committee for the purpose of building a house to the Lord.

I calculate the time one hundred and twenty days for which I think I ought to have one dollar per day for time and expense.

Dec 23rd 1837— Jacob Whitmer.

Two were selected on each side to speak after which G. M. Hinkle spoke.

Decided that the brethren Elisha H. Groves G. M. Hinkle and Jacob Whitmer be allowed one dollar per day and be found while journeying and while at home and in the employment of the committee buisness one dollar per day and find themselves. This to be laid before the Bishop and his Counsellors Adjourned

John Whitmer Clerk W. W. Phelps Chm.

---

[1]The minutes contained in the Far West Record up to this point were copied into the record book from existing original minutes by Ebenezer Robinson, the clerk of the high council of Far West, Missouri. Robinson, who moved with the Church to Illinois in 1839, did his work of copying sometime between April 6, 1838, and October 1, 1842. On October 1, 1842, the Nauvoo high council appointed Hosea Stout, the clerk of the high council, to assist Robinson in completing his assignment, which was to finish copying all minutes of existing high council meetings in Far West, Missouri. Whereas he was only to assist Robinson, evidence shows that Hosea Stout was in fact the recorder or copier of the remaining minutes contained in the Far West Record. (See "Nauvoo High Council Minutes," October 1, 1842, Church Archives.)

[2]Not James McCord who appears on page 186. Dr. McCord was excommunicated on May 11, 1838. (See *History of the Church* 3:31.)

[3]His bill of expenditures.

1838

January 20, 1838

January 20th 1838 Far West

At a social meeting held at the house of Thos B. Marsh. Two of the apostles T. B. Marsh and David W. Patten also High Councellors John Murdock, Simeon Carter Elias Higbee G M. Hinkle Thos Grover Levi Jackman and George Morey were present.

We took into consideration the proceeding of the Presidents in this place viz David Whitmer W. W. Phelps John Whitmer and Oliver Cowdery and we being grieved at their doings after ~~varie~~ various discussions appointed a committee to visit them and enquire into their feelings and determinations viz G. M. Hinkle Thos Grover and George Morey

Resolved that Thomas B. Marsh and John Corril draft a petition, to hand in at the next term of court, for the alteration and regulation of the Town Plot of Far-West. Adjourned meeting till the 26th inst. at 10 o'clock A. M.

January 26, 1838

Far West, January 26, 1838——

Agreeable to adjournment the above named Apostles and High Councilors and Lyman Wight in Company with Samuel Bent, High Priest, and some others met at the house of Br. John Anderson.[1]

John Murdock being the most aged in Council presided and Samuel Bent was chosen clerk of the meeting. The meeting being organized proceeded to buisness and heard the report of the Committee as follows viz. Respecting their selling their lands in Jackson County, they, the Presidents, declared they had not broken revelation ~~or law~~ or Law of God in so doing and further if they were deprived of that privilege they would sell their possessions in Far-West and move out of the place and W. W. Phelps said he would move out of the accursed place and further they declared they would not be controlled by an ecclesiastical power or revelation whatever in their temporal concerns. And respecting the word of wisdom, W. W. Phelps said he had not broken it but had kept it. O Cowdery said he had drank tea three times a day this winter on account of his ill health. David and John Whitmer said they did use tea and coffee but they did not consider them to come under the head of hot drinks.[2]

The Council Resolved as follows:

1st That under existing circumstances we no longer recieve them as Presidents.

2nd That the case be laid before the Church at different meetings held for that purpose by seven of the High Councellors viz. John Murdock, Simeon Carter, Elias Higbee, Levi Jackman, G. M. Hinkle, George Morey, and Lyman Wight but as it was inconsistent for Elias Higbee and Levi Jackman to leave home it was afterward voted that Thomas B. Marsh should take the place of E. Higbee and Thos. Grover that of L. Jackman.[3]

3rd That Elias Higbee and G. M. Hinkle write to the several neighbourhoods and give notice of the times and places of holding meetings.

4th That Thomas B. Marsh give written notice to David Whitmer and W. W. Phelps and John Whitmer of the proceedings of the meeting.

Council Adjourned till February 3rd next

Samuel Bent, Clerk John Murdock, Moderator

---

[1]Here, the high council, this time in the company of two Apostles, met to bring charges against the Missouri presidency. (See pages 107-8.)

[2]David and John Whitmer said tea and coffee were not hot drinks and, therefore, using them was not in violation of the Word of Wisdom. The Saints were still defining the Word of Wisdom. Hyrum Smith's statement on tea and coffee was made in Nauvoo. (See *Times and Seasons* 3[June 1842]:800.)

[3]The council did not wish to accept full responsibility for action against the presidents, and, therefore, called for a vote of the Church membership on this matter, in a general assembly and in meetings with each branch.

February 5-9, 1838

The following are the minutes of the proceedings of a general assembly of the Church of Jesus Christ of Latter Day Saints,[1] assembled at the following places, to transact the buisness of said Church

1st. At Far-West. Feb. 5th, 1838:[2] Thomas B Marsh was chosen Moderator, and John Cleminson Clerk.

The Moderator addressed the throne of grace in prayer, after which he laid before the assembly the object of the meeting, giving a relation of the recent organization of the Church here, and in Kirtland. He also read a certain revelation given in Kirtland, Sept 4th, 1837;[3] which made known that John Whitmer and William W. Phelps were in transgression, and if they repented not, they should be removed out of their places. Also, read a certain clause contained in the appeal,[4] published in the old Star, under the 183rd page, as follows:—"And to sell our lands would amount to a denial of our faith, as that is the place where the Zion of God shall stand according to our faith and belief in the revelations of God."[5]

Elder John Murdock then took the stand, and showed to the congregation why the High Council proceeded thus, was, that the Church might have a voice in the matter; and that he considered it perfectly legal, according to the instructions of President Joseph Smith jr.

Elder G. M. Hinkle then set forth the way in which the Presidency of Far West had been labored with, that a committee of three, of whom he was one, had labored with them. He then read a written document containing a number of accusations against the three Presidents. He spake many things against them, setting forth in a plain and energetic manner, the iniquity of Phelps & Whitmer, in using the moneys which were loaned for the Church. Also D. Whitmer's wrong, in persisting in the use of tea, coffee, and tobacco.

Bishop Partridge then arose, and endeavored to rectify some mistakes of minor importance made by Elder Hinkle. Also, the Bishop spake against the proceedings of the meeting, as being hasty and illegal, for he thought they ought to be had before the common council:[6] and said, that he could not lift his hand against the presidency at present: he then read a letter from President Joseph Smith jr.[7]

A letter was then read by T. B. Marsh from William Smith, who made some comments on the same, and also on the letter read by E. Partridge.

Elder G. Morey, who was one of the committee sent to labor with the Presidency, then spake, setting forth in a very energetic manner, the proceedings of the Presidency as being iniqutous.

Elder Grover also, being one of the committee, spake against the conduct of the Presidency and O. Cowdery, on their visit to labor with them.

Elder David W. Patten, then spake with much zeal against this Presidency, and in favor of Br. Joseph Smith jr and that the wolf alluded to in his letter, was the dissenters in Kirtland.[8]

Elder Lyman Wight next stated that he considered that all other accusations were of minor importance compared to their selling their lands in Jackson County, that they (Phelps & Whitmer) had set an example which all the members were liable to follow: he said that it was a hellish principle, and that they had flatly denied the faith in so doing. Elder Elias Higbee then sanctioned what had been done by the council speaking against the Presidency.

Elder Murdock again took the stand, and stated that sufficient had been said to substantiate the accusations against them

Elder Solomon Hancock plead in favor of the Presidency, stating that he could not rais his hand against them.

Elder John Corrill then spake against the High Council in regard to their proceedings, and labored hard to show that the meeting was illegal, and that the Presidency ought to be had before a proper tribunal, which he considered to be a Bishop and twelve High Priests: he labored in favor of the Presidency, and said that he should not raise his hands against them at present, although he did not uphold them in their iniquity

Elder Simeon Carter, next arose and spake against the meeting as being hasty.

Elder Groves followed brother Carter, in like observations and of like nature.

Elder Patten again took the stand in vindication of the cause of the ~~cause~~ meeting.

Elder Morley then spake against the Presidency, at the same time pleading mercy.

Titus Billings said that he could not vote untill they had a hearing in the common council.

Elder Marsh said that the meeting was according to the directions of Br Joseph. he, therefore, considered it legal

Elder Moses Martin then took the stand & with great energy spake in favor of the legality of the meeting and against the conduct of the Presidency of Zion, alleging that the present corruptions of the church here, were owing to the wickedness and mismanagement of her leaders.

The Moderator then called the vote in favor of the present Presidency. The negative was then called, and the vote against David Whitmer, John Whitmer, and William W. Phelps was unanimous, excepting eight or ten and this minority only wished them to continue in office a little longer, or untill Joseph Smith jr came up.[9]

In S. Carter's[10] settlement, the Saints assembled ~~agreement~~ agreeable to appointment, on the 6th inst[11] When they unanimously rejected the three above named Presidents.

Also, on the 7th inst the Saints assembled at Edmund Durfee's agreeable to appointment, where the above named Presidents were unanimously rejected.

Also, on the 8th, at Nahum Curtis' dwelling house, they were unanimously rejected by the assembly.

Also, at Hauns' Mill, on the 9th the Saints unanimously rejected them.

---

[1]The name of the Church in its complete form indicates that these minutes were recorded in the Far West Record after April 1838, when the official name was given by revelation.

[2]See *History of the Church* 3:3.

[3]This revelation is found in *History of the Church* 2:511. The date in *History of the Church* is September 3, 1837, not September 4, 1837.

[4]See *History of the Church* 2:127 for an additional reference to this appeal.

[5]In reference to this meeting and the selling of their lands in Jackson County, Oliver Cowdery has written: "Messrs W. W. Phelps J. Whitmer and myself had a partial claim to a few lots in Independence, Mo. [which] we sold some time since on some of the Jackson suits costs. We quit claimed our interest in and to the same for a small sum (and glad to get that) which has caused considerable stir. Not long since, Messers D and J Whitmer, W. W. Phelps and myself were waited upon by (as they said) a committee of the High Council who said the church were dissatisfied with our conduct, &c. in selling those lots and not keeping the word of wisdom, and also in not teaching the church to fulfil the consecration law. I told them that if I had property, while I lived and was sane, I would not be dictated, influenced or controlled by any man or set of men by no tribunal of ecclesiastical pretences what ever . . . .

"The . . . council met again and resolved not to have those men (the 3) [David Whitmer, W. W. Phelps and John Whitmer] to be their Presidents, and to call on the church to know if they would consent in the same. They [the High Council] say they have no legal accusation against them, but don't want them to preside over the church any longer. Tomorrow [February 5, 1838] is appointed for the first meeting of the church: the brethren [Whitmers and Phelps] <u>wont go</u>. They will not <u>bend</u> to the principle enough to go and answer to a tribunal which is no tribunal. . . . The council have concluded they have nothing to do with me." (See Oliver Cowdery to Warren Cowdery, February 4, 1838, Cowdery Letters, Henry E. Huntington Library and Art Gallery, San Marino, California; microfilm at Church Archives.)

[6]Note that the bishops (Partridge, Corrill, and Billings) believed that only a common council could try the presidents in Missouri (see Doctrine and Covenants 107:82). The opinion of the high council in Missouri, however, was that it had the authority to try the presidents. This discussion underscores the confusion in the minds of Church leaders regarding the true role of the Missouri presidency.

[7]The letter from Joseph Smith to Bishop Partridge was dated, Kirtland, January 7, 1838.

[8]The Prophet's January 7, 1838, letter to Partridge mentioned the "wolf": "Brother Partridge, Thus saith the Lord, my servant Edward and his house shall be numbered with the blessed and Abraham their father, and his name shall be had in sacred rem[em]brance. And again thus saith the Lord, let my people be aware of dissensions among them lest the enemy have power over them, Awake my shepherds and warn my people! for behold the wolf cometh to destroy them! receive him not. Now I would inform you that my health is good and also that of my family, and it is my earnest prayer to God that health, peace, and pleanty may crown your board and blessings of Heaven rest upon the head of him in whom the Lord hath said there is no guile." (Edward Partridge, Jr., Family Record, page 52, Church Archives.)

[9]Note again the uncertainty of Church leaders on this issue.

[10]Simeon Carter.

[11]February 1838.

February 10, 1838

At a meeting of the High Council, the Bishop & his Council. February 10, 1838, it was moved, seconded & carried, that Oliver Cowdery, William W. Phelps and John Whitmer stand no longer as Chairman & Clerk, to sign and record liceces [licenses].

Also, voted that Thomas B. Marsh, and David W. Patten be Presidents, pro. tempor. of the Church of Latter Day Saints in Missouri, or until Presidents Joseph Smith jr and Sidney Rigdon arrives in the Land of Zion

Also, voted that Thomas B Marsh and David W. Patten be authorized to attend to the afforsaid buisness of Recording and signing licence for the time being.

T. B. Marsh, Clerk. John Murdock, Moderator.

February 24, 1838

At a meeting of the High Council & Bishoprick convened at the new school house in Far West Feb 24th 1838

Present Thos. B. Marsh, President.

Calvin Beebee, Thomas Grover, Isaac Higbee, William Snow, Jefferson Hunt, and John Murdock, on the right of the president.

Simeon Carter, Levi Jackman, George W. Harris, George Morey, G. M. Hinkle and Elias Higbee on the left of the president.

Also, Edward Partridge Bishop and Titus Billings Bishop's councellor.

Council opened by singing and prayer by S. Carter. Prest Marsh then called on the Bishop for a letter[1] written to W. W. Phelps from Prest. Joseph Smith jr, the Bishop then read the letter after which Brs Isaac Higbee, William Snow, ~~and~~ G. W. Harris, G. Morey were appointed to speak on the case, who urged the necessity of assisting the Brethren Joseph Smith Jr and Sidney Rigdon up here.[2] The Bishop and council acquiesed in the same and urged it. Prest. Marsh then urged the same

1st Resolved—~~that~~ by the High Council, Bishoprick and all the assembly, that E. Partridge, G. W. Harris, and Isaac Morly, be a committee to obtain two waggons and teams and money to go and meet the Brethren J. Smith jr & S. Rigdon and assist them on way hither and also to raise three hundred dollars if consistent[3]

2nd. Resolved, by the High Council that it be considered that no High Priest, Elder or Priest (except the Presidency, High Council and Bishoprick) has any right or authority to preside over or take the charge of any Branch, Society or neighbourhood within the bounds of this Stake:[4] but that the teachers, assisted by the deacons, be considered the standing ministry to preside each over his respective branch of the Stake agreeable to the covenants[5]

3rd Resolved that we recommend to all High Priests, Elders and Priests who are in good standing & friends to Joseph Smith jr, the Prophet that they do not take the lead of nor appoint meetings in any branch or neighbourhood of Saints within the bounds of this Stake without the invitation or consent of the Presiding officer of that branch. We also, consider that the teacher, who is the presiding officer, has a right to object to any official character, who may come among them to officiate, who is not in good standing or a friend to the true cause of Christ. And also, that the teacher report, to the High Council, such as are unruly or teach corrupt doctrine among them

4th Resolved that the High Council recommend to each neighbourhood or settlement of Saints, within the bounds of this Stake, to choose for themselves a teacher, who is skilled in the word of God, faithful in his ministry, full of the Holy Ghost, and a friend to Joseph Smith jr, the Prophet of God, to take the wachcare over them, and preside agreeably to the covenants, who shall be assisted by the other teachers and deacons in the Branch.

5th Resolved, that each branch of this Stake send one or more teachers once in three months to the Quarterly conference of this Stake, with a written account of the true situation of his Branch, agreeably to the Covenants.[6]

6 Resolved—that the High Council recommend and consider it the duty of priests to labor from house to house, each in his respective neighbourhood agreeably to the covenants.[7]

7th Resolved, that this High Council recommend to each neighbourhood or settlement of Saints within the bounds of this stake to go to the house of prayer on the Lord's holy day and offer up their sacraments &c. agreeable to the Sabbath's day commandment and also, that they meet together oft for preaching and prayer.[8]

8th Resolved that Bro Elias Higbee, G. M. Hinkle and George Morey, be appointed, a committee to notify the several Branches with in the bounds of this Stake of the above proceedings and furnish each Branch with a copy of the same.

9. Resolved—that this Council adjourn to meet next Saturday at 9 o'clock A. M.

Closed by prayer by Br Calvin Beebee.

John Corrill Clerk

---

[1]This letter was written by the Prophet at New Portage, Ohio.

[2]Oliver Cowdery writes: "They call loudly for help from this place: for many waggons to help them forward. There is a council today [February 24, 1838], I expect, on the subject—what will be the result I am not able to say, but presume messengers will be sent to meet them." (See letter of Oliver Cowdery, February 24, 1838, Huntington Library, microfilm at Church Archives.)

[3]See *History of the Church* 3:8-10. John P. Barnard, a blacksmith, traveled to Huntsville, Missouri, with his carriage to bring Joseph and his family to Far West. (Elden J. Watson, *Manuscript History of Brigham Young* [Salt Lake City: Elden Jay Watson, 1968], page 27.)

[4]This is the first time the word *stake* is used in the Far West Record to refer to a Church unit in Missouri. In this case the stake was located at Far West.

[5]Doctrine and Covenants 20:53-59.

[6]See Doctrine and Covenants 20:81-82. In addition to the membership list called for in Doctrine and Covenants 20, the teachers are now instructed to bring a report of the status of the branch.

[7]See Doctrine and Covenants 20:47. This sixth article was voted null and void on March 15, 1838. (See page 151.)

[8]Doctrine and Covenants 59.

March 3, 1838

At a meeting of the High Council of Zion on the 3rd of March convened according to adjournment.

Present.

Presidents[1]

Bishop Partridge laid the following before the Council for their approval or disaproval namely.

"To the High Council in Zion, Far West Feb 24th 1838

Is the Council willing for me to furnish Br Sidney Rigdon with the North East corner of Block No 6. in Far West, containing Lots No 1, 2, 3, 4, 5, & 6, apprised at $285, free of expense. Also, for me to furnish Br. Joseph Smith jr with the South East corner of Block No 7, containing Lots No 7, 8, 9, 10, 11 and 12 apprised at $220, free of expense. There is a house and a claim upon one of these lots that I may have to buy Also for me to furnish free of expense Br. Joseph Smith jr with the North East corner of Block No 7, containing Lots No 1 & 4 apprised at $100 claim and betterments cost $135 amounting to $235 (in all) Also, for me to furnish, free of expense, Br Hyrum Smith with the North West corner of Block No 8, containing Lots No 2 and 3 apprised at $100

Edward Partridge

Voted by the High Council that they are willing that the Bishop (Partridge) shall hold the above named property for the benefit of the persons therein named and that he remove all incumbrances thereon

E. Robinson Clerk

---

[1]The space here represents a space in the Far West Record manuscript. Hosea Stout had undoubtedly intended to list those present.

March 10, 1838

The High Council of Zion, met in Far West, on Saturday, March 10th, 1838,[1] Agreeable to adjournment;

The council was organized in the following order viz

Thos B. Marsh and David W. Patten Presidents.

1. Simeon Carter	2 Jared Carter
3 Isaac Higbee	4 Thos Grover
5 Levi Jackman	6 Samuel Bent
7 George Morey	8 Newel Knight
9 G. M. Hinkle	10 George W. Harris
11 Elias Higbee	12 John Murdock[2]

Opened by singing and prayer by Elder Grover after which President Marsh read a clause in the Book of Covenants respecting the dutys of Elders in holding Conferences, and made a few remarks upon the same.[3]

Instructions were then given to the Council from Prest Patten and Marsh

1st Resolved—That the H Council recommend to the branches, of this Church, that they receive no members of this Church, who may come among them, unless they bring a certificate of their standing.[4] An appeal case was presented,[5] pending between John Lemons and Solomon Wixom, which was put over untill the last Saturday in April next.

2nd Resolved—That the High Council recommend, by writing, to the various branches of this Church, that all those who wish to receive an ordination, procure a recommend from the branch to which he belongs, & have it pass through the hands of the different quorums for inspection, previous to his ordination.

3. Resolved—That the High Council recommend to all those who hold licences, between the age of 18 and 45, and do not officiate in their respective offices, be subject to military duty.[6]

4. Resolved That the High Council recommend George W. Harris to the office of a High Priest.

Council adjourned one hour till 2 o'clock P. M.

At 2 o'clock Council met persuant to adjournment. opened by singing and prayer[7]

A charge was then preferred against William W. Phelps and John Whitmer, for persisting in unchristian-like conduct.

George M. Hinkle was the plaintiff

It was considered a difficult case therefore six councellors were appointed to speak, namely, Simeon Carter, Isaac Higbee, and Levi Jackman, on the part of the plaintiff.

Jared Carter, Thomas Grover and Samuel Bent, on the part of the defendant. After which the following letter was read by Br. Marcellus Cowdery, bearer of the same, belonging to Thomas B. Marsh, previous to giving it to its rightful owner.

"Far-West, March 10, 1838.

Sir: It is contrary to the principles of the revelations of Jesus Christ, and his gospel, and the laws of the land, to try a person for an offence, by an illegal tribunal, or by men prejudiced against him or by authority that has given an opinion, or decision beforehand or in his absence.

Very Respectfully,
we have the honor to be,
David Whitmer,
W. W. Phelps,
John Whitmer:
Presidents of the Church of Christ in Mo.[8]

To T. B. Marsh,
one of the travelling Councellors.
Attest: Oliver Cowdery,
Clerk of the High Council of the Church of Christ in
in Mo.
I certify the foregoing to be a true copy from the
original.

Oliver Cowdery, Clerk
of High Council."

All the effect the above letter had upon the Council, was to convince them, still more, of the wickedness of these men, by endeavoring to palm themselves upon the Church as her Presidents, after the Church had by a united voice, removed them from their presidential office, for their ungodly conduct; and the letter was considered no more, nor less, than a direct insult, or contempt, cast upon the authorities of God, and the Church of Jesus Christ, therefore, the Council proceeded to buisness[9]

Witnesses

Albert Perry testifies that he loaned some money to W. W. Phelps and J. Whitmer, telling them, he would want it to enter some land with, after a short time

After some time he went to J. Whitmer and told him he wanted to enter a piece of land on which there was some timber; to which he replied that he could enter the land, but the benefit of the timber was all he could have, as it was on the commons; but shortly after this entered the land himself

Br. Newberry testifies that he talked with J. Whitmer respecting the word of wisdom; to which he replied that a man could drink liquor once in a while, but not make a free use of it &c.

Bro. Leonard[10] testifies that he was in company with W. W. Phelps, on his way to Lexington, last fall, when he (W. W. Phelps) remarked that if he (Leonard) wanted to be a man of God in full he must by land of him

Edward Partridge testifies that he spake to those brethren to come in and settle—to which they complied the second invitation, when Br. Phelps said the Bishop should not complain of his not living to his covenant, therefore, endorsed on the mortgage, fifty dollars for his lot: but John Whitmer thought the lots which had been appropriated for the benefit of certain individuals ought to be granted &c. also, that if the house of the Lord was not built, the $2,000 which they had subscribed ought to come to them and they seemed to claim it on the ground that others withdrew their subscriptions. The above sums are the avails of the profits of the Town Plot.[11]

The Bishop further testifies that he understood that the land which was purchased with the Fry money[12] was to be transfered into his hands instead of land purchased with money obtained in the South for "Poor Bleeding Zion" with this reserve that they have pay for their services &c. and that 2,000 dollars be applied to the purpose of building a house to the Lord out of the avails of this land.

They required the Bishop to pay them for their labors in the Church more than six hundred dollars also, to pay the purchase money.

W. Snow testifies that he was at a Council in which the Town Plot was spoken of and concluded to go into the hands of the Bishop, when W. W. Phelps and J. Whitmer said they had subscribed $2,000 for the building a house to the Lord and they had depended upon the profits of the Plot to pay the amount mentioned when one of the Councellors said it was as easy for the Church to pay it out of the profits as for them[13]

A number of charges were sustained against those men; the principal of which, was, for claiming $2,000 Church funds which they had subscribed for the building an house to the Lord in this place, when they held in their possession the City Plot, and were sitting in the Presidential chair, which subscription they were intending to pay from the avails of the town lots; but when the town plot was transfered into the hands of the Bishop, for the benefit of the Church, it was agreed that the church should take this subscription from off the hands of W. W. Phelps & John Whitmer, but in the transactions of the buisness they bound the Bishop in a heavy mortgage,[14] to pay them the above $2,000 in two years from the date thereof; a part of which they have already received, & claim the remainder.

The six councellors made a few appropriate remarks, none of whom felt to plead for mercy, as it had not been asked on the part of the accused, but all, with one consent, declared that justice ought to have his demands.

After some remarks by Presidents Marsh & Patten, setting forth the iniquity of those men, in claiming the $2,000 spoken of, which did not belong to them any more than any other person in the church; it was decided that William W. Phelps and John Whitmer be no longer members of the church of Christ of Latter Day Saints, & be given over to the buffetings of Satan, until they learn to blaspheme no more against the authorities of God, nor fleece the flock of Christ.

The Council were then asked if they concured with the decision; if so, to manifest it by rising, when they all arose. The vote was then put to the congregation which was carried unanimous; the negative was then called but no one voted.

Mr Marcellus Cowdery arose & said he wished to have it understood that he did not vote either way, because he did not consider it a legal tribunal;[15] he also offered insult to the High Council & to the Church, by reading a letter belonging to Thomas B. Marsh before giving it to him, & in speaking against the authorities of the Church.

A motion was then made by President Patten, that fellowship be withdrawn from Marcellus Cowdery,[16] until he make satisfaction, which was seconded and carried unanimous.

Ebenzer Robinson
Clerk of High Council

Thomas B. Marsh,)
) Presidents
David W. Patten,)

---

[1]See *History of the Church* 3:6. Some of this account has been omitted from the *History of the Church* version.

[2]Although John Murdock was the senior member of the high council, he is listed as number twelve. These numbers were assigned, apparently at each meeting, by casting lots.

[3]See Doctrine and Covenants 20:61-62.

[4]Doctrine and Covenants 20:84. Note the desire to bring the Church organization into harmony with the revelations.

[5]This was a case appealed from the elders quorum. Evidence indicates that each quorum had authority to try its own members. Decisions of these quorum cases could be appealed.

[6]B. H. Roberts notes: "The law of Missouri excused from military duty all licensed ministers of the Gospel, and as nearly all the adult members of the Church who were worthy had received ordination to the Priesthood, it left the community in Far West, then a frontier country and liable to be raided by warlike tribes of Indians, without militia companies and state arms for its protection; hence the recommendation of the Council that the brethren within the ages specified, and not actively employed in the ministry, place themselves in a position to accept militia service." (See *History of the Church* 3:6.)

[7]March 10, 1838.

[8]This letter summarizes the position of the presidents. From this point of view they had been treated unjustly. They objected to Marsh and Patten's convening the council in their absence, and claimed that these two Apostles were committed to removing them from the Church.

[9]See *History of the Church* 3:7-8.

[10]Lyman Leonard.

[11]See the explanation given by Thomas B. Marsh in *Elders Journal* 1(July 1838):37-38.

[12]Possibly William Fry.

[13]See page 110.

[14]On April 21, 1838, the Church agreed not to pay the mortgage. (See page 182.)

[15]Concerning this matter Oliver Cowdery wrote: "A day or two since past D and J. Whitmer and W W Phelps were notified by Marsh that a charge had been prepared before the High Council then, and that to day their case would be taken into consideration. Accordingly the following was drawn up, signed & c. And Marcellus is now gone to present it to Marsh in their new fangled council. . . .Whether this little document will cause those hotheaded men to consider their ways I know not, I suppose however they will plead Smith's instructions and justify themselves in trying Presidents of the church before a rabble and call it legal. Be this as it may, when it becomes us to speak we shall probably be heard." (See Oliver Cowdery Letter, March 10, 1838, Huntington Library, microfilm copy at Church Archives.)

[16]This action against Marcellus Cowdery shows the prejudiced nature of the council in this matter. This was a desperate time for the Church. (See F. Mark McKiernan, "Mormonism on the Defensive," *The Restoration Movement* [Lawrence, Kansas: Coronado Press, 1973], pages 121-40.)

March 15, 1838

The High Council of Zion, together with the Bishoprick met in Far West, on ~~Saturday~~ Thursday March the 15th 1838,[1] agreeable to appointment and was organized as follows. President Joseph Smith jr took the charge of the Council.

Simeon Carter	No 1	Jared Carter	No 2
Brigham Young	" 3	Thomas Grover	" 4
Levi Jackman	" 5	Thomas Gates	" 6
Stephen Winchester	" 7	Moses Martin	" 8
George M. Hinkle	" 9	George W. Harris	" 10
Elias Higbee	" 11	John Murdock	" 12

The Council opened by singing "This earth was once a garden place &c." and prayer by Prest Joseph Smith jr.

The minutes of some previous Councils were read by the Clerk

First. The minutes of a Council held on Saturday the 24th of February 1838, when it was voted. First, That the 6th article of the said minutes be null & void & also, that a new article be put in the place of it (which was done)[2]

President Joseph Smith jr gave a history of the ordination of David Whitmer, which took place in July 1834, to be a leader, or a prophet to this Church, which (ordination) was on conditions that he (J. Smith jr) did not live to God himself.[3]

President J. Smith Jr. approved of the proceedings of the High Council, after hearing the minutes of the former Councils.[4]

The Council adjourned for one hour.

---

7 o'clock P. M. The Council and Bishoprick convened agreeably to adjournment and was organized, Joseph Smith jr presiding, when it was opened by prayer by John Murdock,

after which Br John Corrill made some remarks respecting his former conduct, by way of confession, but not to the satisfaction of the Council after which Thomas B. Marsh made a few remarks, followed by George M. Hinkle and others, when Br Corrill made perfect satisfaction.

The Council adjourned untill tomorrow at 1 o'clock.[5]

Benediction by President Joseph Smith jr[6]

Ebenezer Robinson Clk.

---

[1]Joseph Smith and company, including Brigham Young, had arrived in Far West the previous day.

[2]See page 143.

[3]See pages 72-73. See also D. Michael Quinn, "The Mormon Succession Crisis of 1844," *Brigham Young University Studies* 16(Winter 1976):187-233.

[4]Reference is made to (1) dropping the Presidency in Missouri, and (2) the excommunication of Phelps and John Whitmer.

[5]It appears that the conference did not actually convene until two days later.

[6]Joseph Smith opened and closed with prayer and presided in the meeting, indicating the need he perceived to take full charge of affairs in Far West. This was a very important meeting.

March 17, 1838

The High Council and Bishop of Zion met, agreeable to adjournment, in the school house in Far West March the 17th 1838.

The Council was organized as follows:

Thomas B. Marsh, President

Simeon Carter	No. 1	Samuel Bent	No 2
Peter Dustan	" 3	Thomas Grover	" 4
Levi Jackman	" 5	Solomon Hancock	" 6
George Morey	" 7	Newel Knight	" 8
Isaac Higbee	" 9	George W. Harris	" 10
Elias Higbee	" 11	John Murdock	" 12

The council was opened by singing "How firm a foundation" &c. and prayer by N. Knight.

A letter was read, from Charles C. Rich respecting the ordination of Asa C. Earl,[1] who had been ordained a Priest, by his brother, while on a visit to another State, without a Conference, but afterwards gave up his license, there being some dissatisfaction expressed, after he got home, by the branch to which he belonged.

The question was whether ~~the~~ the ordination was legal or not.

The case was not considered difficult, therefore, two Councellors were appointed to speak, viz: George Morey on the part of the Church and N. Knight on the part of the defendant, after which a few remarks by the councellors, it was decided that the ordination was not legal. The Council adjourned untill next Saturday at 9 o'clock.

Closing prayer by Elder John Murdock.

Ebenezer Robinson Clerk

---

[1]A brother-in-law of Charles C. Rich.

March 24, 1838

The High Council of Zion met pursuant to adjournment, Saturday, March 24th 1838.

Council was organized as follows; Presidents Joseph Smith jr. David W. Patten and Thos B. Marsh.

Simeon Carter	No 1	Jared Carter	No 2
Calvin Beebee	" 3	Thos Grover	" 4
Levi Jackman	" 5	Solomon Hancock	" 6
George Morey	" 7	Newel Knight	" 8
George M. Hinkle	" 9	George W. Harris	" 10
Elias Higbee	" 11	Isaac Higbee	" 12[1]

The Council was opened by prayer by Prest David W. Patten.

A Charge was preferred against John Murdock for unchristian-like conduct, in speaking reproachfully of youngsters, by James Newberry.

After a short deliberation it was considered a most difficult case, therefore six councellors were appointed to speak on the case, viz: George M. Hinkle, Elias Higbee and Simeon Carter, on the part of the Church and George W. Harris, Isaac Higbee, and Jared Carter on the part of the accused.

Jacob Gates testifies that Br. Murdock was at his house, the subject of spelling schools, in the evening was introduced, which he[2] disapproved of also, mentioned about a young man's[3] undertaking to hug a girl in an evening meeting but mentioned no names, he disapproved of evening schools and meetings on account of the young people being light minded & tended to draw away their minds from the studies.

Sister Gates[4] testifies that B. Murdock was at her house and disapproved of evening schools &c she concurs with the testimony of her husband.

Br. Outhouse testifies that he labored with Br. Murdock together with Br Newberry when Br Murdock denied making a motion to show James Newberry undertook to hug the girl.[5]

He[6] was then cross examined and says Br. Murdock said in meeting that in making the motion to show how J. W. Newberry undertook to hug the girl, he did not intend to hit Orlando Carter as hard as he did as he was the one to whom he made the motion.

Alonzo Herrick testifies that he was at school one day when the Master[7] & James Newberry got to disputing about hugging the girl, the boy denied undertaking to hug the girl & Mr. Murdock made a motion to show how he done the thing when the boy said it was not so, he also says that he never heard Br Murdock twit[8] the boys of being with the girls, also, that he believes Br Murdock used his best endeavors for the good of the school; also, saw one of the schollars shake his fist at the master; also, that he saw some verses in the hands of James W.

Newberry, Joseph Outhouse & Edward Prindall, which served to tantalize the master.

George P. Dykes testifies that the Elders were called together & Br. Murdock presented a case which was investigated, but he thought proper weight was not put upon the testimony

Edward Prindal testifies that he saw Br Murdock make a motion to show how James Newberry undertook to hug the girl in meeting which James Newberry denied, saying he never done any such thing also that he heard the master say that he did not like to have spelling schools because there was too much going home with the girls also he shook his fist at the master because he thought the master meddled with that which was none of his buisness in correcting them for going home with the girls, also, that he thinks James W. Newberry was not in the habit of running about more than common, also, that it was rumoured about by Br Murdock one or two[9] before being mentioned in school that some of the boys had hugged a girl in meeting. also, Br Murdock said in the meeting of Elders that he had not taken the regular steps with James W. Newberry, and he was sorry that he had not.

A testimony was presented from Orlando Carter, in writing, which was read.

John Lowrie testifies he was at a meeting where Br Murdock requested the Elders to take a separate [room] as he had a matter to have investigated, he made his statement to the Elders & in it he said that he had done wrong in speaking of the matter of James W. Newberry's hugging the girl in meeting before going to him and laboring with him,[10] for which he was sorry, also, testifies that he thought the young men did not treat Br Murdock with that respect with which they ought.

Lyman Leonard testifies that he was at the meeting of the Elders before mentioned when Br Murdock and James W. Newberry laid before them their aggrievances and the matter was investigated. Br Murdock made confession, saying that he had done wrong in mentioning about the young man's attempting to hug the girl, before laboring with him. Also that a decision was had, and a settlement took place between the parties. also, that he[11] did not approve of the treatment of the young men towards Br Murdock and reproved them for it. also, that the Court of Elders was called by mutual consent as far as he knew, and both made their statements.

Sister Leonard[12] concurs with the testimony of her husband and that she was at the meeting in which the young man was accused of attempting to hug the girl & she saw James Newberry wink and smile when the girl went to get water, which she did not like.

Elizabeth Legg testifies that she attended the school & she did not hear Br. Murdock twit the boys of going home with the girls, also, she saw the boys shake their fists at Br Murdock when his back was turned, viz: James W. Newberry and Joseph Outhouse.

Simeon Carter testifies that he was pleased with the conduct of the young men while before him on account of their steadiness.

James W. Newberry testifies that he did not have any hand in writing or composing the verses spoken of in Orlando Herrick's[13] testimony.

The Councellors made a few very~~y~~ appropriate remarks, all of whom thought the charge was not sustained, but rather the accuser was in the fault

Decided that the charge was not sustained, but Br James W. Newberry was in the fault in treating Br Murdock as he did.

The questions was then put to the Council if they concured with the decision if so to manifest it by saying aye. which was done unanimous.

Council adjourned one hour to meet at the Bishops office.

Ebenezer Robinson Clk.

---

6 o'clock P. M. The council met pursuant to adjournment & was organized as follows:

Simeon Carter	No 1	Elisah H. Groves	No 2
Calvin Beebee	" 3	Thomas Grover	" 4
Levi Jackman	" 5	Solomon Hancock	" 6
George Morey	" 7	Newel Knight	" 8
G. M. Hinkle	" 9	George W. Harris	" 10
Elias Higbee	" 11	John Murdock	" 12

The Council opened by prayer by Solomon Hancock.

The subject of absent Councillors was discussed when it was decided that those who cannot attend the Councils, resign their seats and let others fill them who will be able to attend punctually.[14]

Adjourned Ebenezer Robinson Clk.

---

[1]Note that the council changed composition, that is, it had different members, every time it met in this period.

[2]John Murdock.

[3]James Newberry.

[4]Mary Gates.

[5]This whole episode shows the puritanical attitudes of the Saints as well as their serious concern for education.

[6]Joseph Outhouse.

[7]John Murdock.

[8]Means "reproach."

[9]Once or twice.

[10]Note the responsibility of one to speak to an offender before making the issue public knowledge. (See Doctrine and Covenants 28:11.)

[11]Lyman Leonard.

[12]Abigail Leonard.

[13]Also referred to as Alonzo. (See page 154.)

[14]Note that a procedure was established in which high councilors who were frequently absent would be replaced.

April 6, 1838

Far West April 6th 1838[1]

Agreeable to a resolution passed the High Council of Zion, March 3rd, 1838, the Saints ~~of~~ in Missouri assembled at this place, to hold the anniversary of the Church of Jesus Christ of Latter Day Saints[2] and to transact Church buisness.[3]

The meeting was opened by singing and prayer by David W. Patten—After which President Joseph Smith jr read the order of the day as follows;—

"The doors will be opened at 9 o'clock A. M. & the meeting will commence by singing and Prayer.

A sexton will then be appointed for a door keeper & other services in the house of the Lord.

Two historians will then be appointed to write and keep the Church history.[4]

Also a general recorder to keep the records of the whole Church, & be the Clerk of the First Presidency[5]

And a clerk will be appointed for a High Council and to keep the Church records of this Stake.[6]

And three Presidents will be appointed to preside over this Church of Zion.[7]

After which an address will be delivered by the presidency:

Then an intermission of one hour will take place,—

When the meeting will again convene & open by singing & prayer.

The Sacrament will then be administered and the blessing of infants attended to:

The meeting then proceeded to buisness George Morey was appointed sexton & Dimic Huntington assistant. John Corrill and Elias Higbee were appointed historians;

George W. Robinson was appointed general Church Recorder and Clerk for the First Presidency:

Ebenezer Robinson was appointed Church Clerk & Recorder for the Stake of Zion and Clerk of the high Council;

Thomas B. Marsh was appointed President Pro tempore of the Church in Zion, and Brygum Young and David W. Patten his assistant Presidents.

The meeting was adjourned for one hour—& again opened by David W. Patten—After which the bread and wine was administered, & 95 infants were brought froward and blessed.[8]

When on motion the meeting closed.

E. Robinson Clerk

Joseph Smith jr
President.

[1]*History of the Church* 3:13. The practice of holding general conferences semiannually began in 1838. In accordance with Doctrine and Covenants 20:61, regular Church conferences had previously convened quarterly. An abbreviated report of this meeting is found in the Scriptory Book of Joseph Smith, page 29, Church Archives.

[2]Note again the use of the official name of the Church by the clerk prior to April 26, 1838. (See page 140, note 1.)

[3]Here they are consciously holding their conference to coincide with the anniversary of the founding of the Church.

[4]The two "historians" were John Corrill and Elias Higbee.

[5]This record, called "The Scriptory Book of Joseph Smith," was kept by George W. Robinson.

[6]This record, known as the Far West Record, was kept by Ebenezer Robinson.

[7]Thomas B. Marsh, Brigham Young and David W. Patten were chosen as presidents, pro tem. (See page 141.)

[8]Note that the sacrament was administered and children were blessed at this quarterly conference, which was the first such conference held at Far West.

April 7, 1838

Conference Minutes. April 7th 1838[1]

Agreeable to a resolution of the high Council, assembled at Far West, on saturday the 3rd of March, 1838, the general authorities of the Church met, ~~the~~ to hold the first quarterly Conference of the Church of Latter Day Saints of Zion, at Far West on the 7th of April 1838.

Presidents Joseph Smith jr, Sidney Rigdon, T. B. Marsh, D. W. Patten, and B. Young took the stand; after which the several quorums the High Council, the High Priests, the Seventies, the Elders, the Bishop, the Priests, the Teachers, and the Deacons, were organized by their Presidents.[2]

President Joseph Smith jr made some remarks, also gave some instruction respecting the order of the day. The Conference was then opened by singing "O God our hope in ages past" and prayer by Prest B. Young. Also, a hymn was sung "How firm a foundation"—After which President Joseph Smith jr arose and addressed the congregation, at considerable length, on some important items. President Rigdon continued the subject for a length of time, after which, on motion, the meeting adjourned for the space of twenty minutes.

Pursuant to adjournment the Conference convened, and opened by Prayer by D. W. Patten, who also made a few remarks respecting the twelve apostles.

He spake of T. B. Marsh, B. Young, Orson Hyde, H. C. Kimball, P. P. Pratt, and O. Pratt as being men of God, whom he could recommend with cheerful confidence.

He spake somewhat doubtful of William Smith from something which he had heard respecting his faith in the work. He also spake of William E. McLellin, Luke Johnson, Lyman Johnson, and John F. Boynton as being men whom he could not recommend to the Conference.[3]

President[4] John Murdock, then represented the high council. The report was favorable. He stated that the seats of Elisha H. Groves, Calvin Beebee, and Lyman Wight was vacant in consequence of their having moved away so far that they could not attend the Council

Thomas B. Marsh then nominated Jared Carter to fill the seat of Elisha H. Groves which was recieved unanimously.

He then nominated John P. Green, to fill the seat of Calvin Beebee, who was received unanimously.

Also George W. Harris to fill that of Lyman Wight, who was recieved unanimously—

The Presidency then ordained him to the office of High Priest.

On motion Conference adjourned to the 8th at 9 o'clock A.M.

---

[1]See *History of the Church* 3:14.

[2]Charles C. Rich was president of the high priests quorum. Joseph Young was senior president of the seventies; the other six presidents at this time were Levi Hancock, James Foster, Daniel Miles, Josiah Butterfield, Henry

Harriman, and Zera Pulsipher. Harvey Green was president of the elders quorum (124 in number). Edward Partridge was senior bishop and president of the priests quorum. Albert Perry was president of the teachers quorum. The president of the deacons quorum is not known.

[3]Note the custom of speaking in a public meeting about the strengths and weaknesses of the brethren, reflecting the open, democratic nature of the Church. All of the men whom Patten could not recommend, with the exception of William Smith, were excommunicated in 1838, some in Missouri, some in Kirtland.

[4]The use of the title *president* was to indicate Murdock's seniority in the high council.

April 8, 1838

Sunday April 8th[1]—Pursuant to adjournment the conference convened and opened by singing & prayer by President B. Young.

President Joseph jr made a few remarks respecting the Kirtland Bank—who was followed by by Brigham Young, who gave a short history of his travels to Massachusetts and New York

President Charles C. Rich,[2] who ~~was~~ is president of the high priests in Zion: represented his quorum, he read the names of those who belonged to his quorum the principal part of which were in good standing.

The seventies were represented by Presidents Daniel Miles and Levi Hancock.

The quorum of Elders were represented by president Harvey Green—Their number was 124, in good standing.

President Joseph Smith jr next made a few remarks on the word of wisdom, giving the reason of its coming forth, saying it should be observed.[3] On motion, the Conference adjourned for one hour.

The Conference convened, agreeable to adjournment, and opened by singing and prayer, after which Bishop Partridge, represented the lesser Priesthood, and his council.

He gave an account of the incomes and out goes of the Church property which had passed through his hands.

It was then motioned seconded, and carried that the first Presidency be appointed to sign the licences of the official members of the Church—After which on motion, the conference adjourned untill the first Friday in July next.

Ebenezer Robinson Clerk — Joseph Smith, Jr. President.

---

[1]See *History of the Church* 3:15. On this day Joseph Smith sent a letter to John Whitmer in consequence of his withholding Church records.

[2]See page 119 for his appointment.

[3]In the pages of the Far West Record and other early Church records, the Word of Wisdom is frequently questioned and debated. Here, in contrast, the Prophet stresses that it should be observed.

April 12, 1838

The High Council and Bishoprick of Zion, met according to appointment in Far West, April 12 1838[1] Edward Partridge presiding

The Council was organized as follows:

Samuel H. Smith	No 1	Jared Carter	No 2
Thomas Grover	" 3	Isaac Higbee	" 4
Levi Jackman	" 5	Solomon Hancock	" 6
George Morey	" 7	Newel Knight	" 8
George M. Hinkle	" 9	George W. Harris	" 10
Elias Higbee	" 11	John Murdock	" 12

Voted unanimously that John Murdock be a President of the High Council, whose duty it shall be to receive charges and give notice to the defendant, also, to call the Council together and organize them &c.

The Council opened by prayer by E. Partridge

After some remarks by Edward Partridge, several charges

were read by him prefered against Oliver Cowdery which are as follows;

"To the Bishop and Council of the Church of Jesus Christ of Latter day Saints in Missouri.

I do hereby prefer the following charges against President Oliver Cowdery.

1st, For stirring up the enemy to persecute the brethren by urging on vexatious Lawsuits[2] and thus distressing the inocent.

2nd, For seeking to destroy~~ing~~ the character of President Joseph Smith jr by falsly insinuating that he was guilty of adultry &c.

3rd For treating the Church with contempt by not attending meetings.

4th For virtually denying the faith by declaring that he would not be governed by any ecclesiastical authority nor Revelation whatever in his temporal affairs[3]

5th, For selling his lands in Jackson County contrary to the Revelations.[4]

6th For writing and sending an insulting letter to President T. B. Marsh while on the High Council, attending to the duties of his office, as President of the Council and by insulting the whole Council with the contents of said letter[5]

7th, For leaving the calling, in which God had appointed him, by Revelation, for the sake of filthy lucre, and turning to the practice of the Law.

8th, For disgracing the Church by ~~Lieing~~ being connected in the 'Bogus' buisness as common report says.

9th For dishonestly Retaining notes after they had been paid and finally for leaving or forsaking the cause of God, and betaking himself to the beggerly elements of the world and neglecting his high and Holy Calling contrary to his profession.

Far West April the 7th 1838. Seymour Brunson"

It was not considered a difficult case, therefore, ~~two~~ one spake on a side, viz Samuel H. Smith on the part of the Church and Jared Carter on the part of the defendant.[6]

A letter was then read by Edward Partridge from O. Cowdery which reads as follows:[7]

Far West Mo April 12th 1838

Dear Sir,

I received your note of the 9th inst on the day of its date, containing a copy of nine charges preferred ~~against~~ before yourself and Council, against me, by Elder Seymour Brunson.

I could have wished, that those charges might have been defered untill after my interview with President Smith; but as they are not, I must waive the anticipated pleasure with which I had flattered myself of an understanding on those points which are grounds of different opinions on some ~~Chur~~ Church regulations, and others which personally interest myself

The fifth charge reads as follows: "For selling his lands in Jackson County contrary to the revelations" so much of this charge, "For selling his lands in Jackson County" I acknowledge to be true, and believe ~~a~~ that a large majority of this Church have already spent their Judgements on that act,[8] and pronounced it sufficient to warrant a disfellowship; and also that you have concured in its correctness—consequently, have no good reason for supposing you would give any decision contrary

Now sir the lands in our Country are allodial[9] in the strictest construction of that term, and have not the least shadow of feudal tenours attached to them, consequently, they may be disposed of by deeds of conveyance without the consent or even approbation of a superior.

The fourth charge is in the following words, "For virtually denying the faith by declaring that he would not be governed by any ecclesiastical authority nor revelation whatever in his temporal affairs."

With regard to this, I, think, I am warranted in saying, the judgment is also passed as on the ~~fifth~~ matter of the fifth charge, consequently, I have no disposition to contend with the Council; this charge covers simply the doctrine of the fifth, and if I were to be controlled by other than my own judgment, in a compulsory manner, in my temporal interests, of course, could not buy or sell without the consent of some real or supposed authority. Whether that clause contains the precise words, I am not certain—I think however they were these "I will not be influenced, governed, or controlled, in my temporal interests by any ecclesiastical authority or pretended revelation whatever, contrary to my own judgement" such being still my opinion shall only remark that the three great principles of English liberty, as laid down in the books, are "the right of personal security; the right of personal liberty, and the right of private property" My venerable ancestor[10] was among that little band, who landed on the rocks of Plymouth in 1620—with him he brought those maxims, and a body of those laws which were the result and experience of many centuries, on the basis of which now stands our great and happy Government: and they are so interwoven in my nature, have so long been inculcated into my mind by a liberal and intelligent ancestry, that I am wholly unwilling to exchange them for any thing less liberal, less benevolent, or less free.

The very principle of which I conceive to be couched in an attempt to set up a kind of petty government, controlled and dictated by ecclesiastical influence, in the midst of this National and State Government. You will, no doubt say this is not correct; but the bare notice of those charges, over which you assume a right to decide, is, in my opinion, a direct attempt to make the secular power subservient to Church dictation—to the correctness of which I cannot in conscience subscribe—I believe that principle never did fail to produce Anarchy & confusion.

This attempt to controll me in my temporal interests, I conceive to be a disposition to take from me a portion of my Constitutional privileges and inherent rights. I only, respectfully, ask leave, therefore to withdraw from a society assuming they have such right.

So far as relates to the other seven charges, I shall lay them carefully away, and take such a course with regard to them, as I may feel bound by my honor, to answer to my rising posterity.

I beg you, sir, to take no view of the foregoing remarks, other than my belief on the outward government of this

Church. I do not charge you, or any other person who differs with me on those points, of not being sincere; but such difference does exist, which I sincerely regret.

With considerations of the highest respect, I am,

Your obedient servent.

O Cowdery.

Rev.[11]
Edward Partridge
Bishop of the
Church of Latter
Day Saints

John Corrill testifies that some time last fall Marcellus Cowdery came to him and requested him to pay certain notes, against Joseph Smith jr but he declined, soon after a writ was served on him; he supposed that it was through the influence of O. Cowdery that the writ was served. From circumstances, he is of the impression that O. Cowdery has used his influence to urge on lawsuits, which have taken place of late in this place. Also, that O. Cowdery said to him "the law is my theme.

John Anderson testifies that, from circumstances, he believes that O. Cowdery had been influential in causing lawsuits in this place, as a number more lawsuits have taken place since he came here than before

Dimic B. Huntington, testifies, that O. Cowdery called to him one ~~day~~ evening as he was passing through the street, and said that he smelt a skunk (an enemy &c.) and if he knew who it was he would put the screws to him, and also informed D. B Huntington if he heard any guns fired in town to put the screws (I.E. the law) to him who done it, this was after he was appointed to attend the suits of the Corporation[12] and also went on to urge lawsuits as even to issue a writ on the Sabbath day also, that he heard him say that he intended to form a partnership with Donaphon who is a man of the world and a wicked man[13]

George M. Hinkle, testifies that O. Cowdery wanted to

become a secret partner in the store as he would be able to collect the debts & act as an Aterny[14] and thereby be able to get his fees or living which was verbally agreed to, when he traded a considerable and finallly they got sick of him and got rid of him the best way they could, which they did do, but still solicited for buisness in the law line, and has frequently solicited for buisness in collecting debts, as he was an Aterny in the place, also testifies that he has seen him urge on lawsuits with others.

George W. Harris testifies that one evening last fall[15] O. Cowdery was at his house together with Joseph Smith jr, and Thomas B. Marsh, when a conversation took place between Joseph Smith jr & O. Cowdery, when he seemed to insinuate that Joseph Smith jr was guilty of adultery, but when the question was put, if he (Joseph) had ever acknowledged to him[16] that he was guilty of such a thing; when he[17] answered No. Also he believes him to be instrumental in causing so many lawsuits as had taken place of late

David W. Patten testifies, that he went to Oliver Cowdery to enquire of him if a certain story was true respecting J. Smith's committing adultery with a certain girl,[18] when he turned on his heel and insinuated as though he[19] was guilty; he[20] then went on and gave a history of some circumstances respecting the adultery scrape stating that no doubt it was true. Also said that Joseph told him, he had confessed to Emma, Also that he has used his influence to urge on lawsuits.

Thomas B. Marsh testifies that while in Kirtland last summer, David W. Patten asked Oliver Cowdery if he Joseph Smith jr had confessed to his wife that he was guilty of adultery with a certain girl, when Oliver Cowdery cocked up his eye very knowingly and hesitated to answer the question, saying he did not know as he was bound to answer the question yet conveyed the idea that it was true. Last fall[21] after Oliver came to this place he heard a conversation take place between Joseph Smith and Oliver Cowdery when J. Smith asked him if he[22] had ever confessed to him that he was guilty of adultery, when after a considerable winking &c. he said <u>No</u>. Joseph then asked him if he ever told him that he confessed to any body, when he answered No.

Joseph Smith jr testifies that Oliver Cowdery had been his bosom friend, therefore he intrusted him with many things.[23] He then gave a history respecting the girl buisness. Also that Oliver Cowdery took him one side and said, that he had come to the conclusion to get property and if he could not get it one way he would another, God or no God, Devil or no Devil, property he must ~~must~~ have and since that he has dealt dishonest with him that he has taken a printing press and type from Kirtland for which he was to give up some notes which he had against Joseph Smith jr and Sidney Rigdon which he did not do, nor had to this day.

The Council adjourned one hour.

The Council convened according to adjournment opened by prayer by B. Young.

Sidney Rigdon testifies that in January 1837 Oliver Cowdery offered to sell out his share in the printing office at Kirtland Ohio, which they Joseph Smith jr & Sidney Rigdon bought and gave their notes, after which say in the spring following he wished to get a press & some of the type which they granted him on conditions that he should give up the notes above refered to, he then went into the office and took whatever he pleased & so completely stripped the office, as he (Rigdon) was informed by D. C. Smith,[24] that there was scarcely enough left to print the "Elders Journal," whereas, before there was a sufficient quantity to print a weekly and monthly paper, the book of Covenants, Hymn Book, Book of Mormon &c. but the notes he did not give up

F. G. Williams testifies that Oliver Cowdery told him that there was a certain man in the Church who could compound metal and make dies, that he could make money so that it could not be detected and if it was the case it was no harm to take that money and pass it. The man's name was Davis. Also three men came to him to take out a writ to take some persons who had passed some Bogus (counterfeit) money, viz: John Boynton, Warren Parrish and Burton H. Phelps. Also that it was reported that Oliver was engaged in the Bogus money buisness. Also he did not disapprove of the principle of Davis' making the dies and money.

Joseph Smith jr testifies that Mr Sapham a man who did not belong to the Church came to him and told him that a warrant was about to be isued against Oliver Cowdery for being engaged in making a purchase of Bogus money & dies to make the counterfeit money with. after which himself and President Rigdon went to see him, (Oliver) and talked with him about it, when he denied it after which they told him if he was guilty he had better leave the country; but if he was inocent to stand a trial & he should come out clear; but that night or the next he left the country.

Sidney Rigdon concurs with the foregoing testimony.

John Corrill testifies that Oliver Cowdery has neglected attending meeting.

George W. Harris concurs in the same

The fourth and fifth charges were rejected by the Court. The 6th charge was withdrawn.

After some remarks by the Councellors, it was decided by the Bishop and his Council that the 1st, 2nd, & 3rd charges were sustained, the 7th was sustained, also the 8th charge was sustained satisfactoryly by circumstantial evidence. The ninth charge was sustained. he was, therefore, considered no longer a member of the Church of Jesus Christ of Latter Day Saints.[25]

The decision was sanctioned by the High Council.

The Council adjourned untill tomorrow at 9 o'clock.

Closed in prayer by Isaac Morley.

Ebenezer Robinson Clerk

---

[1]See *History of the Church* 3:16-18. The *History of the Church* notes that the bishop and high council assembled at the bishop's office. This tribunal, with Bishop Partridge presiding, was constituted as a common council, appropriately organized to try Oliver Cowdery, one of the presidents of the Church. George W. Robinson included an abbreviated account of this trial in the Scriptory Book of Joseph Smith, pages 29-31, Church Archives.

[2]There was a Church moratorium on collecting debts incurred by the failure of the Kirtland Safety Society. Cowdery, in violation of this moratorium, pressed civil lawsuits against Church members concerning indebtedness.

[3]This charge was finally rejected by the council.

[4]The council also dropped this charge.

[5]This charge was withdrawn.

[6]It is interesting that this case was not considered difficult and, therefore, only two councilors spoke, in view of Cowdery's prominent role in the Church. Cowdery's view of this matter follows: "The circumstances under which I left Far West, in June 1838, and immediately following are familiarly known to you all, no doubt. Those circumstances connected with myself and family are always painful to reflect on; but you will be reminded again that I do not charge or believe that either of you contributed anything to render my situation or circumstances, then or afterwards, in the least afflicting; and for this reason, I speak the more freely.... There is another circumstance to which I must now refer in which you as members and principals in a great and increasing society, are interested; and in which also, whether in or out of that society, I must continue to feel sensibley and keenly.... Now what I have to say concerning all the difficulty between myself and your church ... is simply this: I believed at the time, and still believe, that ambitious and wicked men, envying the harmony existing between myself and the first elders of the Church, and hoping to get into some other men's birthright, by falsehoods, the most foul and wicked, caused all this difficulty from the beginning to end. They succeeded in getting myself out of the Church; but since they themselves have gone to perdition, ought not old friends—long tried in the furnace of affliction, to be friends still, even laying out of view any and all religious considerations." (See letter of Oliver Cowdery to Brigham Young, December 25, 1843, Huntington Library, microfilm copy in Church Archives.)

[7]This letter of Oliver Cowdery, while relegated to a footnote in *History of the Church* is an eloquent statement of constitutional law, property rights, and Cowdery's English heritage.

[8]Here Cowdery expressed his feeling that the council was prejudiced against him and had already determined his guilt.

[9]In law, land owned independently; freehold state as opposed to feudalism.

[10]Edward Fuller.

[11]Possibly Cowdery is taunting Partridge in using the title Reverend.

[12]The corporation of the city of Far West. (See page 119.)

[13]Although generally regarded by present day Latter-day Saints as a hero and friend of the Saints, Alexander W. Doniphan was regarded by some members in Missouri as an enemy of the Church.

[14]Attorney.

[15]November 6, 1837. (See page 119.)

[16]Cowdery.

[17]Cowdery.

[18]The girl referred to here is Fanny Alger, Joseph Smith's first plural wife. (See Oliver Cowdery to Warren Cowdery, January 21, 1838, Huntington Library, microfilm copy at Church Archives and Benjamin F. Johnson to Elder George S. Gibbs," 1911, typewritten copy, Brigham Young University.) The fact that the Prophet was practicing polygamy in Kirtland provides insight into Oliver's accusation of adultery. There are at least three possibilities for Cowdery's charges:

1. Oliver did not know about plural marriage and, therefore, assumed Joseph Smith was committing adultery.

2. Oliver did know about plural marriage but was not granted permission to practice it, and, seeking revenge, charged the prophet with adultery.

3. Oliver knew about plural marriage and entered the practice himself without authorization. (See George Q. Cannon, *Juvenile Instructor* 16 [September 15, 1881]:206, and 20[December 1, 1885]:360; Joseph F. Smith, *Journal of Discourses* 20:29; and Danel W. Bachman, "A Study of the Mormon Practice of Plural Marriage before the Death of Joseph Smith," M.A. thesis, Purdue University, 1975.)

[19]Joseph Smith.

[20]Oliver Cowdery.

[21]November 1837.

[22]Joseph Smith.

[23]Specifically, plural marriage.

[24]Don Carlos Smith.

[25]Cowdery was rebaptized November 12, 1848.

April 13, 1838

The High Council of Zion met in Far-West on Friday April 13th 1838[1]

Thomas B. Marsh, David W. Patten and Brygham Young Presiding.

The Council was organized as follows:

Simeon Carter	No. 1	Jared Carter	No. 2
Thomas Grover	" 3	John P. Green	" 4
Levi Jackman	" 5	Solomon Hancock	" 6

George Morey	" 7	Newel Knight	" 8
George M. Hinkle	" 9	George W. Harris	" 10
Elias Higbee	" 11	John Murdock	" 12

The Council was opened by singing and prayer by President David W. Patten after which several charges were preferred against Lyman E. Johnson which are as follows:

"To the Council of the Church of Christ of Latter day Saints in Missouri.

I prefer the following charges before your honorable body against Lyman E. Johnson.

1st, For persecuting brethren by stiring up people to prosecute them, and urging on vexatious lawsuits against them and thereby bringing distress upon the inocent.[2]

2nd For virtually denying the faith of the Church of Christ of Latter Day saints, by vindicating the cause of the enemies of this Church, who are dissenters from us, now in Kirtland, and speaking reproachfully of the Church and High Council, by saying their proceedings were illegal and that he never would acknowledge them to be legal, these assertions were without foundation and truth, also, treating the Church with contempt by absenting himself from meetings on the sabbath, by not observing his prayers in the season thereof and by not observing the word of wisdom.

3rd. For seeking to injure the character of Joseph Smith jr by reporting that he had a demand against him of one thousand dollars, when it was without foundation in truth

4th For laying voilent hands on our Brother Phineas Young, and by kicking and beating him, thereby throwing contempt on the Church of Christ of Latter-Day Saints in Missouri

5th. And by saying that he would appeal the suit between him & Brother Phineas Young and take it out of the County, saying that he could not get justice done him, thereby speaking reproachfully of the authority of Caldwell County.

6th For telling a falshood.

7th For taking whiskey and making Weldon[3] drink & then cheating him out of his property

A Ripley"[4]

After which a letter was read from the defendant by John Murdock as follows:

"Far West, Mo April 12th 1838

Sir Yours of the 9th inst. containing a copy of six charges, preferred, before the Council by A. Ripley, against me has been received, and it appears to me to be a novel document, assuming a right to compel me under pain of religious sensure and excommunication not to appeal a lawsuit or change the venue of the same in which I am deeply interested, without the consent of a religious body.

This assumption of power being manifest in the fifth Charge, I should not condescend to put my constitutional rights at issue upon so disrespectful a point; as to answer any other of those charges until that is withdrawn & untill then shall withdraw my self from your society and fellowship.

Yours

Lyman E. Johnson

Mr John Murdock

The case was not considered difficult, therefore, two spake on the case; viz Thomas Grover, on the part of the Church and John P. Green on the part of the defendant.

George M. Hinkle testifies he knew Lyman E. Johnson has been active in urging on lawsuits, also, that L. E. Johnson told him he had a note against him (Hinkle) which he procured in Clay County, which was not the case, as he had no note of the description, therefore, he had lied.

Thos Grover testifies that Mr Gilbert had a claim upon a piece of land, after which Lyman E. Johnson entered it from under him, after being told that Mr Gilbert had claim upon it.

Alanson Ripley testifies, that Lyman E. Johnson had been

told that there was a claim upon the piece of land which was referred to above, also he heard Lyman E. Johnson say he had a note against J. Smith jr.

Simeon Carter, testifies, that Lyman E. Johnson inquired of him if there was any land to be entered, when he told him he thought there was none except it was some which poor brethren had a claim on, and that he must not enter that, as it was contrary to the decision of the High Council; afterwards he did enter a forty upon which one of the brethren had made some improvement.

Arthur Morrison testifies that it was the understanding that Lyman E. Johnson acted as an Atterney for Mr. Bennor in commencing a suit against George M. Hinkle, & took a very active part in the case.

David W. Patten testifies, that Lyman E. Johnson had told him in conversation at different times, that while God sat upon his throne or his face the color it now was, he never would sanction the proceedings of the High Council in this place, because he said they were illegal and as for coming to this Council he would not, also he used tea and coffee while living at D. W. Patten's and did not tend family prayers while living at his house, also had used his influence against certain brethren especially against the Smith family, also he had a correspondence with the dissenters at Kirtland and vindicated their cause and spoke against the First Presidents of the Church, also made light of the word of wisdom, also Lyman E Johnson reported he had a thousand dollar note against Joseph Smith jr

Joseph Smith jr testifies that he, Lyman E. Johnson vindicated the cause of the dissenters, both in publick and private and spoke against the Saints while in Kirtland, also heard Lyman E. Johnson say that while God sat upon his throne and his face was the color it now was he never would sanction the proceedings of the Church and Council, in this place also Lyman E. Johnson told him he had a thousand dollar note against him (J. Smith) which was not the case, but the note which he pretended to have was one given to Joseph Smith jr while acting as cashier in the Kirtland Bank

Absolom Scritchfield testifies, that he has seen Lyman E. Johnson come to Mr. Musick's[5] (tavern) and drink liquor, say brandy.[6]

George W. Harris testifies that he has neglected to attend meeting on the Sabbath days.

George Morey concurs with the above testimony.

The Council adjourned for one hour.

The Council convened agreeable to adjournment.

Opened in prayer by President B. Young.

Brigham Young, testifies that Phineas Young came to Br. Green's[7] a few mornings since, with his head cut the blood running out of his ears, also his stomach was injured, & Phineas said Lyman E. Johnson had fought him; which was proved in court afterwards.

John P. Green concurs with the above testimony.

Dimic B. Huntington, testifies that Lyman E. Johnson told him that he had given Phines Young a pounding, because he had given him the lie, and if any other man should give him the lie, he would not promise that he would not get the same sauce.

Also testifies that Lyman E. Johnson told him, previous, to a decision, being had by civil authority, that he would not begrudge paying five dollars for whipping a man as he did Phineas, but if the judgment was any wise high, he would change the venue and take it out of the County.

David W. Patten, testifies that Lyman E. Johnson told him that he would change the venue and take the suit out of the County, previous to the time that the warrant was issued.

George Morey, testifies, that previous to decision being given on the case of Phineas Young, Lyman E. Johnson told him he intended to get bail and take a change of venue and take it out of the County.

Thomas B. Marsh testifies that Lyman E. Johnson told him, that he had learned the nack of traveling on Steam Boats without paying his fare, by slipping from place to place in the

Boat when they were calling for the fare, and when they would ask him for his pay, he would tell them he had paid it, when he had not.[8]

Edward Partridge, testifies that in purchasing a lot for father Smith, he turned out a note against Lyman E. Johnson, which he rather declined paying at the first presentation, but afterwards said, he had paid taken it up when he had, therefore, told a falshood.

George M. Hinkle testifies that Lyman E. Johnson told him, after he returned from the North, when he purchased his farm of Weldon, the history is as follows: "Before we got there, as we understood, he was fond of liquor, so we got some, lumborum (as Bump[9] called it) and went to Mr Weldon's and got him tolerably well shaved, before we introduced the trade, when we purchased a large farm with great improvements together with five hundred head of hogs, a good stock of horses and cattle, also, a flock of sheep, the plows belonging to the farm &c. for twenty-two hundred ~~dollars~~ and fifty dollars."

Thomas B. Marsh concurs with the above testimony and, also David W. Patten.

After some few appropriate remarks, by the Councellors, it was decided by the President that Lyman E Johnson be no longer considered a member of the Church of Christ of Latter Day Saints, nor a member of the quorum of the twelve Apostles of the Lamb and also be given over to the buffetings of Satan untill he learns to blaspheme no more against the authorities of God.

Ebenezer Robinson Clerk

A charge was then prefered against David Whitmer,[10] by Alonson Ripley, as follows:

"To the High Council of the Church of Latter day Saints in Missouri.

I prefer the following charges before your Honorable body against David Whitmer.

Charge First. For not observing the word of wisdom, for unchristian-like conduct[11] in neglecting to attend to meetings, in uniting with, and possessing the same spirit with the Dissenters, in writing letters to the Dissenters in Kirtland unfavorable to the cause and to Br Joseph Smith jr.

3rd[12] For neglecting ~~his~~ the duties of his calling.

4th. For seperating himself from the cause and the Church while he has a name among us.

5 For signing himself President of the Church of Christ in an insulting letter to the High Council.

A. Ripley."

After which a letter was read from D. Whitmer in words as follows:

"Far West Mo April 13th 1838.

John Murdock

Sir I received a line from you bearing date the 9th inst. requesting me as a High Priest to appear before the High Council and answer to five several charges on this day at 12 o'clock.

You sir with a majority of this Church have decided that certain Councils were legal by which it is said I have been deprived of my office as one of the Presidents of this Church I have thought and still think they were not agreeable to the revelations of God,[13] which I believe and by my now attending this Council, and aswering to charges as a High Priest, should be acknowledging the correctness and legality of those former assumed Councils, which I shall not do.

Believing as I verily do, that you and the leaders of the Councils have a determination to persue your unlawful course at all hazards, and bring others to your standard in violating of the revelations, to spare you any further trouble I hereby withdraw from your fellowship and communion—choosing to seek a place among the meek and humble, where the revelations of Heaven will be observed and the rights of men regarded.

David Whitmer."

After the reading of the above letter it was not considered necessary to investigate the case,[14] as he had offered contempt to the Council by writing the above letter; but let the Councellors speak what they had to say ~~and~~ upon the case and pass decision

The councellors then made a few remarks in which they spoke warmly of the contempt offered to the Council in the above letter, therefore, thought he was not worthy a membership in the Church.

When Prest Marsh made a few remarks and decided that David Whitmer be no longer considered a member of the Church of Christ of Latter day Saints.

Voted by the high Council that Oliver Cowdery be no longer a Committee—man to search out locations for the gathering of the saints.

Council adjourned untill tomorrow morning 9 o'Clock.

Closed in Benediction by President Joseph Smith jr

Ebenezer Robinson, Clerk.

---

[1]See *History of the Church* 3:20. Also the Scriptory Book of Joseph Smith, page 31, Church Archives.

[2]This is the same charge as the one preferred against Oliver Cowdery. Early Church leaders were suspicious of lawyers.

[3]Possibly Micah B. Welton.

[4]Alanson Ripley.

[5]Samuel Musick.

[6]Sabbath violation, neglect of prayers, drinking brandy, and so on would now be subjects of a temple recommend interview, not grounds for excommunication.

[7]John P. Greene.

[8]Note the Church's interest in honesty.

[9]Jacob Bump.

[10]April 13, 1838. An abbreviated account of these proceedings is found in the Scriptory Book of Joseph Smith, page 31, Church Archives.

[11]This charge covered a multitude of sins.

[12]Note that the second charge may have been omitted.

[13]Doctrine and Covenants 107.

[14]Considering the stature of David Whitmer in the Church, the failure of the council to investigate the charges and hold a court is remarkable. (See

Ebenezer Robinson, "Items of Personal History of the Editor," *The Return* [Davis City, Iowa], September 1889.)

April 14, 1838

The High Council of Zion met agreeable to adjournment on Saturday the 14th of April 1838.

Being organized as follows:

Joseph Smith jr Thomas B. Marsh and Brigham Yound, Presiding.

Simeon Carter	No 1	Jared Carter	No 2
Thomas Grover	" 3	Isaac Higbee	" 4
Levi Jackman	" 5	Solomon Hancock	" 6
George Morey	" 7	Newel Knight	" 8
George M. Hinkle	" 9	George W. Harris	" 10
Elias Higbee	" 11	John Murdock	" 12

Council opened in prayer by Elder John Murdock.

An appealed case was then presented to the Council, pending between Eders Wait and West,[1] from the Elders quorum, when the proceedings of the Elders quorum were read also the charges which reads as follows:

"Far West March 27th 1838.

To the High Council,

I, in appealing the case between me and Elder West, to the High Council, prefer the first charge contained in the original charges, namely; A spirit of dissension, in that he declared publickly that he did not believe in the vote of the General Assembly, last Nov. 7th, "not to support stores and shops selling spiritous liquors, tea, coffee, and tobacco."[2] And also I shall bring any testimony I can find to the same effect and connect it with the foregoing charge.

And also, the first item of the second charge contained in the original, namely; Teaching incorrect doctrine in that he said the word of wisdom did not concern our Spiritual Salvation.[3]

Truman Wait, Complainant."

The case was not considered difficult, therefore, two Councellors were to spak on the case, viz: George Morey, on the part of the Church, and Newel Knight, on the part of the part of the defendant.

Some remarks were made by the defendant, in which he acknowledge a part of the first charge.

Darwin Chase, testifies that he heard Nathan West say that he would not believe the decision of the High Council if it did not coincide with the Book of Covenants.

Also, he heard Mr West say that he did not covenant to not uphold stores and shops, which sold liquor, tea, coffee and tobacco, because he had already made as many covenants as he kept &c but if any persons had made any such covenants, he would say to them 'for God's sake to keep them.'

William Hulet, testifies that he heard Elder West say that if he had his mind made up on ~~any~~ a certain item of Revelation and the High Council should decide contrary his mind upon that item, he would not believe the decision except they would bring proof to substantiate it. Also that he never did hear Elder West say any thing against Joseph Smith jr but heard him say that he considered him the Prophet as much as ever.

The Council adjourned one hour.

Council convened according to adjournment.

Silas Maynard testifies, that he heard Elder West say one evening last winter that he did not acquiece in the proceedings of the High Council and Church in cutting off W. W. Phelps & John Whitmer from the Presidents office.

Thomas Grover, testifies, that at the General Conference last winter, when the case of W. W. Phelps & John Whitmer was investigated, Elder West voted to have them continue in the office of Presidents.

Elder West confesses, that at the time of the Conference above referred to, he did think the move ~~two~~ too hasty and did not coincide with them the proceedings of the Council at that time, but now saw the matter different and does coincide with them &c.

Elder Wait, testifies that Elder West said in a Conference of Elders that he did not consider the word of Wisdom given by Commandment or Constraint.

After a few remarks by the Councellors and parties it was decided by the President, that considering the case, Br. West had erred in spirit, therefore, feel to admonish him, but do not find anything in him worthy of death or bonds.

Council adjourned untill next Saturday at 9 o'clock.

Closed in prayer by ~~President~~ Br Harris.[4]

Ebenezer Robinson Clerk

---

[1]Truman Wait and Nathan West.
[2]See page 124.
[3]Another case of the Word of Wisdom being challenged and tested.
[4]George W. Harris.

April 21, 1838

High Council met according to adjourment on Saturday the 21st of April 1838.

After singing a hymn, a prayer was offered by Br. Joseph Smith jr.

A charge was then preferred against Lyman Wight by John Anderson which, charge was put over until Thursday the 24th of May next, at 9 o'clock A. M.

1st Resolved, that the "Elders Journal" be published monthly as it was commenced.

2nd Resolved that President Thomas B. Marsh be the publisher of the "Elders Journal."

3rd Resolved, that the printing press, type and furniture which was purchased of John Whitmer with all the furniture pertaining to the establishment, be sold by the Committee to Edward Partridge, and that he be authorized to pay for the same out of the avails of the City lots or donations

4th Resolved, that Edward Partridge do not pay to W. W. Phelps and John Whitmer a certain mortgage,[1] which they hold against him, and that this Council uphold him in not paying the the above mortgage.

5th Resolved—that this Council authorize Edward Partridge to assist, in making houses on, and fencing the lots in this City which are appropriated to the use of Joseph Smith jr. and Sidney Rigdon, with the avails arising from the town plot.

6th Resolved—that Edward Partridge make an appropriation of not more than one hundred dollars to this Schoolhouse, out of the avails of the town plot.[2]

7th Resolved that this Council support Thomas B. Marsh as the publisher of the "Elders Journal" and use their influence to obtain subscriptions for the same.

8th Resolved that this Council, the Bishop and his Council use their influence to cause the people to consecrate to the Lord, for the support of the poor and needy.

9th Resolved that the Bishop be authorized to obtain or build a sufficient storehouse or houses to recieve all the ~~concie~~ consecrations of the people, to be paid for out of the avails of the town plot

10th Resolved that this High Council and Clerk publish the minites of the High Council, from time to time as they shall deem proper[3]

11th Resolved that the aforesaid record commence at the time of the last Council held in Clay County.

Adjourned till Saturday the 28th inst

John P. Green Clk pro. tem.

---

[1]See pages 109, 147-49.

[2]Much of the business of the high council was secular in nature, such as decisions to publish, to buy property, and to appropriate money for schools.

[3]Some high council minutes had previously been published in the *Elders Journal.*

April 28, 1838

The High Council of Zion met in Far West April 28 1838[1] agreeable to adjournment.

Thomas B. Marsh and David W. Patten, Presiding.

The Council was organized as follows:

Simeon Carter	No. 1	Jared Carter	No. 2
Levi Jackman	" 3	Zechariah Wilson	" 4
Sidney Rigdon	" 5	Joseph Smith jr	" 6
George Morey	" 7	Newel Knight	" 8
George M. Hinkle	" 9	George W. Harris	" 10
Elias Higbee	"11	John Murdock	" 12

After which it was voted that Joseph Smith jr and Sidney Rigdon act in the places of NO. 9 & 10.

The Council was opened by in prayer by in Prest Marsh

An appeal case[2] was presented pending between Jackson and Lyons, when the minutes of an Elder's meeting was read by Councellor Hinkle in which the above case had been tried, also the charges and the appeal. The several charges were read when the accused confessed the 1st, 2nd 3rd 4th the 5th he denied also the 6th, 7th 8th, 9th, 10th & 11th.

The Case was considered difficult, therefore, four were to speak on it viz: George M. Hinkle and Sidney Rigdon on the part of the Church and George W. Harris and Joseph Smith jr on the part of the defendant.

The Council adjourned for one hour.

The Council met agreeable to adjournment.

Opened in singing "This Earth was once a garden place" &c and Prayer by President David W. Patten.

Peter Dustan was appointed to fill the seat of No. 2 pro. tempore.

Voted by the High Council that the proceedings of the Elder's Conference held to investigate the case of J. Lemons and

S. Wixom[3] are null and void, as they kept no regular minutes or records of them.

Br. Best[4] testifies that he heard Br Lyons[5] prophecy at Br Wheeler's[6] that some one would be heard to mourn, after that Lyons told him that he had a wife selected and she was in the house, they were then at Br Curtis',[7] and she was Sister Jackson and Lyons requested him to tell her that her husband was dead, also, Lyons told him, the Lord had shown her to him for his wife, also heard Lyons say that if she broke her covenant she would be miserable, because he had seen her future state, also, when he told Sister Jackson what Lyons requested him, she cried and said she hoped the Lord would be merciful to her in her afflictions

At another time, he heard Sister Jackson say that Lyons told her the Lord had revealed to him that she was to be his wife and she believed that she had a testimony that he told the truth. Sister Jackson had been absent from her husband about five months, but he returned soon after, which was some time in November last. Also, was knowing to Lyons walking to and from meetings with her, both in night and day time, as she lived at his house.

Shadrach Roundy—testifies that Lyons had some conversation with him respecting getting a wife, saying he was going to have a wife and that by revelation, because the Lord was going to let him have a wife with whom he could live in peace &c.

At another time Lyons told him that he enquired of the Lord respecting a companion, when Sister Jackson was presented before him, when he said to the Lord "She is pregnant by another man;" when the Lord replied "wait my time & it will all come right" Lyons generally took the lead of meetings in that Branch.[8]

John P. Barnam[9] testifies that, Lyons told him he had a revelation and it was of God, he should be married in a few days, but seemed to almost doubt of its truth, but soon after he enquired of the Lord to know whether it was of God or not, when the reply was, "I know all things," therefore Lyons

Concluded it was of God, also that Lyons was a man of great influence in the Church, and when he spoke in the name of the Lord, the brethren had great confidence in it &c

Thomas Guyman concurs in the testimony previously given, also he heard Sister Jackson say she was afraid of the curses of God falling upon her, therefore she consented to have Br Lyons but was soon sorry for it also after Lyons said her husband was dead she was considerably troubled about it and frequently requested the Church to pray for her husband that he might return &c but after some time she expressed her fears that he was dead & was inclined to think she had a testimony to that effect, also Lyons told him Brother Best had given him liberty to come to his house to see Sister Jackson.

Br Jackson testifies that his wife was not pregnant when he returned (See Sister Jackson's letter on Pages 157 and 158 & 159.[10])

Br Benjamin testifies that, Calvin Reed, a boy of about 15 years of age, said he had a revelation or vision, in which he saw, Br Jackson dead or preaching to the spirits in prison &c.

After some lengthy remarks by the Councellors, and very good instruction given by Councellor Smith,[11] the accused made confession to the satisfaction of the Council, when it was decided that Br Lyons be retained in the Church, but his license be taken from him, as it is ~~not~~ considered that he is not qualified to hold an office in this Church

The Council concurred with the foregoing decision.

The Council adjourned untill two weeks from today.

Closed in prayer by Sidney Rigdon.

Ebenezer Robinson Clerk

---

[1]See *History of the Church* 3:25-26.

[2]Another account of this trial, in the hand of George W. Robinson, is found in the Scriptory Book of Joseph Smith, pages 34-37, Church Archives. This record notes that this appeal case came from a branch of the Church near Guymon's Mill, Missouri. See also *History of the Church* 3:25.

[3]John Lemon and Solomon Wixom.
[4]Henry Best.
[5]Aaron Lyons.
[6]Possibly Baldwin Wheeler.
[7]Probably Nahum Curtis.
[8]Known as the Salem Branch.
[9]Probably John P. Barnard.
[10]See pages 206-8.
[11]Joseph Smith.

May 13, 1838

The High Council of Zion met in Far West May 13th 1838.[1]
Thomas B. Marsh presiding.
The Council was organized as follows:

Simeon Carter	No 1	Isaac Higbee	No 2
James McCord[2]	" 3	John P. Green	" 4
James Emmett	" 5	Solomon Hancock	" 6
Simeon Gardner	" 7	Ebenezer Robinson	" 8
George M. Hinkle	" 9	George W. Harris	"10
Elias Higbee	" 11	John Murdock	"12

The Council was opened by prayer by Prest. T. B. Marsh

A case was then presented pending between Samuel Kimball, plaintiff and John L. Butler, James Emmett, and James Hendrix defendant, which was put over untill the last Thursday in June next.

1st Resolved—That the High Council hold monthly sessions, to be the last Thursday in each month, the first to commence the last Thursday in June next[3]

2nd Resolved—That Sidney Rigdon be appointed to correct the matter for the "Elders Journal" (that is) the Orthography and Prosody of the different letters &c.

3rd Resolved That the High Council authorize the Bishop to set apart eighty acres of land for the benefit of Sidney Rigdon and also, 80 acres for Joseph Smith jr.[4]

4th Resolved That the High Council use their influence to have the Church consecrate their properties for the benefit of the poor.

5th Resolved That Elias Higbee, Simeon Carter, & George W. Harris be a committee to converse with Joseph Smith jr and Sidney Rigdon, to agree upon some particular price or wages for their services in the printing office & their saleries for the coming year.[5]

6th Resolved That the Committee be authorized to instruct the Bishop to pay the First Presidency, J. Smith, & Sidney Rigdon, whatever sum they agree with them for.[6]

The Council adjourned untill a week from next Thursday, the 24th inst

Ebenezer Robinson Clerk

---

[1]See *History of the Church* 3:31-32. In *History of the Church*, the date of this meeting is given as May 12, 1838.

[2]Probably not Dr. McCord who left the Church on May 11, 1838. See *History of the Church* 3:31.

[3]The high council had been meeting at random. Now a decision was made to have it meet on a regular schedule.

[4]These large parcels were located outside the original city plot.

[5]A more detailed account of this meeting, found in the Scriptory Book of Joseph Smith (pages 41-42), gives insight into this resolution: "The presidency laid before the high Council, their Situation, as to maintaining their families in the Situation & relation they Stood to the Church, Spending as they have, for eight years, their time and tallents & property in the Service of the Church, and are now reduced as it were, to absolute begery, and Still were detained in Service of the Church, and it now become[s] necessary that Something Should be done for their Support either by the Church, or else they must do it themselves, of their own labour, and if the Church Said help yourselves they would thank them, and immediately do So, but if the Church Said Serve us then Some provision must be made for them. The Subject was taken into concideration, by the Council (who acts for the Church), and thoroughly investigated. Thereupon the Council voted to authorize the Bishop to give or make over to Prest. Joseph Smith Jr. & Sidney Rigdon each an eighty of land Situated adjacent to the City Corporation which land is the property of the Church allso voted that a committee of three be appointed of the Council, to contract with Said presidency to their sattisfaction, for their Services this present year not for preaching or for receiving the word of God

by revelation neither for instructing the Saints in righteousness, but for Services rendered in the printing establishment in translating the ancient records &c. &c. The committee, which consisted of Geo. W. Harris, Elias Higbee & Simeon Carter who agreed that Prest Smith & Rigdon should be entitled to & receive for this year [$1,100 each] as a just remuneration for their services." (See also *History of the Church* 3:32.)

[6]See Ebenezer Robinson, "Items of Personal History of the Editor," *The Return* (Davis City, Iowa), October 1889. Robinson stated that such an uproar followed the decision to pay the First Presidency annual wages that the request was finally dropped.

May 24, 1838

The High Council of Zion met in Far-West on Thursday the 24th of May 1838

Brygum Young, Presiding.

The Council was organized as follows:

Reynalds Cahoon	No 1	Jared Carter	No 2
Thomas Grover	" 3	John P. Green	" 4
Daniel Carn	" 5	Solomon Hancock	" 6
James McCord	" 7	Ebenezer Robinson	" 8
George M. Hinkle	" 9	George W. Harris	" 10
Brigham Young	" 11	John Murdock	" 12

The Council was opened in prayer by Prest Young.

A Charge was then read by John Murdock against Lyman Wight, which had been prefered by John Anderson.[1]

After which another charge was read against Lyman Wight prefered by Daniel Avery.

Also another charge was read against Lyman Wight prefered by William Wirick, which were all put over untill the last Thursday in June.[2]

Council Adjourned untill the last Thursday in June next.

Ebenezer Robinson, Clerk.

---

[1]See page 195.

[2]See page 196.

June 23, 1838

The High Council of Zion met in Far West June 23rd 1838.[1]
Presidents Marsh and Patten Presiding
The Council was organized as follows

Simeon Carter	No 1	Jared Carter	No. 2
Thomas Grover	" 3	John P. Green	" 4
Levi Jackman	" 5	Sampson Avard	" 6
John Greg	" 7	Guyman[3]	" 8
Reynalds Cahoon	" 9	George W. Harris	" 10
Chase[2]	" 11	Sylvester Hulett	" 12

The Council was opened by singing by Prest Marsh
After much consultation it was,

1st Resolved That Thomas B. Marsh be sole proprietor of the printing establishment.

2nd Resolved—That every order, sent from Kirtland upon Joseph Smith jr, Sidney Rigdon, and Hyrum Smith, shall be rejected, untill a bill of particulars be recieved from their agents at Kirtland.[4]

3rd Resolved That the Clerk be authorized to inform those agents, of the proceedings of the Council, by writing.

4th Resolved—That the High Council authorize the Bishop, to give President David W. Patten an acre of land upon which he now lives, also, give up the obligation he now holds against him.[5]

5th Resolved—That the Bishop take the Musick house from off the hands of Joseph Smith jr and dispose of it as he pleases.

6th Resolved That a committee be appointed to labor with John Burke, Adam Lightner, and Joseph Smith jr, keepers of publick houses, that they keep ~~a~~ good orderly houses, and have no drinking, swearing, gambling, and debauchery carried on therein.

7th Resolved—That Benjamin Benson & Daniel Shearer, be the aforesaid committee.[6]

8th Resolved That the High Council use their influence to

have Br Marsh dispose of his land,[7] to obtain money to further on the printing buisness.

The Council adjourned.

E. Robinson Clerk.

---

[1]On the previous Sabbath, June 17, 1838, Sidney Rigdon had preached his "Salt Sermon" which admonished local dissenters to withdraw from Far West, Missouri. The Scriptory Book of Joseph Smith, page 47, gives the context for the speech: "I [George W. Robinson] would mention or notice something about O. Cowdery David Whitmer Lyman E. Johnson and John Whitmer who being guilty of bace iniquities and that to manifest in the ages of all men, and being often entreated would continue in their course Seeking the Lives of the First Presidency and to overthrow the Kingdom of God which they once testified off, Prest Rigdon preached one Sabbath upon the Salt that had lost its Savour that it is henceforth good for nothing but to be cast out, and troden under foot of men, And the wicked flee when no man pursueth. These men took warning, and Soon they were Seen bounding over the prairie like the Scape Goat to carry of[f] their own Sins we have not Seen them Since, their influence is gone, and they are in a miserable condition. So also it with all who turn from the truth to Lying Cheating defrauding & Swindeling."

[2]Stephen or Darwin Chase.

[3]Thomas Guyman.

[4]The agents were Newel K. Whitney, Oliver Granger, and William Marks.

[5]See page 115.

[6]See page 191.

[7]Marsh had extensive landholdings in and around Far West.

June 28, 1838

Far-West June 28th 1838

The High Council of Zion met according to adjournment.

Thomas B. Marsh President

Simeon Carter	No 1	Jared Carter	No 2
Harlow Redfield	" 3	John P. Green	" 4
Levi Jackman	" 5	Solomon Hancock	" 6
Isaac Higbee	" 7	Newel Knight	" 8
John Killion	" 9	George W. Harris	" 10
Elias Higbee	" 11	John Murdock	" 12

The Council was opened by singing "~~How~~ Now let us rejoice in the day of Salvation," &c. and prayer by President Patten.

The following report was then read by the Clerk & accepted by the Council.

"To the Presidency and High Council of the Church of Jesus Christ of Latter Day Saints in Zion, Greeting.

We the undersigned, being a committee to wait upon the publick houses and groceries in this place, Far West, and inform the keepers of the same, of the determination and desire of the spiritual authorities of this Stake to improve the moral condition of the same, do respectfully report, that we attended to that duty, and found Mr J. Smith jr, Mr. J. Burke and families manifested a perfect willingness to comply with the request of your Honorable body. Mr Adam Lightner,[1] grocer manifested the same spirit and agreed that if it was requested he would not keep any more ardent spirits in the place &c. June 28th 1838."

Daniel Shearer.
Benjamin Benson."

The following charges were then ~~read~~ prefered and read

"To the Presidency and High Council.

This may certify that I prefer a charge against James Emmett, John L. Butler and James Hendrix for forbiding me to commune under a pretence that I was not a member of the Church, and for trying to defraud me in deal, and for lying & slander &c. April 23rd 1838.

Samuel Kimball."

The case was not considered difficult, therefore, two councellors spake, ~~on~~ viz: Simeon Carter on the part of the accuser, and Don C. Smith pro. tem. on the part of the accused.

Simeon Gardner, testifies that he heard Emmett say, in preaching that there was thieves in the Church & he would forbid some from partaking the sacrament & call some names after awhile but did not call any names in his hearing. Emmett seemed to convey the idea that he knew this thing by spirit. Some time after this he heard Emmett forbid, Kimball to partake the sacrament.

H. Gardner testifies that he heard Emmett say, in preaching, that there were thieves in the Church and hereafter he should mention names, this he knew by the Spirit of God, the next Sunday he was at meeting again, and heard Emmett say that there was theft in the family of Kimball, he also said that Butler knew there was iniquity in the Church and he (Butler) had neglected to see to it but would hereafter. He heard Emmett forbid Kimball to partake of the sacrament also that he is acquainted with the family of Kimball & knows nothing against them, also, knows nothing against the defendants.

Charity Butler testfies that she heard Emmett say Kimball had forbid his boys going to meeting and it would be well for the brethren to keep their children from Kimball's, as he kept them from meeting, also, she had heard Kimball speak hard against John Butler and James Hendrix, but his family was respectable people

Julia Hendrix testifies that Emmett and her husband entered a forty of land and were to share equally in the timber, also, Kimball and Butler entered a forty apiece, and the understanding was, that they were to share equally in the timber, but she does not know as they have divided the timber, also, she was at a meeting where fellowship was withdrawn from Kimball by the members of the branch to which he belonged and he was not as yet restored.

Isaac Higbee testifies that he was one of the company who was appointed to divide the timber between four brethren above named, which they did, as he thought to their satisfaction. The time they attended to this buisness was after the parties had been before the Bishop, in which decision they justified Kimball instead of criminating him.

Also heard Emmett forbid Kimball to partake the sacrament and he understood it was because he did not comply with the Bishop's decision.

Simeon Gardner concurs with the foregoing testimony.

Council adjourned one hour.

Council convened agreeable to adjournment.

Opened by singing "The Spirit of God like a fire is" &c. and prayer by President Patten.

As the parties had agreed to join issue and come to trial and prove what they could against each other, therefore, it was voted that two more speak upon the case, viz: Harlow Redfield, on the part of the accuser and John P. Green on the part of the accused, after which the following charges were prefered against Samuel Kimball by John L. Butler.

"I prefer a charge against Samuel Kimball for slandering myself and others, and destroying other people's property, and rendering his family unhappy.

June 28th 1838

J. L. Butler."

Julia Hendrix testifies that she has heard Kimball call his family lazy & trifling &c.

Charity Butler, testifies that she has heard Kimball say he would never consecrate to Bishop Edward Partridge, also heard him say his children were lazy.

Malinda Porter testifies that she has heard Kimball scold at his family (i.e.) children, also has heard him speak against Emmett & Butler, calling them rascals, villians, scape gallows, &c., also heard him speak against the Bishop, saying his Council would counsel for hire and he would judge for reward

Jerome Benson testifies that he has heard Kimball say that the Bishop give in a partial decision in his case.

Warner Porter testifies that he heard Kimball say that Emmett and Butler had acted the rascal and scounderal long enough, &c

Lavina Gardner testifies that Kimball scolds his family at a harsh rate and will say that he will leave them, if they do not obey him he will never come back, but they might starve for ought he cared, also accused his family of being priestridden, because they would go to meeting when Emmett and Butler took the lead; also testifies that he is a very industrious man, and provides for his family as well as he possibly can, and always taught his children to act in righteousness, and not lie nor commit any sin of the kind & be industrious

Rebecca Kimball testifies that her father is rather fretful, but his children did not mind him as they had ought, and when he was most fretful, it would be when he would get most discouraged about getting along and supporting his family, and that his children did not help him as they might, also, he taught his children to be industrious.

The Council decided that the decision, of the Bishop, was illegal, consequently, null and void, and therefore that Samuel Kimball was a member of the Church.[2]

After some remarks by the Councellors, and the plaintiff, the Council adjourned untill tomorrow morning at 8 o'clock.

---

[1]Lightner's willingness to comply with this request is interesting since he was a nonmember.

[2]Note that an appeal to a higher court resulted in overturning the lower court's decision.

June 29, 1838

June 29th 1838 Far West Mo

The High Council met according to adjournment and was organized. President Marsh opened by prayer.

James Emmett then came forward and plead his own cause, by justifying himself also John L. Butler and James Hendrix.

President Marsh then arose and addressed the Council and decided that Hendrix was not criminated.

He then addressed Emmett by chastising him for his course of conduct and condemned the Spirit he was of.

He then chastised Kimball for speaking against the Bishop

and his Council and then proceeded to give the following decision.

"That Samuel Kimball confess his faults to those individuals whom he has slandered, and walk before his family as a man of God, or he could not have a standing in the Church: this confession to be made in the publick congregation.

That James Emmett should confess to the Council that he had insulted them, and should make satisfaction to them, and also that he should publickly confess, that he had been exercised with a delusive spirit, and that he come out publickly and denounce it forever, also confess that he had unlawfully slandered the family of Samuel Kimball, and that unless he humbly confess these things, he could not hold a standing in the Church.

That John L. Butler was in the fault and he was also requested to confess to Samuel Kimball."

The Council unanimously sanctioned the decision of the President

Adjourned for one hour.

High Council met according to adjourment.

George M. Hinkle took his seat in the place of John Killion, pro. tem.

President Marsh opened by prayer.

The charge against Lyman Wight by John Anderson (prefered the 24th of May) was then presented by John Anderson, viz:

"For fellowship, for unjust deal and for abuse to me and for defamation of character.

Voted that two speak on a side, viz: Jackman[1] and I. Higbee for the plaintiff and Hancock and Knight for the defendant.

Henry Sabrisky, states that Anderson sold Wight a certain mill seat for the benefit of the Church and that Wight was to give one hundred dollars for the mill seat, to be paid in one year.

The President decided that the above charge could not bear in this Council, the plaintiff then withdrew his suit.

A charge was then taken up against Lyman Wight for intoxication and thereby disgracing the Church (prefered the 24th of May) by ~~Daniel Avery~~. William Wirick

Edward Larkey states that he was going by the house of the defendant and saw him leaning over the fence and had the appearance of intoxication, but did not see him drink any thing, also that he was in Liberty[2] and saw Wight call for liquor, but saw him drink nothing.

Daniel Avery states that he saw the defendant leaning over the fence and hardly able to speak and to appearance intoxicated

Arthur Morrison says he went to Liberty with the defendant and that his breath smelt of whiskey and was hardly capable of managing himself and he considered him intoxicated with liquor.

L Gibbs[3] says last summer Wight called at his shop a number of times and drank wine, but did not know that he was drunk

After the foregoing testimony a number more was presented in writing, after which the defendant agreed that he was intoxicated.

The President then decided that Lyman Wight must confess this sin with in one month or not be considered a member of the Church[4]

---

[1]Levi Jackman.
[2]Liberty, Clay County, Missouri.
[3]Luman Gibbs.
[4]Note that Wight was not taken directly to court, but given a period of time to confess his error.

July 6, 1838

The High Council and Bishop of Zion met in Far West. July 6th 1838,[1] to transact certain Church buisness.

George M. Hinkle laid before the Council the circumstances of his moving to De Witt,[2] therefore he wished to sell his house to Bishop Partridge for President Joseph Smith jr when it was,

1st Resolved—That the High Council instruct the Bishop to purchase Br Hinkle's house for Prest J. Smith jr

2nd Resolved, That the Bishop be instructed to purchase a cook stove for Prest Joseph Smith jr.

3rd Resolved That the Bishop be instructed to prepare the house, aforesaid, and make it comfortable to dwell in.

Council adjourned.

Ebenezer Robinson, Clerk

---

[1]On July 4, 1838, two days earlier, Sidney Rigdon delivered his inflammatory Fourth of July speech, which aroused the ire of the Missourians. George W. Robinson, the Prophet's clerk, recorded the following in the Scriptory Book of Joseph Smith: "This day was Spent in Cellebrating the 4th of July in commemoration of the declaration of Independence of the United States of America, and also to make our decleration of Independence from all mobs and persecutions which have been inflicted upon us time after time untill we could bear it no longer being driven by ruthless mobs and enimies of the truth. from our homes our property confiscated our lives exposed and our all jeopardized by such conduct. We therefore met on this day in Far West Mo. to make our declaration of independance, and to lay the cornerstones of the house of the Lord agreeably to the commandment of the Lord unto us given April 26th 1838. . . . An address was delivered by Prest. S. Rigdon . . . . The order of the day was most splendid and beautiful Several thousand of Spectators were present to witness the S[c]ene. The address was delivered on the public square under the hoisted flagg representing the Liberty and independence of these United States of America."

[2]George M. Hinkle and John Murdock, high councilors in Far West, were sent by the high council to establish a Mormon settlement in DeWitt, Carroll County, Missouri. The site, located at the confluence of the Grand and Missouri Rivers, was an ideal port of entry for Mormon goods to be shipped to Adam-Ondi-Ahman. Hinkle and Murdock purchased half of the town plat from Henry Root on June 23, 1838, for $500. Bishop Partridge signed the note. In July 1838 families began gathering to DeWitt, and by October 1838 some seventy Mormon families were residing there. The increasing Mormon population, however, excited the citizens of Carroll County, and by October 1838 they were forced to leave. In February 1839 both Hinkle and Murdock sold their interest in the town plat.

July 6, 1838

Conference

Far-West Mo. Friday July 6th 1838.

The authorities of the Church of Jesus Christ of Latter Day Saints, opened at this City to hold the Second Quarterly Conference, in this City of Zion and to transact Church buisness.

The conference opened by singing "The Spirit of God like a fire is burning" and prayer by President D. W. Patten, after which another hymn was sung, "Now let us rejoice in the day of Salvation."

Presidents Joseph Smith jr. & Sidney Rigdon, Presiding.

The Presidents of the different Quorums proceeded to organize their respective Quorums, as follows:

First the High Council.

Second, the High Priests.

Third the Seventies by King Follett acting as President as the Presidents were absent.

Fourth, the Elders, by Ralph Cox, acting President in the absence of the President.

Fifth the Bishop and Council.

Sixth the Priests.

Seventh the ~~Deacons~~ Teachers by T. B. Clark[1] acting President of the day.

Eighth, the Deacons, by Isaac Hamblin acting President for the day.

When the following hymn was sung "Oh happy souls who pray."

The Conference adjourned for one hour.

The Conference convened agreeable to adjournment, opened by singing, "He died the great Redeemer died."

After which President Sidney Rigdon made a few remarks

respecting the officers in the Church saying, each officer must stand in his place, and perform his duty as it is required at his hand, and in so doing, he would be willing to predict, that there would be no difficulty in the Church untill the coming of Christ, also that the foundation of the happiness of the Church rests upon the heads of the Teachers and Deacons, whose duty it is to go from house to house and see that each family in the Church is kept in order, and that the children are taught the principles of righteousness; and also that the time had come when it was required at the hands of the Deacons, Teachers, & Priests to render an account of their stewardship, the standing of the various branches to which they belonged, &c.[2] he also gave much good instruction to the Upper Priest-hood—He then addressed all the quorums present on the subject of speaking lightly of each other, thinking, perhaps, he had not much influence, when at the same time some one might be present who had great confidence in you, and it would soon lead to a great difficulty, because all the Officers in the Church has more influence ~~in~~ than he may suspect, therefore, when you speak, let your words be seasoned with grace.

He then addressed the Elders, saying they were called to convert the world, and admonished them to put away ambition and go and perform the duty which is required at their hands—he compared the Elders to quarriers of stone, who merely quarried the stones and brought them to the building, where the Priests, Teachers, and Deacons, are polishers, whose duty it is to prepare them for the building.

After which several recommends were read and passed the Conference, viz:

Elisha Everett To the office of a Teacher

William Davis & John Buckhannan also Deacons

Norvil Head to the office of an Elder.

Allen Rathburn to the office of a Deacon.

John Lytle, who had been ordained a Priest was reordained by the Conference.

Ahisa Young was recommended to the office of Teacher.

Truman Brace, was ordained a Deacon in Jackson County but has not as yet received his licence, therefore, it was voted, by the Conference that he receive a licence.

Voted that Hezekiah Peck receive a licence as a Priest. Voted that William Gregory receive a renewal of his licence.

Voted that Alvin C. Graves recieve a new licence as a Teacher.

Voted that John S. Higbee recieve a new licence as a Deacon.

Voted that Jackson Smith recieve a new licence as an Elder.

Voted that Robert B. Thompson recieve a new licence as an Elder.

Voted that Orin Rockwell recieve a licence as Deacon

The Bishop, Edward Partridge represented the Lesser Priesthood, also gave an account of the temporal affairs of the Church.

President Marsh gave some instructions to the Teachers, respecting their returns of their branches.

President Rigdon made some remarks respecting the names of the different Creeks in this vicinity, in which he altered the names of some, as follows:

Steer Creek, he called Silver Creek, Log Creek he called Walnut Creek, Marrow-bone Creek he called Ambrosia. Poor Tom Creek he called Prairie Creek.[3]

After which he confessed the sins of George Walters,[4] who is considered a dangerous man in society, as being a man who harbors wicked and ungodly men in his house both night & day.

The Conference adjourned untill tomorrow at 10 o'clock A.M.

Benediction by Prest Joseph Smith jr

Ebenezer Robinson Clerk.

---

[1]Timothy B. Clark.

[2]In his discourse on duties of officers of the Church, Sidney Rigdon gave good counsel to "hometeachers."

[3]Sidney Rigdon, in an attempt to introduce dignity and refinement into frontier Missouri, renamed local streams. This attempt, however, failed, because the streams now bear the former names.

[4]Walters, a temporary convert, owned large tracts of land in Caldwell County and remained there after the Mormons' expulsion.

July 7, 1838

Far-West, Mo. Saturday July 7th 1838.[1]

The Conference convened agreeable to adjournment.

Opened by Prayer by President Sidney Rigdon.

When the following brethren, who came up in the Camp in 1834 received their blessing, also ordained as Seventies:

Horace Evans,	James Dunn,	Alanson Ripley,
Chandler Holbrook,	Justus Morse,	John Fawsett,
Jackson Smith,	Thomas Turner,	Ebenezer Miller,
Joseph Holbrook	Lewis Sabriskie	Horace Cowan,
James R. Ivie	John C. Annis	

After which several recommends passed the Conference as follows:

William Martin, presented but rejected by the Conference.

Johnathan T. Packer, to the office of Teacher.

Pleasant Ewell to the office of Deacon

Uziel Corey to the office of Deacon.

George Walters came forward ~~and~~ to make confession but did not give satisfaction.

After some remarks by President Rigdon, & On Motion, the Conference adjourned untill the first Friday in October next.

Benediction by President Rigdon.

Ebenezer Robinson, Clerk.

---

[1]During this conference, on Sunday, July 8, 1838, the revelation concerning the law of tithing was received, as well as several other revelations, some not published. (See Doctrine and Covenants, sections 117-120, and unpublished revelation to William W. Phelps and Frederick G. Williams in Kirtland Revelation Book, Church Archives.)

July 26, 1838

The High Council of Zion met in Far-West, Thursday, July 26th 1838[1]

When it was ordered by the Council, that the Bishop be authorized, to furnish the Clerk of this Stake with a Blank Book for him to keep the record of the names of the members of this Stake in.

Ebenezer Robinson, Clk.

---

[1]A more detailed account of this meeting is found in the Scriptory Book of Joseph Smith, pages 59-60:

> This day the first presidency, High Council & Bishops Court, met to take into concideration, the disposing of the publick properties in the hands of the Bishop, in Zion, for the people of Zion have commenced liberally to consecrate agreeably to the revelations, and commandments of the Great I Am of their Surpluss properties &c.
>
> It was agreed that the first presidency keep all their properties, that they can dispose of to their advantage and Support and the remainder be put into the hands of the Bishop or Bishops, agreeably to the commandments, and revelations.
>
> 1st Mooved Seconded & carried unanymously, That the first presidency Shall have their expences defrayed in going to Adam Ondi Awman, and also returning therefrom That the Bishop of Zion pay one half, and the Bishop of Adam Ondi Awman the other half
>
> 2nd Mooved Seconded & carried unanymously that all the traveling expences of the first presidency Shall be defrayed in traveling at any time or place
>
> 3rd Mooved Seconded & carried unanymously That the Bishop be authorised to pay orders coming from the East inasmuch as they will consecrate liberally, but this to be done under the inspection of the first presidency
>
> 4th That the first presidency Shall have the prerogative to say to the Bishop whose orders Shall or may be paid by him in this place or in his jurisdiction. Carried unanymously
>
> 5th Mooved Seconded and carried That the Bishop of Zion receive all consecrations, East, West, & South, who are not in the Jurisdiction of a Bishop of any other stake.
>
> 6th Mooved & carried that we use our influence to put a stop to the Selling of Liquor in the City Far West or in our midst. That

our streets may not be filled with drunkness and that we use our influence to bring down the price of provisions.

7th Mooved Seconded & carried unanymously that br. Wm. W. Phelps, be requested to draw up a petition to remove the County Seat to Far West.

August 31, 1838

The High Council of Zion met in Far West, Thursday, August 31st 1838.

Presidents Sidney Rigdon and Hyrum Smith, Presiding.

The Council was organized as, follows:

Simeon Carter	No. 1	Jared Carter	No 2
Orson Hyde	" 3	John P. Green	" 4
Isaac Higbee	" 5	George W. Robinson	" 6
George Morey	" 7	Amasa Lyman	" 8
Harlow Redfield	" 9	George W. Harris	" 10
Elias Higbee	" 11	Samuel Bent	" 12

The Council was opened by prayer by President Hyrum Smith

An application was made by Orson Hyde in favor of Br Russel;[1] to receive a City lot in Far-West, gratis, which was not granted.

Also an application for a lot in the City Far-West, to be give to Almon Babbitt, which was not granted

An appealed case was presented by John Patten against certain Brethren as follows:

"To the Presidency and High Council of Far-West, Greeting.

The undersigned, feeling very much agrieved, by the report of a committee of Elders, appointed by the quorum of Elders, of Far-West, to investigate a cause of complaint presented to said quorum, by David Frampton, aginst the subscriber, and now, whereas said committee (composed of Daniel Shearer, Ralph Cox, and David Juda) have made a report which I consider very unjust and oppressive and intolerable, contrary to most positive testimony, both oral and written, and which I consider setting a precident dangerous if imitated and subversive of the rights and liberties of free men, and deciples of our Lord and Saviour: I therefore, appeal to your sacred quorum to take unto reconsideration the above; refered to matter of complaint; and also to call to account the above named committee for reporting such a harsh and uncalled for decree, contrary to all known and justly established usages of law and equity in civilized nations and the subscriber as in duty bound will ever pray for the salvation of men.

Dec. 18th 1837. John Patten."

The above appeal having been not attended to by the then existing Presidency of Far West, for a number of causes the above appeal is made to the present Presidency for their investigation

August 11th 1838. John Patten."

After which the report of the above committee was read by the Clerk, as follows:

"To the President, Council and Quorum of Elders in Zion, assembled in Far-West,

We, the undersigned, being appointed a committee to attend at the house of John Patten, to hear and investigate the cause of complaint, that was lodged before this quorum by David Frampton against John Patten, beg leave to, and do, report that we did attend to that duty, and found John Patten and Sheffield Daniels, and Abigail Daniels under transgression and are of the opinion that they ought not to be admitted to the Sacrament untill there is a better understanding and more union between them, and we further believe, that the ground work of all this contention originated from John Patten, directing those men, to wit: Daniels, Johnson, Pettigrew, Fairchild &c to purchase claims to cover a certain 40 acres of land, and then, before they laid their claims before the

Committee, he, the said Patten secured to himself the land, and wanted those men to have their claims laid on some other piece or parcel of land & herein they were dissatisfied, & thus the contention arose, and we further believe, that Br John Patten's conduct is of such a nature towards Br Sheffield Daniels and his wife, and others, that unless he makes satisfaction to this Conference at our next meeting, that his licence be called for by the President and be requested to give them up."

Dec 16th 1837. Daniel Shearer
Ralph Cox Committee
David Judy

After some consultation, the record of former Councils were read which were had on the head of John Patten in 1837. Also the proceedings of the Elders quorum were read by the Clerk of the Elders quorum.

After some consultation, it was decided by the High Council, that the proceedings of the Elders quorum were not legal, therefore the matter was quashed and John Patten have his standing as before the decision of the Committee of the Elders quorum:

Resolved That Seymoure Brunson fill the seat of Harlow Redfield, and William Snow fill the seat of Amasa Lyman during the remainder of this session

Several charges were read, prefered by Alexander Williams, against sundry individuals, also one prefered against Alexander Williams by Josiah Fuller.

The charges generally were rejected, by the Council as it was buisness belonging to the Bishop, however there was a charge against Elder Williams for teaching erronious doctrine which he confessed that he had done in a degree.

It was decided by the Council that Elder Williams be no longer a member of the Church of Jesus Christ of Latter Day Saints.[2]

Resolved—That the charges prefered by Alexander William be not considered worthy of notice by any Court of this Church.

Resolved That the Bishop, Edward Partridge be instructed

to pay a certain debt of 14 dollars & 50 cents which President Rigdon has been under the necessity of borrowing to purchaseing provisions with. Council adjourned untill the last Thursday in September next. Closed in prayer by Samuel Bent.

Ebenezer Robinson, Clerk.

---

[1]Isaac Russell.

[2]Note that Alexander Williams was excommunicated for teaching false doctrine. This action seems harsh by present standards.

April 28, 1838

The following letter of Sarah Jackson should have been inserted on Page 139, in the minutes of a Council, on the 28 of April 1838, but was not in consequence of its being mislaid and did not come to hand until the recording had been done thus far. (See page 139)[1]

"It came to pass in the year of our Lord 1837, That I having lately came into this work, my husband sent me to this country some time months previous to his coming.[2] I was here some time and he did not come.

I, believing Elder Lyon to be a man of God, asked him to inquire of the Lord concerning my husband and what ~~had~~ was the cause of his not coming.

Sometime after that, he held a prayer meeting at Br Wheelers here he prophesied and said some one now in the room shall be led to mourn before three weeks unless there was a speedy repentance, & who it was he did not know. So on returning from meeting, he told me, that he had inquired of the Lord, and that my husband was dead and preaching to the spirits in prison, and that I was the one that should be led to mourn.

The next morning he passed by where I was and began to tell of his restlessness and that the Lord had appointed him a wife, by revelation, and he knew her name, and if he did not have her in less than six months he would never prophesy in the name of Jesus again.

At another time, he told me that he would tell me the whole of his mind, saying that when he inquired of the Lord, that the Lord told him that my husband was dead and preaching to the spirits in prison, and that I was presented before him, and that the Lord told him that I was to be his wife. "Lord is it so?" "Yes for I know all things." He said he went again to inquire of the Lord and I was presented before him again "Why Lord she won't have me." "Yes she will" said the Lord, "and if she don't I'll place another in her stead that shall be more beautiful to the eye than she is.

He told me that if I refused this I should be forever miserable, for he had a complete view of my future state and he would write it down, for he knew, just how it would be. Said he you are young and I am old I am afraid some one will try to persuade you off.

Moreover if this is not all true I will deny that there is a God in Heaven. I said, I doubt it. He then accused me of unbelief saying when a man of truth told me anything I was hard to believe when it is of God.

Furthermore he said, he was then in the same spirit that he was when he cursed that man and he died, and when he saw the death of his wife,[3] and that he had proved it by living testimony and why should you not as well believe me now as to believe that, for I would not tell you anything to injure you, for them that are ordained to this high authority are ordained of God and you have as much right to believe me as to believe Paul; yes, and a better right for it is not handed down so far.

He said Br Joseph told him to be cautious who he cursed in the name of the Lord, for who he cursed was cursed, and who he blessed was blessed.

And at another time he told me that Lord had told him, that I did not care as much for him as he thought I did and that I need not try to hide anything from him, for the Lord would reveal it to him.

And he led me to believe that the vengeance of God was about to be poured speedily upon me if I did not agree to his evil designs.

This I send to the honorable High Council of Far-West, as testimony against Elder Lyon as being true testimony.

Given under my hand, this 27th day of April 1838."

Sarah Jackson.

---

[1]See page 185; 139 is the manuscript page.

[2]Sarah Jackson had come to western Missouri from Alton, Illinois. See the Scriptory Book of Joseph Smith, page 35, Church Archives.

[3]Roxana Palmer Lyon.

October 5, 1838

Conference.

The 3rd Quarterly conference of the authorities, of the Church of Jesus Christ of Latter Day Saints, assembled in Far-West on Friday, October 5th 1838.[1]

President Brigham Young presiding.

Conference opened by singing, "O! happy souls who pray." &c and prayer by the President—

After which the following hymn was sung: "Now let us rejoice in the day of salvation." &c

As there were not a sufficency of members present to make a quorum to do buisness, therefore, the Conference adjourned untill 2 o'clock P.M.

The Conference convened agreeable to adjournment.

Opened by singing and prayer by Elder Kimball.

Presidents Young and Marsh presiding.

As there were not a sufficient number of the High Council

and other ordained members, to form quorums, to do buisness as a quarterly Conference, yet there were some ~~some~~ recommends for ordination which were read and one passed the Conference in the name of the Church, viz: Brother Isaac Laney, as he was about to go on a visit to his friends in the South.

Br Horace Alexander made a request to have an Elder accompany him to Indiana and Ohio, also requested an ordination to the office of an Elder, which was granted by the Conference & Elder Ebenezer Page was appointed to accompany him.

A recommend was handed to the Conference by the Clerk of the Elder's Quorum, recommending Stephen Chase to be ordained as President of the Elder's Quorum which was read by the Clerk and passed unanimously.

Emanuel M. Murphy made a request to have an Elder accompany him to South Carolina this season, when Almon Babbitt was appointed to be his Companion, if it met his feelings.

After some remarks by various members of the Conference, it was, Moved, Seconded and Caried—

That Brs Isaac Morley, John Buchanan, and James Allred be ordained or not to the Bishopric, by the First Presidency, as they see proper.

The Conference adjourned untill tomorrow at 10 o'clock.

Closed in prayer by Isaac Morley.

---

[1]See *History of the Church* 3:156.

October 6, 1838

Saturday, October 6, 1838.[1]

Conference convened agreeably to adjournment.

Opened by singing, "To him that made the sun and moon and stars" &c. and prayer by President B. Young.

Prests Marsh and Young presiding.

Elder Benjamin L. Clapp gave a statement of this travels in Kentucky, as he had just returned from there, many doors were opened in that part of the country, and calls for preaching continually. He wished some Elders to go to that country.

A call was then made for volunteers to go forth and preach the gospel, when several Elders offered themselves, also a call for ~~volunteer~~ members, who wished to be ordained and go into the vineyard to make it manifest, when Br. Albert Sloan made a request to be ordained to the office of an Elder, after some remarks it was moved, seconded, and carried that he be ordained as aforesaid.

The following are the names of the Elders who volunteered to go forth into the vineyard this season.

James Carroll, James Galliher, Luman A. Shirtliff, James Dunn, Ahaz Cook, Isaac Decker, Cornelius P. Lott, and Alphius Gifford.

President Marsh gave some very good instructions to the Elders who have volunteered requesting them not to go forth boasting of their faith, or of the judgments of the Lord; but to go in the Spirit of meekness and preach repentance unto the children of men.[2]

Elder John Taylor, from Canada, by request, gave a statement, of his feelings respecting his being appointed as one of the Twelve.[3] He said he was willing to do anything, which God would require of him, by the assistance of the Lord.

After which it was voted by the Conference that Br John Taylor fill the vacancy of one of the Twelve.

After which Stephen Chase came forward and was ordained a President to preside over the Quorum of Elders, in this Stake of Zion.

The following persons then came forward and were ordained to the office of Elders under the hands of the Presidents, viz: Isaac Laney, Horace Alexander, and Albert Sloan.

Voted by the Conference that Samuel Bent and Isaac

Higbee fill the seats of John Murdock and George M. Hinkle, in the High Council who have moved to De Witt.

Elder Kimball made a few appropriate remarks to the Elders respecting their duty.

Bishop E. Partridge made a Report of the temporal affairs of the Church.

Conference adjourned until the first Friday and Saturday in January next at 10 o'clock A. M.

Closed in benediction by Prest Marsh.

Ebenezer Robinson, Clerk.

---

[1]See *History of the Church* 3:153-55.

[2]Marsh's advice may have resulted from the difficulties they had experienced in Missouri.

[3]See Doctrine and Covenants 118.

December 10, 1838

Note by the Recorder. It was thought proper to insert the following memmorial,[1] of the citizens of Caldwell County, Missouri, in this place, as it contains a Synopsis of our unparalleled suffering and the persecution which was waged against us, by the authorities, as well as the citizens, of that State. The memmorial was not granted by the Legislature, therefore, it will also show the reason why we have come to this place. (Nauvoo, January 30th, 1843. Hosea Stout, Recorder.)

"To the Honorable Legislature of the State of Missouri, in Senate and house of Representatives, convened.—

We the undersigned petitioners, inhabitants of Caldwell County Missouri, in consequence of the late calamity that has come upon us, taken in connexion with former afflictions, feel it a duty we owe to ourselves and our country, to lay our case before your Honorable Body for consideration.

It is a well known fact, that a Society of our people commenced settling in Jackson County, Missouri in the summer of 1833,[2] where they according to their ability purchased lands and settled upon them, with the intention and expectation of becoming permanent citizens in common with others.

Soon after the settlement began, persecution began, and as the society increased, persecution also increased; untill the society at last was compelled to leave the County. And ~~others~~ although an account of these persecutions has been published to the world, yet we feel that it will not be improper to notice a few of the most prominent items in this memmorial.

On the 20th of July 1833, a mob convened at Independence a committee of which called upon a few of the leading men of our Church there, and stated to them, that the store, printing office, and indeed all other machanick shops, must be closed forthwith; and the society leave the country immediately; these propositions were so unexpected, that a certain time was asked for, to consider upon the subject before an answer should be returned, that being refused and our men being individually interrogated, each one answered, that he could not consent to comply with their propositions. One of the mob replied, that he was sorry, for the work of destruction would commence immediately. In a short time, the printing office, which was a two story brick building, was assailed by the mob and soon down and with it much valuable property destroyed. Next they went to the store for the same purpose, but Mr. Gilbert, one of the owners, agreeing to close it, they abandoned their design. Their next move was their dragging off Bishop Partridge from his house and family, to the publick square, when surrounded by hundreds, they partially stripped him of his cloths and tared and feathered him from head to foot. A man, by the name of Allen, was also tared and feathered at the same time. This was Saturday, and the mob agreed to meet on the following Tuesday, to accomplish their purpose, of driving or massacreing the society. Tuesday came and and the mob also bearing with them a red flag, in token of blood. Some two or three of the principal men of the society offered their lives if that would appease the wrath of the mob, so that the rest of the society might dwell in peace upon their lands: answer was that, unless the society would consent to leave en masse, every man should die for himself. Being in a defenceless situation, to save a general massacre, it was agreed that one half of the society should leave the county by the first of next January, and the remainder by the first of the following April; a treaty was entered into and ratified and all things went on smoothly for awhile; but sometime in October the wrath of the mob began again to be kindled, insomuch that they shot at some of our people, whipped others, and threw down their houses and also committed many other depredations: indeed the society of Saints, were harrassed for sometime both day and night, their houses were brickbatted and broken open, women and children insulted &c—the store house of A. S. Gilbert & Company was broken open, ransacked and some of the goods strewed in the street these abuses with many others of a very aggravated nature so stired up the indignant feeling of our people that a party of them, say about 30 met a company of the mob, of about double their number, when a battle took place in which, some two or three of the mob and one of our people were killed. This raised as it were the whole County in arms, and nothing would satisfy them but an immediate surrender of the arms of our people, and they forthwith to leave the County. Fifty-one guns were given up, which have never been returned, or paid for to this day. The next day parties of the mob, from 30 to 70, headed by priests, went from house to house threatening women and children with death if they were not off before they returned. This so alarmed them, that they fled in different directions, some took shelter in the woods, whilst others wandered on the prairies, till their feet bled; in the mean time the weather being very cold, their sufferings, in other respects, were very great.

The society made their escape to Clay County, as fast as they possibly could, where the people received them kindly & administered to their wants, After the society had left Jackson County, their buildings, amounting to about 200, were either burned or otherwise destroyed; much of their crops, as well as stock, furniture &c. were also destroyed.

The loss of property, added to the trouble and expence of moving, if properly estimated, would make a large sum for which they have not yet, received any remuneration.

The society remained in Clay County, nearly 3 years, when, at the suggestion of the people there, they removed to that section of country, now known as Caldwell County. Here the people purchased out most of the former inhabitants and also entered much of the wild lands, many soon owned a number of Eighties each, whilst there was scarcely a man but what secured to himself at least a Forty. Here we were permitted to enjoy peace for a season; but as our society increased in numbers and settlements were made in Davis[3] & Carroll Counties, the mob spirit showed itself again.

For months previous to our giving up our arms to Genl Lucas' army, we heard little else, than rumors of mobs being collecting in different places, and threatening our people. It is well known, that the people of our Church, who had located themselves at De Witt, had to give up to a mob, and leave the place, notwithstanding the milita were called out for their protection.

From De Witt the mob went towards Davis County and whilst on their way there, they took two of our men prisoners, and made them ride upon the cannon, and told them, that they would drive the Mormons from Davis to Caldwell, and from Caldwell to H E L L; and that they would give them no quarters, only at the canon's mouth.—The threats of the mob induced some of our people to go to Davis to help to protect their brethren, who had settled at Diahman on Grand River.—The mob soon fled from Davis County & after they were dispersed, and the canon taken during which time no blood was shed, the people from Caldwell returned to their homes in hopes of enjoying peace and quiet; but in this they were disappointed, for a large mob was soon found to be collecting on the Grindstone, from ten to fifteen miles off, under the command of C. Giliam;[4] a scouting party of which came within about four miles of Far-West, and drove off stock belonging to our people in open day light.—About this time word came to Far-West, that a party of mob had come ~~to~~ into Caldwell County to the South East of Far-West, that they were [stealing] horses and Cattle,—that they were burning houses, and ordering the inhabitants to leave their homes immediately; and that they had then actually in their possession three men prisoners; this report reached Far-West in the evening and was confirmed about midnight.—A company of about sixty men went forth under the command of David W. Patten, to disperse the mob, as they supposed.—A battle was the result, in which Captain Patten and two of his men were killed & others wounded; Bogart,[5] it appears, had but one killed,[6] and others wounded and notwithstanding the unlawful acts committed by Capt Bogart's men previous to the battle, it was now asserted and claimed that he was regularly ordered out as a Militia Captain to preserve the peace along the line of Ray and Caldwell Counties.—That battle was fought four or five days previous to the arrival of General Lucas[7] and his army.—About the time of the battle with Capt Bogart a number of our people, who were living near Haun's mill, on Shoal Creek, about 20 miles below Far West; together with a number of emigrants, who had been stopped there in consequence of the excitement, made an agreement with the mob, which was about there, that neither party should molest the other but dwell in peace.—Shortly after this agreement was made, a mob party of from 2 to 300 many of whom are supposed to be from Chariton County, some from Davis, and also those who had agreed to dwell in peace, came upon our people there, whose number in men were about 40, at a time they little expected any such thing; and without any cerimony, notwithstanding they begged for quarters, shot them down as they would Tigers or Panthers; some few made their escape by fleeing. Eighteen were killed & a number more severely wounded.

This tragedy was conducted in the most brutal and savage

manner. An old man,[8] after the massacre was partially over, threw himself into their hands & begged for quarters, when he was instantly shot down, that not killing him, they took an old corncutter and litterally mangled him to pieces.—A lad of seven years of age,[9] after being shot down also begged to be spared; when one of them placed the muzzle of his gun to his head and blew out his brains.—The slaughter of these people, not satisfying the mob, they then proceeded to rob and plunder the people.—The scene that presented itself after the massacre, to the widows and orphans, of the killed, is past discription!!!

It was truly a time of weeping, of mourning, and of lamentation!!!!—As yet, we have not heard of any being arrested for these murders, notwithstanding, there are men boasting about the country, that they did kill, on that occasion, more than one Mormon, whereas all our people who were in the battle with Capt Patten against Bogart, that can be found, have been arrested, and are now confined in jail, to await their trial for murder.

When Genl Lucas arrived near Far West, and presented the Governor's order,[10] we were greatly surprised, yet we felt willing to submit, to the Authorities of the State.—We gave up our arms without reluctance, we were then made prisoners and confined to the limits of the town, for about a week; during which time the men from the country were not permitted to go to their families many of whom were in a suffering condition, for the want of food and fire-wood; the weather being very cold and stormy.—Much property was destroyed by the troops in town, during their stay there; such as burning house-logs, rails, corncribs, boards, &c. the using of corn and hay, the plundering of houses; the killing of cattle, sheep and hogs, and also the taking off horses not their own; and all this without regard to owners; or asking leave of any one.—

In the meantime men were abused, women insulted and ravished by the troops; and all this, while we were kept prisoners.—Whilst the town was guarded, we were called together by the order of General Lucas, and a guard placed close around us; and in that situation were compelled, to sign a deed of trust, for the purpose of making our individual property all holden, as they said, to pay off the debts of every individual belonging to the Church, and also to pay for all damages, the old inhabitants of Davis may have sustained, in consequence of the late difficulties in that County.—[11]

Genl Clark[12] was now arrived, and the first important move by him was the collecting our men together on the square and selecting out about 50 of them; whom he immediately marched unto a house and confined close, this was done, without the aid of the sheriff; or any legal process. The next day 46 of those taken, were driven like a parcel of menial slaves, off to Richmond, not knowing why they were taken; or what they were taken for. After being confined in Richmond more than 2 weeks, about one half were liberated the rest after another week's confinement, were most of them recognized to appear at Court and have since been let to bail. Since Genl Clark withdrew his troops from Far-West, parties of armed men have reconoitered the County, driving off horses, sheep, and cattle, and also plundering houses.—The barbarity of Genl Lucas' troops ought not to be passed over in silence, they shot down our cattle and hogs merely for the sake of destroying them, leaving them for the ravens to eat. They took prisoner an aged man by the name of Tanner[13] and without any reason for it, he was struck over the head with a gun, which laid his skull bare.—Another man by the name of Carey,[14] was also taken prisoner by them, and without any provocation, had his brains dashed out with a gun; he was laid in a waggon, and there permitted to remain, for the space of 24 hours, during which time no one was permitted to administer to him comfort and consolation; and after he was removed from that situation, he lived but a few hours.—The destruction of property, at, and about Far-West, is very great, many, ~~yes a large portion~~ are stripped bare as it were, and others partially so; indeed take us as a body, at this time, we are a poor and afflicted people; and if we are compelled to leave the State in the spring many; yes a large portion of our society, will have to be removed at the expense of the State, as those who otherwise might have helped them, are now debarred that privilege, in consequence of the deed of trust we were compelled to sign, which deed so operates upon our real estate that it will sell for but little or nothing at this time.—

We have now made a brief statement of the most prominent features of the troubles that have befallen our people since their first settlement in this State; and we believe that these persecutions have come in consequence of our religious faith; and not for any immorality on our part.—

That instances have been of late, where individuals have trespassed upon the rights of others, and thereby broken the law of the land, we will not pretend to deny; but yet we do believe, that no crimes can be substantiated against any of the people who have a standing in our Church of an earlier date than the difficulties in Davies County. And when it is considered, that, the rights of this people have been trampled upon from [time] to time with impunity, and abuses heaped upon them almost innumberable; it ought in some degree, to paliate for any infraction of Law which may have been made on the part of any of our people.

The late order of Governor Boggs to drive us from this State, or exterminate us, is a thing so novel, unlawful, tyrannical and oppressive, that we have been induced to draw up this memmorial and present this statement of our case to your Honorable Body, praying that a law may be passed resinding the order of the Governer to drive us out of from the State; and also giving us the sanction of the Legislature to inherit our lands in peace we ask an expression of the Legislature, disapprobating the conduct of those who compelled us to sign a deed of trust and also disapproving of any man or set of men, in taking our property in consequence of that deed of trust, and appropriating it to the payment of debts not contracted by us; or for the payment of damages sustained in consequence of tresspasses committed by others.

We have no common stock; our property is individual property, and we feel willing to pay our debts as other individuals do; but we are not willing to be bound to pay other people's debts also.

The arms which were taken from us here, which we understand to be about 630, besides swords and pistols we care not so much about, as we do the pay for them; only we are bound to do military duty, which we are willing to do, and which we think was sufficiently manifested; by the raising of a volunteer Company last fall at Far-West, when called upon by General Parks[15] to rais troops for the frontier.

The arms given up by us, we considered were worth between twelve and fifteen thousand dollars; but we understand they have been greatly damaged since taken, and at this time probably would not bring near their former value; and as they were both here and in Jackson County taken by the Militia; and consequently by the authority of the State; we therefore, ask your Honorable Body to cause an appropriation to be made by law, whereby we may be paid for them; or otherwise have them returned to us, and the damages made good.

The loss sustained by our people, in leaving Jackson County, are so situated, that it is impossible to obtain any compensation for them by law because those who have sustained them are unable to prove those trespasses upon individuals.

That the facts do exist that the buildings, crops, stock, furniture, rails, timber, &c. of the society have been destroyed in Jackson County, is not doubted by any at this time acquainted in this upper country; and since those trespasses cannot be proved upon individuals, we ask your Honorable Body to consider this case; and if in your liberality and wisdom, you can conceive to be proper, and make an appropriation by law to compensate those sufferers.—The State we think would never feel the loss, whereas those sufferers, many of whom, are still pressed down with poverty, in consequence of those losses, would be enabled to pay their debts, and also in some degree relieved from poverty and woe, whilst the widow's heart would be made to rejoice & the orphan's tear measureably dried up, and the prayer of a grateful people ascend on High with thanksgiving and praise to the author of our existence of that beneficient act.—

In laying our case before your Honorable Body, we say that

we are willing and ever have been to conform to the Consitution and laws of the United States and of this State. We ask, in common with others, the protection of the laws. We ask for the privileges guaranteed to all free citizens of the United States and of this State, to be extended to us; we may be permitted to settle and live where we please, and worship God according to the dictates of our own consciences, without molestation;—And whilst we ask for ourselves this privilege, we are willing all others should enjoy the same

We now lay our case at the feet of your Legislature & ask your Honorable Body to consider it, and do for us after mature deliberation, that which your wisdom, patriotism and Philanthropy may dictate.—And as in duty bound will ever pray.

Far West Caldwell County,
Missouri. Dec. 10th 1838

Edward Partridge	A committee
Heber C. Kimball	appointed by
John Taylor	the citizens of
Theodore Turley	Caldwell County
Brigham Young	to draft this
Isaac Morley	memmorial and
George W. Harris	sign it in their
John Murdock	behalf
John M. Burk	

---

[1]See *History of the Church* 3:217-24 for a printed version of the memorial. A handwritten manuscript copy is located in the Joseph Smith Collection, Church Archives. This memorial was presented to the Missouri legislature by John Corrill on December 19, 1838. (See *History of the Church* 3:238, 242.) The Missouri Legislature appointed a committee to investigate the matter. The committee reported on May 4, 1840, well after all Mormons had left Missouri. The decision of the committee was that the Mormons could not be helped by the legislature. (See *History of the Church* 4:90.) Since this memorial has been published elsewhere, only limited editing has been done here.

[2]Should be 1831.

[3]"Davis" should read "Daviess."

[4]Cornelius Gilliam.
[5]Samuel Bogart.
[6]Moses Rowland.
[7]Samuel D. Lucas.
[8]Thomas McBride.
[9]Sardius Smith, who is usually listed as ten years of age.
[10]Governor Lilburn W. Boggs.
[11]Although many of the Saints did sign away their property, the State of Missouri did not follow through on this intention.
[12]John B. Clark.
[13]John J. Tanner.
[14]William Carey.
[15]Hiram G. Parks.

December 13, 1838

Far West Wednesday (Dec. 13 1838[1]

Agreeable to appointment the standing High Councillors met, when it was found that several were absent, who, (some of them) have had to flee for their lives, therefore it being necessary that those vacancies be filled the meeting was called for that purpose, and, also, to express each others feelings respecting the word of the Lord.

President Brigham Young Presiding.[2]

The Council was opened by prayer by Elder Kimball

After prayer Prest Young made a few remarks saying he thought it all important to have the Council reorganized, and prepared to do buisness. He advised the councellors to be wise and judicious in all their movements and not hasty in their transactions; as for his faith it was the same as ever, and he fellowshiped all such as loved the gospel of our Lord and Savior Jesus Christ in act as well as ~~deed~~ word.

Elder Kimball arose and said he felt as formerly for he had endeavored to keep a straight forward course; but wherein he had been out of the way, in any manner, he ment to mend in that thing, and he was determined to do as much as possible, as he would be done by, and his faith was as good as ever, he was in fellowship with all who wanted to do right.

Simeon Carter said as to his faith in the work it was the same as ever, he did not think that Joseph was a fallen prophet;[3] but he believed in every revelation that had come ~~from~~ through him: Still he thought that perhaps Joseph had not acted in all things according to the best wisdom yet how far he had been unwise he could not say; he did not think that Joseph would be removed and another planted in his stead; but he believed he would still perform his work, he was still determined to persevere and act in righteousness in all things so that he might at last gain a crown of glory and reign in the Kingdom of God

Jared Carter responded with Prest Brigham Young's feelings and wished still to walk with the brethren

Thos Grover said that he was firm in the faith and he believed the time would come when Joseph would stand before kings and speak marvelous words &c.

David Dort expressed his feelings in a similar manner. Levi Jackman says his faith is the same as ever and he has confidence in Br Joseph as ever.

Solomon Hancock says he is a firm believer in the Book of Mormon and Doctrine & covenants and that Br. Joseph is not a fallen Prophet, but will yet be exalted and become very high.

John Badger says his confidence in the work is the same as ever, and his faith, if possible is stronger than ever he believes that it was necessary that these scourges should come.

George W Harris says that as it respects the scourge which has come upon us that the hand of God was in it &c.

Samuel Bent says that his faith is as ever and that he feels to praise God in prisons and in dungeons and in all circumstances whatever he may be found.

After some consultation it was thought expedient to nominate High Priests to fill the vacancies.

The Council was organized as follows:

Simeon Carter	No 1	Jared Carter	No 2
Thos Grover	" 3	David Dort	" 4
Levi Jackman	" 5	Solomon Hancock	" 6

John Badger	" 7	John Murdock	" 8
John E. Page	" 9	George W. Harris	" 10
John Taylor	" 11	Samuel Bent	" 12

Voted that John Murdock fill the vacancy of John P. Green No. 4. and David Dort the place of Elias Higbee No. 11. and John Badger the place of George Morey No. 7. and Lyman Shearman the place of Newell Knight untill he returns

Council adjourned till Friday evening at 6 o clock

Closed in prayer by Prest Young.

E Robinson, Clerk.)

---

[1]See *History of the Church* 3:224-26. After Far West was taken by the Missourians (October 31, 1838), no meetings were to be held. Therefore, there is a break in meetings from October 6, 1838, to December 13, 1838. (See Anson Call Journal, Church Archives.)

[2]Thomas B. Marsh had left the Church, and David W. Patten had been killed in battle, and the First Presidency was in jail. Brigham Young assumed command, conducting a reorganization of the high council.

[3]The fall of Far West, the imprisonment of the Prophet, and other problems led to the disaffection of many of the Saints and the charge that Joseph Smith was a fallen prophet.

December 19, 1838

The High Council of Zion met in Far West Wednesday December 19th 1838.[1] The Council was organized as follows:

Ebenezer Robinson	No. 1	Jared Carter	No 2
Thomas Grover	" 3	Reynolds Cahoon	" 4
Theodore Turley	" 5	Solomon Hancock,	" 6
John Badger	" 7	John Murdock	" 8
Harlow Redfield	" 9	George W. Harris	" 10
David Dort	" 11	Samuel Bent	" 12

The Council was opened by prayer by President B. Young who presided over the Council

Harlow Redfield gave a statement of his feelings—he said his faith was as good as it ever was, notwithstanding, he did not feel to fellowship all the proceedings of the brethren in Daviess County. He thought they did not act as wisely as they might have done &c

Voted by the Council that John E. Page and John Taylor be ordained to the apostleship to fill vacancies in the Quorum of the Twelve.

When they came forward and received their ordination under the hands of Brigham Young and Heber C. Kimball.[2]

Voted that we send a petition to the general Government and send it by mail

Voted that Edward Partridge and John Taylor be a committee to draft the above mentioned petition; also it is their privilege to chose another person to assist them.

Council adj untill next Wednesday at 1 o'clock at this place

E. Robinson Clerk).

---

[1]See *History of the Church* 3:240.

[2]Here the high council is conducting general Church business, that is, matters which are now handled only by General Authorities.

December 26, 1838

The High Council of Zion met agreeable to adjournment, in Far West on Wednesday Dec. 26th 1838[1] and was organized as follows:

Simeon Carter	No. 1	Jared Carter	No 2
(No 3, 4, and 5 absent)		Solomon Hancock	" 6
John Badger	" 7	John Murdock	" 8
Harlow Redfield	" 9	George W. Harris	" 10
David Dort	" 11	Samuel Bent	" 12

The Council was opened by prayer by Prest B Young who presided over the Council, after which a hymn was sung.

Voted that the Council are satisfied with Br Redfield.[2]

Voted that E. Robinson be appointed to write communications to an Editor in Michigan, who has requested it.

Council adjourned untill next Wednesday at 10 o clock A. M.

E. Robinson Clerk

---

[1]See *History of the Church* 3:242.

[2]*History of the Church* 3:242 identifies this man as David Redfield. However, a later reference (*History of the Church* 3:287) indicates that this might be Harlow Redfield.

1839

January 2, 1839

Far-West, Mo. January 2nd 1839.

The High Council of Zion assembled according to adjournmt

Simeon Carter (1) Jared Carter (2) Solomon Hancock (6) John Badger (7) John Murdock (8) George W. Harris (10) David Dort (11) and Samuel Bent (12)

The Council was opened by prayer by Simeon Carter

The Council adjourned untill two weeks from today at 10 o'clock P. M

E. Robinson Clerk.

January 16, 1839

The High Council of Zion met Far West, January 16th 1839.[1]

The Council was organized as follows

Simeon Carter (1) Jared Carter (2) Solomon Hancock (6) John Badger (7) John Murdock (8) George W. Harris (10) and Samuel Bent (12)

The Council was opened by prayer by the Clerk

Resolved That the vote be recinded which was passed last spring (   ) ~~which was passed last~~ appointing Isaac Morley, Recorder of Patriarchal Blessings.

The Council adjourned untill two weeks from to day at 10 o clock A. M.

Council Closed in prayer by the prest B Young

E. Robinson Clerk.

---

[1]These are the last minutes from Missouri in the Far West Record.

1844

June 1, 1844

Nauvoo June 1st 1844[1]

The High Council of the Church of Latter day Saints met at the Seventies Hall[2] agreeably to adjournment on the 1st of June 1844 at 2 o clock P. M.

Present William Marks President

Counsellors	George W. Harris	Peter Haws in place Sal Bent
	James Allread	Henry G. Sherwood
	Alpheus Cutler	Lewis D. Wilson
	William Huntington	William C. Perry in place of D. Fullmore
	Leonard Sobey	
	Aaron Johnson	Newell Knight
		Robert Stone in place of Thos. Grover

Prayer by President William Marks——Voted unanimously on Motion of William Marks that Joseph M. Cole be and is hereby appointed Clerk of the High Council[3]—
Case 1st Complaint brought by James Ivins against Alphonzo Green for damages done by said Greens horses to J Ivins' grass field—By advice of President Marks the parties agreed to submit their differences to arbitrators and proceeded to choose said arbitrators[4]—J Ivins chose Josiah Ells, and A. Green choose brother Gates these two were to choose the third person by whose descision the parties agreed to abide———

Case 2d Moses Daily vs Conference of Highland Branch

At a conference of the Highland Branch on the 3rd day of May 1844 Moses Daily was cut off from said Branch, from which said Daily took an appeal before this Council. H. W. Miller stated that Daily refused to be tried by said conference in consequence of the difficulty then before the conference having been submitted to arbitrators by whose descision he was willing to abide H Kimball Testified to the same in substance——John W. Archey Testified in substance the same as the other two and further said that the ~~other~~ said Conference withdrew the hand of fellowship from said Daily by reason of his having refused to be tried by said Conference—— H. W. Miller stated that said Daily and Brt over } Willkins both agreed to abide the descision of the above named arbitrators; said Miller was one of the arbitrators.

Michael Stoken saith that he was one of the arbitrators as above named by H. W. Miller that Daily refused to be tried by said conference for several reasons; first they had no right to try him but he would submit to a trial before the high Priest Quorum. 2d that he had not the proper witnesses and 3d that he had agreed to submit ~~his~~ said difference to arbitrators—— Kenedy states the same in substance as Stoken

The case was duly sumed up by Counsellor Sobey of the part of Moses Daily and Couselor Sherwood for the Conference decided by a unanimous vote of this council that the descision of the highland Conference against Moses Daily be reversed and said Daily be restored to a standing in the church——[5]

On motion of George W. Harris Resolved That John Scott and Younger Green be cut off from this church for Apostacy——

Case of Samuel C Brown
vs
Branch at New Orleans[6]

Fellowship having been withdrawn from Samuel C. Brown by a conference held at New Orleans on the 14th day of January 1844 from which descision said Brown took an appeal to this council——Resolved that this council sustain the descision of the New Orleans Conference against said Samuel C Brown——

Signed William Marks President
Joseph M. Cole Clerk

---

[1]These high council minutes differ from the others in the Far West Record in that they were not transcribed at a later date, but apparently were recorded at the time of the meetings. They are also unique in being a record of events that transpired in Nauvoo as opposed to Missouri or other places. These notes were not included in the official typescript of the Far West Record, and are available only in handwritten manuscript form.

[2]Note that the high council had a more suitable meeting place than they had in Missouri, where they met in homes, stores, and so on.

[3]Joseph M. Cole, who served as a recorder of baptisms for the dead, was appointed as clerk of the high council and began his minutes at this time. The minutes in the Far West Record are in his hand.

[4]Here the high council is using an alternative to Church court action by referring the case to impartial mediators.

[5]Here the high council, acting as a court of appeals, actually reversed a decision of a lower court, a high priests' court.

[6]The high council was acting as a court of appeals, not only for Nauvoo, but for the entire Church.

June 15, 1844

Nauvoo June 15th 1844[1]

High Council Met agreeably to adjournment at the Seventies Hall on the 15th of June 1844 at 2 o clock P. M.

Present William Marks President

Councellors	Shadrach Roundy	James Allread
	Lewis D. Willson	Alpheus Cutler
	Josiah Smith for D. Fullmore	George W Harris
		Aaron Johnson
	Edmund Fisher " Grover	William Huntington
	Ezra Parrish " Knight	
	Leonard Sobey Henry G. Sherwood	

Case 1st ~~David M. Gamet~~ ~~vs~~ Libius T. Coons	S. Roundy counsellor for L. T. Coons Jas. Allread Councellor for ~~D. M. Gamet~~ Joseph Pennock L. T. Coons
vs Joseph Pennock	made some introductory remarks upon the charges prefered against

Pennock which were Lying, dishonesty, rude contempt. L. T. Coons introduced some affidavits which were not received by the Council—David M Gamet. stated that if the branch would give him Joseph Pennock three days time he could bring witnesses to impeach ~~witnesses~~ the Testimony of the two Binghams the time was granted and at the next meeting Joseph Pennock denied having asked for an adjournment on the account of witnesses.[2]

Daniel E Loveland states the same things as D M Gamet Charles Webb stated that J Pennock said he thought he could produce witnesses that would impeach the Binghams. that he Pennock did not deny asking for an adjournment—At this stage of the proceedings for the want of Witnesses and by an agreement of the parties the case was adjourned till Saturday two weeks from today at 2 oclock P. M.

Case 2d Ethan Pettit vs Elder David Bennett } For want of certain witnesses the case togeather with the council be adjourned till next Saturday at ~~2 oclock P. M~~ June 22d at 2 oclock P. M.

J M Cole Clk

---

[1]These final notes were recorded just twelve days prior to the Prophet's death. This was a momentous period in Church history. The whole *Nauvoo Expositor* incident, which led to the incidents at Carthage, transpired in the days surrounding this meeting.

[2]The procedures of the high council court were becoming more formalized as time went on. There is possibly a borrowing from the Church's involvement in the municipal court process.

Appendix A

Oliver Cowdery to Joseph Smith
Independence, Missouri
January 28, 1832
Original located in Joseph Smith Collection,
Church Archives

Bro. Joseph

According to promise I transmit to you the proceedings of the confrences held 23-24, and 27th. which are as follows.

Minuets of a General Confrence held in the land of Zion (Kaw Township Jackson County Mo.) at the dwelling house of bro. Newel Knight 23 First Month (Jan.) AD. 1832. 3 o clock P.M.

Names of Elders Present who were ordained to the H.P.H.

Edward Partrage
John Carrell
Isaac Morley
John Whitmer
John Murdock
Wm W Phelps
Lyman Wight
Harvey Whitlock
Newel Knight
Parley Pratt
Oliver Cowdery

Names of Elders who were not ordained to the H.P.H.

Levi Hancock

Zebedee Coltrin
Selah J. Griffin
Calvin Bebee
Peter Dustin
Joshua Fairchild
Daniel Cathcart

Priests

Hezekiah Peck

Teacher

Isaac Bebee

Edward Partrage appointed moderator and Oliver Cowdery Clerk. Prayer by bro. John Murdock.

By joint resolution commandments read relative to various subjects. Resolution offered by bro. Lyman Wight to take into consideration the circumstances of two brethren present. (Isaac & George Bebee) who desired to preach the Gospel.

Commandment read by the Clerk certain remarks made by him and bro. Wm W. Phelps relative to the subject.

Commandment read and remarks made by bro. Edward Partrage concerning the duties of Priests Teachers and deacons their duties read by bro. John Whitmer from the Articles and Covenants. remarks by bro. John Carrell stating the office of a Priest Teacher or Deacon to be as important as that of a High Priest. Resolved therefore that there be no person ordained in the churches in the land of Zion to the office of Elder Priest Teacher or Deacon without the united voice of the Church in writing in which such individual resides.

The above Resolution adopted by unanimous vote. Records of the church which came from Chardon Geauga Co. ohio received and laid on the Table. Presented by their Teacher Isaac Bebee.

The Bishop brought forward a statement of the lands purchased for inheritances for the saints amounting to nearly twelve hundred acres. After a long discussion upon the expediency of mechanics immediately moving to this land for the benefit of the Church, the following resolution was proposed.

Resolved that the Bishop be instructed to request the Churches in the east to send to this land a blacksmith, two shoemakers, a carpenter one joiner and mason one waggon and plow maker one tanner and currier one millwright one hatter one chair & cabinet maker, one silver Smith and one wheelwright. The last Resolution adopted by unanimous vote upon motion of the Clerk. Confrence adjourned until half past 8 o clock A.M. closed.

Prayer by brother Daniel Cathcart. Oliver Cowdery Clerk of Confrence 4 O clock. eve
[January 24, 1832]

Confrence convened according to adjournment names called and prayer by the Clerk. Minuets of yesterdays proceedings read. The Bishop brought forward his acount of moneys received from the churches and also a statement of the expenditures of the same. The Bishop made certain remarks relative to the subject now before the Confrence stating that in consequence of not making minuets at the time of paying out moneys last summer while traveling to this land and after arriving he could not account for nearly sixty dollars and after presenting the account bro. Wm W Phelps arose and said that he was knowing to the Bishops paying at one time, more than thirty dollars last summer for passage to this land which was not on the account presented. By unanimous vote the above sum allowed the Bishop. The following is a list of the Bishops account.

Amount of funds paid over to the Bishop to Jan 24 1832 including moneys of his own	$9508.24
Amount of disbursements on the lands and other necessares for the church up to January 24, 1832	$8449.90
Total amount of funds now remaining in the Bishops hands at this date Jan 24. 1832	$1058.24

By unanimous vote the above account accepted.

Resolved that the Bishop lay before each General con held by the Elders in this land a regular account of moneys and properties received and expended for the use and benefit of this church. The above carried by unanimous vote. The con. then proceeded to take into consideration the subject of Schools. After deliberate discussion the following Resolution passed by unanimous vote. Resolved that this Confrence appoint Brs. Oliver Cowdery William W. Phelps and John Correll to superintend Schools in the Churches in this land. The records of the Church which came from Colesville N.Y. received and laid on the Table. presented by their Priest Hezekiah Peck. Upon motion of bro John Murdock bro John Carrell appointed by unanimous vote to keep the General Church Record of names of the Desiples in this land. According to the Church Covenants. Resolved that the Bishop be instructed to establish a house of entertainment in the Town of Independence to accommodate the traveling Elders of this Church and other brethren whose circumstances may require. Also inquirers from a distance &c. to be supported out of the General Church fund a regular return of its expenditures and income to be made to each General Confrence held in this land Said establishment to be put in operation as soon as circumstances may permit. Carried by unanimous vote. Confrence adjourned until 3 oclock P.M. Oliver Cowdery Clerk of Confrence.

Con. convened according to adjournment 3 oclock P.M. Quotation from the Lord. "And it shall come to pass that the Bishop of my church after that he has received the properties of my Church that it cannot be taken from the Church" &c. The Confrence therefore Resolved that the Bishop of this Church at the time of receiving moneys or other properties for the use and benefit of this Church of any member of the same shall give a receipt to the person at the time covenant for himself and his heirs that such moneys or properties shall be expended for the use and benefit of this church according to the covenants and Laws of the same and that whatever amount of such moneys or properties may be in his possession should he be removed from his said office of Bishop by death or otherwise shall be handed over to his successor By unanimous vote the above resolution passed.

Bro. Edward Partrage brought forward certain letters written by bro. Sidney Rigdon one addressed to himself bearing date Kirtland September 10th 1831. another addressed to bro. John Carrell and Isaac Morley, bearing date Hiram Portage Co. Ohio 14th Nov. 1831. After a few remarks a motion was carried to have the said letters read by the Clerk After deliberate discussion it was Resolved that Wharas this Confrence has been made acquainted with certain difficulties existing between the Bishop of this Church (Edward Partrage) and bro. Sidney Rigdon and Wharas the said Sidney has prefered certain charges against the said Bishop (Edward Partrage) detrimental to his character and standing as a Bishop in the church of Christ. Therefore we the Confrence having no legal right to proceed to a trial of the same in the absence of one of the parties Recommend that the Elders stationed in this land converse with the said Bishop (Edward Partrage) on this subject and write the said Sidney a friendly humiliating letter advising that this difficulty be settled and thereby the wound of the Church be healed. By unanimous vote. General Confrence adjourned to tuesday the 3d of 4 month (April) 1832. Closed. Singing Prayer by bro. Edward Partrage. Oliver Cowdery Clerk of Confrence.

In consequence of the ill health and crowd of business our bro. Sidney Gilbert was unable to attend the General Confrence for which cause we thought proper to hold a special one to examine his accounts &c. by his request.

Minuets of a Special Confrence held at the dwelling house of bro. Sidney Gilberts Independence Jan. 27, 1832 (evening) Edward Partrage appointed moderator., and Oliver Cowdery Clerk

Names of Elders present

John Whitmer	Sidney Gilbert
William W. Phelps	Selah Griffins
Edward Partrage	John Correll
John Carrell	Oliver Cowdery

Prayer by Bro John Carrell. Brother Sidney Gilbert brought forward the following account of moneys received of N.K.

Whitney & co. Received of N.K. Whitney agent of the churches at the east and sundry brethren on the way to this land $1692.00. The following is the amount of disbursements

Paid out for Gilbert & Whitney for goods and transportation to this place	$ 827.94
Paid for transportations for families and bagage from ohio to this place	$ 804.89
Other necessaries for the use and benefit of the Church	$1045.00
	$2677.83

	$1002.70
	1692.00
Total amount received	$2694.70
Total amount paid out	$2677.83
Sums remaining	16.87

By unanimous vote the above account accepted.

After certain remarks from bro. Sidney Gilbert relative to the store in this place it was Resolved that a letter be addressed by brs. Edward Partrage Sidney Gilbert and Oliver Cowdery on the subject of the store in this place to the Agent of the Disiples in the east (NK Whitney) requesting a special confrence to sit upon the contents of said letter. By unanimous vote. Singing. Prayer by bro. Wm Phelps. Closed. Oliver Cowdery Clerk of Confrence

The following items I insert to accompany the foregoing documents by request of the Bishop which I copy from his own hand. "Although the Bishop has reported that there is nearly twelve hundred acres of land purchased that you may have a better understanding we think propper to state that it is mostly woodland & not in a situation to be improved this season even if it should be thought advisable to clear it faster than what is wanted for timber. And further we would state that one piece of the land is not as yet paid for which when added to what has been now paid to the Elders who go east will reduce the amount of funds in the Bishops hands more than 200 dollars. We would further state that provisions are scarce & dear nearly double what they were one year ago. We have not a large supply on hand probably not more than enough for the brethren here. The store not getting opened as soon as we expected has injured us verry much in the purchase of provisions. According to instructions sent here it was expected to be opened about the middle of Oct. & thinking that purchases might be made with goods & the money saved in the Church we neglected to buy expecting bro. Gilbert would certainly be here soon. From the funds in the Bishops hands you will redily perceive that we are not in a situation to buy much more land & procure a stock of provisions & cows for those who are coming here this spring. For the foregoing reasons we have sent only for mechanics knowing that others are commanded to come & believing that others will come without a command not knowing but what that they may. We donot expect that all the mechanics will be found & sent but we have sent for those most needed." Among the mechanics sent for it is expected that one blacksmith one shoemaker and one mason will come in the Church from Nelson. and brother Elliott Babit Kingsberry and Stebbens, and a brother from Winchester Indiana who is a tanner. Advise the brethren by all means to come by land and thus obey the command of the Lord. We think that it would be well for the brethren to bring one barrell buckwheat, and one of clover seed, or half a bbl clover seed if possible.

Ten of our brethren have started to proclaim the Gospel namely (John Murdock & Lyman Wight) (Parley Pratt & Levi Hancock) these four are going on the south side of the Missouri to St. Lewis Cincinnati and Bethany Virginia. (Calvin Bebee & Peter Dustin) through the more settled parts of Illinois & Indiana Michigan into Ohio. Daniel Cathcart & Joshua Fairchild through the north part of this state through Ill. Indi. to Ohio.

Say to brother Oliver Olney that if he can send a carding machine and clothiers tools this spring by water we think that it will be well, which can be put in operation as soon as circumstances may permit. Also say to brother Ashley of Strongsville that the Bishop says if he can send the leather up to this land as he talk to me last Oct as Confrence in Orange it will be of great worth to the Desiples.

The brethren are generally well and rejoicing in the Lord. The Bishop and all the Elders with all the brethren send love to the eastern churches.

I remain your brother in the Lord
Oliver Cowdery

Joseph Smith Jun.

P.S. We expect soon to be ready to print and hope that brother Martin can supply with paper at present you can tear off the bottom of this sheet which will serve him for a bill you see if ten thousand copies are struck it will take double the amount of the first mentioned Ream and we feel anxious that it may be so for I think there is no fear of sale O.C.

Appendix B
Church Courts

Latter-day Saints have always regarded their Church court system as the most equitable judicial system in the world. Speaking in a nineteenth-century conference session, Heber C. Kimball said, "I believe that there never was a more correct organization of a court on earth than our High Councils."[1]

The origins of the Church court system antedated the organization of the Church. In the revelation presently known as Doctrine and Covenants section 20, teachers of the Church were instructed in a judicial role. Less than one year later, an elders' hearing with a bishop present was added. By August of that year, bishops were designated as judges in Israel. At Kirtland, Ohio, on February 13, 1833, a council of high priests met to investigate charges against Burr Riggs. Within two weeks, another council of high priests had excommunicated Riggs from the Church. In May 1833, the First Presidency acted in the capacity of a court of review or appeals court. In the next month, judicial activities were engaged in by a council of high priests, the First Presidency, and a council of elders. The first formal bishop's court was organized in December 1833.

With all of these developments as background, the first high council was organized February 17, 1834, superseding the council of high priests as a court. As the revelation on Church courts, section 102, says, "the high council was appointed by revelation for the purpose of settling important difficulties." (V.2.) Building on the basic high council court jurisdiction, other courts were developed. By March 1835, the following additional judicial bodies were operational:

1. The bishop's court.
2. Priesthood quorum courts.
3. The standing high council. (See Doctrine and Covenants 107.)
4. The traveling high council. (See Doctrine and Covenants 107.)
5. The First Presidency and twelve high priests as an appellate court.
6. The bishop's court for the First Presidency.

Thus, within five years of the organization of the Church, a well-developed court system had been established.[2]

As the Church court machinery developed, legal principles and procedures also took shape. In section 42 of the Doctrine and Covenants, one of the earliest principles of Church law was established, namely: any member who sincerely repented and corrected his conduct was, and is, usually pardoned. In the same revelation another principle was established. Two witnesses were required before a person could be brought to trial in a Church court. In Doctrine and Covenants 102, the high council court was not to act as three judges and jury of twelve, but as a judge with two assistants (his counselors) and a panel of six spokesmen for the defendant and six for the Church in any case. The procedure was that lots would be drawn to ascertain who would speak for whom, and to determine the order of speaking. The odd numbers 1, 3, 5, 7, 9, and 11 were to speak on behalf of the Church, while the even numbers 2, 4, 6, 8, 10, 12 were to speak on behalf of the accused. In reaching a decision, the majority of the council concurring with the president was sufficient, but dissenting counselors could require a new trial in the light of new evidence.

Within the context of Church history, it is obvious that Church courts were once held more frequently than they are today. Many of the early Church members, including their leaders, faced discipline at the hands of the courts. Reminiscing on his early experiences in the Church, George A. Smith recalled, "We had High Council upon High Council, Bishop's trial upon Bishop's trial; and labor and toil constantly to settle difficulties and get our minds instructed in principle and doctrine, and in power that we had to contend with."[3]

Courts in the early Church had more options in terms of possible types of discipline than they have now. Church courts at the time the Far West Record was being recorded could:

1. Dismiss the charges.
2. Forgive.
3. Admonish.
4. Allow a probationary period.
5. Revoke one's license.
6. Disfellowship.
7. Excommunicate.

In contrast to the options open to a court in those days, Church courts today have only four options available:

1. Exoneration.
2. Probation.
3. Disfellowshipment.
4. Excommunication.[4]

It is apparent that the Church courts of the early nineteenth century had more courses of action available to them than do Church courts of today. While it is true that a greater percentage of Church members were involved in Church courts then, the courts had more freedom in dealing with the cases that came under their jurisdiction.

At the time the events recorded in the Far West Record were taking place, many important and long-lasting precedents relating to Church courts were being established. The Far West Record is at once a historical record of those events and a reference book on Church courts. Those involved in holding Church courts today may certainly benefit from studying the court proceedings contained in the Far West Record.

---

[1]*Journal of Discourses* 10:63.

[2]Several excellent studies on the history of the Church court system are available. See, for example: James R. Moss, "Historical Development of the

Church Judicial System, 1830-1835," *The First Annual Church Education System Religious Educators' Symposium; CES Church History Symposium* (August 19, 20, 1977, Brigham Young University); Joseph B. Keeler, *The Bishop's Court* (n.p. 1902); C. Paul Dredge, "Dispute Settlement in the Mormon Community: The Operation of Mormon Courts," unpublished paper dated January 31, 1972, Church Archives; Stephen J. Sorensen, "Civil and Criminal Jurisdiction of L.D.S. Bishop's and High Council Courts, 1847-1852," *Task Papers in L.D.S. History,* no. 17 (April 1977).

[3]*Journal of Discourses* 11:7.

[4]Letter of the First Presidency (June 1, 1979) and accompanying handbook supplement: "8. The Church Judicial System," especially pages 6-7.

Biographical Appendix

Sources Used in Preparing the Biographical Appendix

Books

Andrus, Hyrum L., and Bennett, Richard E. *Mormon Manuscripts to 1846*. Provo, Utah: Harold B. Lee Library, 1977.

Arrington, Leonard J. *Charles C. Rich*. Provo, Utah: Brigham Young University Press, 1974.

Bitton, Davis. *Guide to Mormon Diaries and Autobiographies*. Provo, Utah: Brigham Young University Press, 1977.

Brooks, Melvin R. *L.D.S. Reference Encyclopedia*. Salt Lake City: Bookcraft, 1965.

Esshom, Frank. *Pioneers and Prominent Men of Utah*. Salt Lake City: Utah Pioneers Book Publishing Company, 1913.

Flake, Lawrence W. *Mighty Men of Zion*. Salt Lake City: Karl D. Butler, 1974.

Jenson, Andrew C. *Latter-day Saint Biographical Encyclopedia*. 4 vols. Salt Lake City: Deseret News, 1936.

Jessee, Dean C., ed. *Letters of Brigham Young to His Sons*. Salt Lake City: Deseret Book Company, 1974.

Smith, Heman C., and Smith, Joseph III. *The History of the Reorganized Church of Jesus Christ of Latter Day Saints*. 4 vols. Independence: Herald House, 1951.

Smith, Joseph. *History of the Church of Jesus Christ of Latter-day Saints*. Edited by B. H. Roberts. 7 vols. Salt Lake City: Deseret Book Company, 1964.

Smith, Joseph Fielding. *Essentials in Church History*. Salt Lake City: Deseret Book Company, 1963.

Watson, Elden J., ed. *Manuscript History of Brigham Young*. Salt Lake City: Elden J. Watson, 1968.

Watson, Elden J., comp. *The Orson Pratt Journals*. Salt Lake City: Elden J. Watson, 1975.

Whitney, Orson F. *History of Utah*. 4 vols. Salt Lake City: George Q. Cannon and Sons, 1892-1904.

Periodicals

Evening and Morning Star

Messenger and Advocate

The Return

Times and Seasons

Utah Genealogical and Historical Magazine

Manuscripts

Salt Lake City. Church Archives. Journal History.

Salt Lake City. Church Archives. Kirtland Council Minute Book.

Salt Lake City. Church Archives. "Lists of Residents of Jackson County, Missouri."
Salt Lake City. Church Archives. Patriarchal Blessing File.
Salt Lake City. Genealogical Department, The Church of Jesus Christ of Latter-day Saints. Early Church Information Card Index.
Salt Lake City. Genealogical Department, The Church of Jesus Christ of Latter-day Saints. Patron Section, Family Group Sheets.

Ebenezer ABBOTT (?-?) was present at a Church conference on June 3, 1831, held at Kirtland, Ohio. He is listed as having "denied the faith" by later scribes.

Hazen ALDRICH (*Andrew Hazen Aldrich*) (?-?) joined the Church in 1832 in New Hampshire. He marched with Zion's Camp and afterward was called to the First Quorum of Seventy. He joined with dissidents in Kirtland and left the Church.

Horace ALEXANDER (1812-81), a native of Virginia, was ordained an elder in Far West, Missouri, in 1838. He marched with the Mormon Battalion and later served a mission to the southern states.

Charles ALLEN (1806-?), a native of Pennsylvania, was tarred and feathered with Edward Partridge during the Jackson County, Missouri, disturbances.

James ALLRED (1784-1876), born in North Carolina, marched with Zion's Camp and lived through the expulsion of the Saints from Far West and Nauvoo. He was kidnapped in Nauvoo and held in Missouri, but was eventually released. He settled Spring City, Utah.

Martin Carroll ALLRED (1806-40), a native of Kentucky, marched with Zion's Camp in 1834 and was among those arrested at the fall of Far West.

John ANDERSON (1796-?) was born in Connecticut and married Lydia Kellog. He is said to have died in Nauvoo, Illinois.

John C. ANNIS (1784-?), born in Vermont, served as a Lieutenant in the Nauvoo Legion.

Major Noble ASHLEY (1798-?) was born in Sheffield, Massachusetts, and was ordained a high priest in 1831. He resided in Jackson County, Missouri, from 1832 to 1833, but left the Church by 1838.

Sampson AVARD (1809-?), a native of the Isle of Guernsey, was baptized in 1835. During the Far West period he was the leader of a retaliatory group that came to be called the Danites. He became a witness against Church leaders, implicating them in the institution of the Danites. He was subsequently excommunicated. He was living in Illinois in 1850.

Daniel AVERY (1793-?), a native of New York, was kidnapped in December of 1843 and carried to Missouri on a charge of horse stealing. He escaped and returned to Montrose, Iowa, where he served as president of the elders quorum.

Almon W. BABBITT (1813-56), born in Massachusetts, joined the Church in 1833. He was a member of Zion's Camp and was ordained a seventy in 1835. He served as president of the Kirtland Stake. He was killed by Indians while serving the State of Deseret in congress.

John BADGER (1800-40) was born in Waterford, Vermont, baptized in June 1832, and ordained an elder the following month. He died in 1840 in Lee County, Iowa Territory.

Caleb BALDWIN (1791-1849), a native of Nobletown, New York, joined the Church in 1830 and soon thereafter moved to Jackson County, Missouri, where he took part in the Battle of the Big Blue. In 1838 he was among those arrested by General Clark, spending the winter in Liberty Jail with Joseph Smith and other Church leaders. He lived in Illinois and settled in the Salt Lake Valley.

Caleb BALDWIN, *Jr.* (1817-?) was baptized in 1837 and ordained a seventy in 1840.

Nancy Kingsbury BALDWIN (1799-?), a native of Ohio, was married to Caleb Baldwin, Sr.

Wheeler BALDWIN (1793-1887) was ordained an elder in 1831 in Ohio, and a high priest later that same year. He joined with the Reorganized Church in 1863.

John P. BARNARD (1803-74) was born in New Hartford, New York, and was baptized in June of 1835. He died in 1874 in Box Elder County, Utah.

Lorenzo Dow BARNES (1812-42) was born in Toland, Massachusetts, and joined the Church in 1833. He was a member of Zion's Camp and later served several missions. He died in England, the first missionary to die while preaching the gospel in a foreign land.

William BATSON (1790-?), a native of New Jersey, lost his priesthood license during the Hulet Branch trial. It was apparently restored, however, since he received a mission assignment in 1844.

Calvin BEEBE (also *Bebee* and *BeeBee)* (1800-?) was born in Paris, New York, and served on the Far West high council. He was excommunicated by the Zarahemla Stake, Iowa Territory, for keeping a "tippling house."

George BEEBE (1811-81), a native of Oswego, New York, was baptized in October of 1830. He died in Provo, Utah.

Isaac BEEBE (1800-?), a native of Paris, New York, moved with his family to Jackson County, Missouri, in 1833.

BENJAMIN (?-?) was possibly Nahern or Timothy Benjamin, both of whom owned land in Caldwell County, Missouri.

BENNAR (?-?) was possibly Elias Benner, a Mormon who owned land in Caldwell County, Missouri, and was a member of Zion's Camp.

David BENNETT (1801-53) was born in New York. He was wounded in Jackson County, Missouri, during the expulsion of the Saints in 1833. He migrated to Utah and died in Mount Pleasant.

Benjamin BENSON (1779-1846), a native of Maple, New York, was baptized in 1832. He died in Mendon, Illinois, but his wife, Kazia Messenger, migrated to Utah.

Jerome BENSON (1810-73), a native of New York, was the son of Benjamin Benson. He went to Utah in 1852 and was sent to settle San Bernardino, California.

Samuel BENT (1778-1846) was born in Barre, Massachusetts, and joined the Church in 1833. He was a member of Zion's Camp and later moved to Missouri in 1836. He was a member of the Nauvoo high council and the Council of Fifty. He presided over the settlement at Garden Grove, Iowa, where he died.

Brother BEST (?-?) was possibly Henry Best, one of those filing affidavits concerning the expulsion from Missouri. He had resided there from 1834.

Titus BILLINGS (1793-1866), a native of Greenfield, Massachusetts, was baptized in 1830 and moved to Missouri in 1832. He was ordained a counselor to Bishop Partridge in 1837. He served as president of the branch in Lima, Illinois, until 1845.

Lilburn W. BOGGS (1792-1860) was an enemy of the Saints in Jackson County, Missouri. Later, as governor of the state, he issued the "extermination order," expelling the Saints from Missouri. Orrin Porter Rockwell was accused of an attempt on Boggs's life in 1842. Boggs recovered and later operated a business in California.

William BOLTON (?-?) was an elder residing in Jackson County in 1832.

Ezra BOOTH (1792-) was a Methodist preacher before joining the Church. He was ordained a high priest in 1831 but was excommunicated later that year. He subsequently wrote nine anti-Mormon letters that appeared in the *Ohio Star*, thus becoming the first Mormon apostate to publish anti-Mormon literature.

John F. BOYNTON (1811-90) was born in Bradford, Massachusetts, and joined the Church in 1832. In 1835 he was ordained one of the original Apostles of the Church, but he became disaffected in the financial crisis in Kirtland of 1837. He was dropped from the Twelve and was later excommunicated.

Truman BRACE (1783-1855), a native of Torrington, Connecticut, was also referred to as "Father Brace" because of his age. He was a member of the Colesville Branch, the first to move to Jackson County, Missouri, in 1831. He signed the covenant to assist the poor in the exodus from that state in 1838-39.

Joseph BRACKENBURY (1788-1832) a native of Lincolnshire, England, was converted to the Church in 1831. The same year he left on a mission to New York. While on the mission he died suddenly from the effects of poison administered by enemies.

Benjamin BRAGG (?-?) was an early member of the Church in Warrensville, Ohio. He was silenced by the vote of the conference held in Kirtland on September 12, 1831.

Samuel BROWN (1801-82) was born in Altstead, New Hampshire, and temporarily lost his priesthood license in 1834 in the Hulet Branch trial. He marched in Zion's Camp and served as a doorkeeper in the Kirtland Temple. He settled in Payson, Utah.

Samuel C. BROWN (1820-?), the son of David and Mary Brown, was born in Fredrick County, Virginia.

Seymour BRUNSON (1799-1840) was baptized and made an elder in January 1831. He served missions in 1832 with Daniel Stanton and Luke Johnson, and he was later appointed a temporary member of the high council in Far West.

John BUCKHANNAN (also *Buchanan*) (1786-1839) was born in Ireland. He was baptized in 1835, but died in Lima, Illinois, in 1839.

Jacob BUMP (1791-?), a native of New York, served with Zion's Camp in 1834 and later was among those who defended the actions of Joseph Smith as leader of that group. However, in 1838, Bump was among those who left the Church and participated in mob action against Church members.

John M. BURKE (1793-1853) was an early resident of Kirtland, later moving to Missouri, where he was among those who petitioned for redress to the U. S. Congress in 1839. He later settled in Ogden, Utah.

George BURKETT (1788-1871) was born in Bedford, Pennsylvania. He joined the Church in 1831 and soon after moved to Jackson County. He was eventually expelled from Missouri with the other Saints. He died in Ogden, Utah.

Sarah Smith BURKETT (1787-?) was wife of George Burkett and joined the Church with her husband in 1831. She died during the Nauvoo period in Augusta, Iowa.

Serenes (also *Sirenes*) *BURNETT* (?-?) was among the original settlers of Chagrin Falls, Ohio. At his home in Orange, Ohio, a conference of the Church was held on October 25, 1831.

Stephen BURNETT (1814-?), a native of Ohio, was baptized in 1830 and ordained an elder in 1831. Later that year he was ordained a high priest. He apostatized by 1838.

Charity Lowe BUTLER (1782-1851) was born in North Carolina and joined the Church in 1835. She died in North Pidgeon, Iowa.

John Lowe BUTLER (1808-60), a native of Kentucky, was baptized in 1835 and soon settled with the Saints in Missouri. He was forced from Missouri and Illinois with the rest of the Church. He served as bishop in Spanish Fork, Utah.

Reynolds CAHOON (1790-1861), a native of Cambridge, New York, was baptized in 1830 and ordained a high priest in 1831. He was a counselor to Bishop Whitney in Kirtland and a member of the stake presidency in Adam-Ondi-Ahman and in Iowa. He died in Salt Lake City, Utah.

William Farrington CAHOON (1813-93), the son of Reynolds Cahoon, was born in Harpersfield, Ohio. He marched with Zion's Camp and became a member of the First Quorum of Seventy. He followed the Church to Illinois and eventually to the Great Salt Lake Valley.

Daniel CARN (also *Garn*) (1802-72), a native of St. Clair, Pennsylvania, was called as bishop of the first German-speaking branch of the Church in Nauvoo. In 1851 he was called as mission president in Germany. He died in Salt Lake City.

Benjamin CARPENTER (?-?) was possibly the Benjamin Carpenter who built the first grist mill on the present site of Chagrin Falls, Ohio. A conference of the Church was held in Carpenter's house in Norton, Ohio, April 21, 1834.

James CARROLL (1795-?) was born in England and was active during the Kirtland period of the Church, working for Oliver Cowdery as a scribe and in the printing office. He moved to Missouri, but he was excommunicated in Nauvoo.

Gideon Haden CARTER (1798-1838) was born in Killingworth, Connecticut, and was baptized in 1831 and served a mission to Vermont in 1832. He was killed in 1838 at the Battle of Crooked River in Ray County, Missouri.

Jared CARTER (1801-ca.1849), brother of Gideon Carter, was baptized in 1831. He was a member of the high council in Kirtland and Far West. After his disaffection in 1838, he remained only a nominal member of the Church.

Orlando Henry CARTER (1820-60), a native of Vermont, was endowed in the Nauvoo Temple, December 24, 1845.

Simeon Dagget CARTER (1794-1869), a native of Killingworth, Connecticut, was ordained a high priest in 1831 and was a member of the high council in Clay County and in Far West, Missouri. He served a mission to Germany in 1841. He died in Brigham City, Utah.

William CARTER (?-?) lost his elder's license in September 1831.

Daniel CATHCART (1803-?) was born in New Jersey, and served in Zion's Camp during the summer of 1834. He was expelled with the Saints from Missouri in 1838. He had lived at Adam-Ondi-Ahman.

Jacob CHAMBERLAIN (1779-?) was born December 26, 1779, in Dudley, Massachusetts.

Solomon CHAMBERLAIN (1788-1862), a native of Old Canaan, Connecticut, was among the first to settle in Jackson County, Missouri. At the time of the exodus from Nauvoo, he was chosen a member of the original pioneer party that arrived in the Great Salt Lake Valley in 1847.

Darwin CHASE (1816-63) was born in Ellisburg, New York, and was baptized with his father's family in 1831. He was ordained a seventy in 1839. He was imprisoned in Richmond, Missouri, following the fall of Far West. He followed the Church to Utah.

Stephen CHASE (1799-?), a native of New York, held several positions in the Church, including president of the elders quorum in Far West. He served as a member of the high council in Iowa.

John Maddison CHIDESTER (1809-93) was born in Pompey, New York, and joined the Church in 1832. He was a member of Zion's Camp in 1834. At the time of the exodus from Nauvoo, he built and ran one of the ferries that crossed the Mississippi Riber. He helped colonize Washington County, Utah.

Benjamin L. CLAPP (1814-61), a native of Alabama, was baptized a member of the Church in 1835 and settled with the Mormons in Missouri. In 1838, he was called on a mission to Kentucky. He returned to take part in the battle of Crooked River and was forced to flee to Iowa to escape imprisonment at the fall of Far West. While residing in California, he was excommunicated.

John B. CLARK (1802-85), a native of Kentucky, was a brigadier general of militia in the Black Hawk War. He was elected major general in 1836. He was given the assignment in 1838 by Governor Boggs to force the Saints from the state or exterminate them. He served Missouri in the U. S. Congress.

John Wesley CLARK (1808-40) was born in Durham, Connecticut, and was among those who gathered at the temple site in Far West to witness the departure of the Twelve Apostles for England. He died in Illinois in April 1840.

Timothy B. CLARK (1773-1848), a native of New Haven, Connecticut, was generally referred to as "Father Clark" by the Saints in Missouri. He died May 29, 1848.

John CLEMINSON (?-?) served in a number of positions in Far West, including clerk of the circuit court and official recorder, but by the time of the disorders in that place, he was apparently in sympathy with the state, since he was offered free passage with his family out of the city before General Clark entered. He was subsequently excommunicated.

Henry Alanson CLEVELAND (1809-67) was born in Scohaine, New York, and was baptized in 1830. He was wounded during the difficulties at Far West. He went west and settled in Centerville, Utah.

Emily COBURN (?-?) attended the baptism of the Colesville Saints in New York in June 1830. Her minister tried to force her to remain a Presbyterian, but she was baptized. Her sister, Sally Coburn Knight, was Newel Knight's wife.

Joseph COE (1785-), a native of New Jersey, was ordained a high priest in 1831. He helped lay the foundation stone of the Kirtland Temple in 1833, and he was a member of the Kirtland High Council. He left the Church, however, in 1837.

Barnet COLE (1796-1860) was born in Gruedhall, Vermont, and received a patriarchal blessing in 1846 in Nauvoo. He died in Box Elder County, Utah, in 1860. He is listed in the Far West Record only as "Brother" Cole.

Zebedee (also *Zebidee*) *COLTRIN* (also *Coultrin*) (1804-87) was a member of Zion's Camp and was afterward ordained a member of the First Quorum of Seventy. He also served as a member of the stake presidency in Kirtland. He settled in Spanish Fork, Utah.

Libius Thaddeus COONS (1811-72), a native of Plymouth, New York, was baptized in 1832. In 1834 he marched with Zion's Camp to Missouri. He was an original member of the First Quorum of Seventy. He lived in Richfield, Utah.

John CORRILL (1794-?), a native of Massachusetts, was baptized in 1831 and ordained a high priest and assistant to Bishop Partridge. He was a prominent leader in Jackson County, but he was excommunicated in 1839 in Far West when he joined with other dissenters.

Horace COWAN (?-?) joined the Church in 1833 in Kirtland and traveled to Vermont, where he was ordained an elder. He marched with Zion's Camp and later moved to Missouri. He was incarcerated briefly with Joseph Smith in the Liberty Jail in March 1839.

Marcellus COWDERY (?-?), brother of Oliver Cowdery, was a member of the Church. He testified for Oliver Cowdery in Far West. He was disfellowshipped in April 1838.

Oliver COWDERY (1806-50), a native of Wells, Vermont, with Joseph Smith received the Aaronic and Melchizedek Priesthood in 1829. He was one of the three witnesses to the Book of Mormon and was a charter member of the Church. He was excommunicated in Far West, but was rebaptized in 1848 in Kanesville, Iowa. He died in Richmond, Missouri.

Ralph COX (?-?) was a member of the Church in Far West. He served as acting president of the elders quorum.

Nahum CURTIS (1784-) was the son of Moses and Molly Curtis and was born in Franklin County, Massachusetts. His wife was Millicent Waite.

Alpheus CUTLER (1784-1864), a native of Plainfield, New Hampshire, was baptized in 1833 and was ordained a high priest in 1836. He was appointed a member of the Nauvoo high council in 1839. He later rejected Brigham Young's leadership and organized the True Church of Jesus Christ.

Moses DALEY (also *Daily* or *Dailey*) (1794-1865) was born in Wallbill, New York, and served on a committee to purchase land in Kirtland for the Church. He later moved to Missouri, settling at Adam-Ondi-Ahman. He died in California.

Abigail DANIELS (1800-?), a native of Maine and the daughter of Daniel and Sarah Warren, was married to Sheffield Daniels.

Sheffield DANIELS (1787-1855) was born in Keene, New Hampshire, and was ordained an elder shortly after the exodus of the Saints from Missouri. He died in Iowa in 1855.

William DAVIS (1794 or 1795-1883) was born in Union, Pennsylvania, and was baptized in December 1832. He eventually settled in Brigham City, Utah.

Isaac DECKER (1800-1873), a native of the Netherlands, migrated to Utah with the first pioneer company in July 1847. His family home was in Utah County. Two of his daughters, Lucy and Clarissa, married Brigham Young.

Philo DIBBLE (1806-95), a native of Berkshire, Massachusetts, joined the Church in its infancy, in September

1830. He was wounded in the mob attack in Jackson County, Missouri, but stayed with the Saints through the Missouri and Illinois periods, eventually migrating to Utah.

Alexander W. DONIPHAN (1808-84) represented the Saints as a lawyer on several occasions. He introduced the bill in the Missouri legislature that created Daviess and Caldwell Counties, where the Saints lived for a period of time. He served as a general in the state militia of Missouri, and drew praise from the Saints for refusing to shoot Joseph Smith at the time of the fall of Far West.

David DORT (1790-1841), a native of Gilsum, New Hampshire, was a charter member of the Kirtland Safety Society and a member of the high council in Kirtland, Far West, and Nauvoo. He died in Nauvoo in 1841.

Samuel DROLLINGER (1801-34), a native of Hamilton, Ohio, was baptized into the Church in 1831 with his wife, Rachael. He died in Clay County, Missouri.

James DUNN (1787-?) was born in Pennsylvania and served as assistant steward in Zion's Camp.

Edmund DURFEE (1788-1845), a native of Rhode Island, joined the Church in 1831. In 1837 he moved to Caldwell County, Missouri, only to be expelled with the other Saints the next year. He settled in Illinois, where he was murdered by a mob in 1845.

James DURFEE (1795-1844) was ordained an elder in 1833. He was one of the leaders of the Mormon forces at the battle of Crooked River. He died in 1844 and was buried in the old Nauvoo cemetery.

Peter DUSTIN (1781-?) was born in Grafton, New Hampshire, and served as president of the Blue River Branch in Jackson County, Missouri, where he was ordained a high priest in 1833. He later served on the Missouri high council.

George Parker DYKES (1814-88), a native of Illinois, was ordained a seventy in 1839, laboring afterward as a missionary in Illinois. He enlisted in the Mormon Battalion in 1846. He died in Arizona.

Ellis EAMES (?-?) was ordained an elder in Jackson County, Missouri. He was later president of a conference in Clay County, August 6, 1834. Eames received a mission call while in Nauvoo in the summer of 1844.

Asa C. EARL (1810-91), a native of New York, was baptized in 1833 in Illinois, along with a number of his neighbors, including Charles C. Rich and Hosea Stout. Earl married Rich's sister, Minerva, who died in 1840. Earl later migrated to Utah.

Sylvester Henry EARL (1815-72) was born in Ohio and baptized in 1837. After his baptism, he moved to Far West, Missouri. He served a mission in 1838 and served as guard of the temple in Nauvoo before he was forced to leave with the other Saints. He was a member of the first company of pioneers to arrive in Utah.

Josiah ELLS (1806-85), a native of England, was baptized by Benjamin Winchester in October 1838. Although he was prominent in Nauvoo, he later associated with the apostate organization of William Law and eventually became an apostle in the Reorganized Church.

Ruggles EMES (?-?) was baptized and ordained a priest before October 1831. He resided in Medina, Ohio, at that time.

James EMMETT (1803-52), a native of Kentucky, joined the Church in 1831. He was disfellowshipped temporarily in 1837 and found himself in trouble again when he led a company of one hundred Saints away from Nauvoo against the counsel of Church leaders. He died in the Mormon settlement of San Bernardino, California.

Charles ENGLISH (?-?) was a member of the Church in Clay County, Missouri, where he owned property. He testified in the Hulet Branch trial in 1834.

Horace EVANS (1810-?) was born in Dalton, New Hampshire. He was ordained a seventy in Illinois.

Elisha EVERETT (also *Averett*) (1810-90), a native of Tennessee, was baptized in 1835. He migrated to Utah and died in Glendale, Washington County.

Pleasant EWELL (1788-1852), a native of Virginia, joined the Church in 1837 and was ordained an elder in 1839 and a high priest in 1844. He migrated with the Saints to Utah, settling in Lehi.

Joshua FAIRCHILD (1797-1891), a Canadian, was the son of Joshua Fairchild and Elizabeth Cooley. He moved to the Great Basin with the Church and settled in Cassia County, Idaho.

John FAWSETT (1804-73) was born in Illinois. He served in later years as bishop in Midway, Utah.

Daniel Babcock FILLMORE (1819-94) was born in Camillers, New York, and was baptized in 1842 and then moved to Nauvoo. He was among those sent to Wisconsin to obtain timber for the Nauvoo buildings. He died in Payson, Utah.

Edmund FISCHER (?-?) served in Zion's Camp and later was ordained to the First Quorum of Seventy.

King FOLLETT (1788-1844), a native of Vermont, joined the Church in 1831. He moved with the Saints to Missouri and was one of those arrested in 1838. He was jailed through the winter of 1838-39, first in Richmond and later in Columbia. After he was released he settled in Nauvoo. His name is still remembered for the funeral oration delivered for him by Joseph Smith in 1844.

Isaac FOLLIS (also *Follice* and *Fallace*) (?-?), an elder in Jackson County, Missouri, was among those driven from the county in 1833.

David FRAMPTON (1796-1843), a native of Derry, Pennsylvania, was among those arrested at the time of the fall of Far West, although he was released in a few days. He made his way to Illinois with the body of the Saints, but died in that state in 1843.

Edson FULLER (?-?) was baptized and ordained an elder before June 3, 1831. He was soon after sent on a mission to Missouri, but was troubled by evil spirits and excommunicated later that same year.

Josiah FULLER (?-1838) was possibly the same Josiah Fuller whose name was mentioned in conjunction with work on the Kirtland Temple. He was killed in the mob attack on Haun's Mill in 1838.

David FULLMER (1803-79), a native of Chillisquaque, Pennsylvania, joined the Church in 1836 and resided in

Caldwell County, Missouri, by 1837. He was later ordained a high priest in Nauvoo. He served on the Nauvoo high council, the Council of Fifty, and in the Salt Lake stake presidency.

James GALLAHER (?-?) was a Mormon property owner in Caldwell County, Missouri, and was among those who signed a covenant to assist the poor in the removal of the Church from the state.

David M. GAMET (1812-84) was born in Otsego, New York, and was baptized in 1835. Although many of his children settled in Utah, he remained in the midwest and died in Iowa.

Simeon GARDNER (?-?) served as a member of the high council in Far West. Gardner was among those excommunicated by the Twelve Apostles in Far West, April 26, 1839.

Jacob GATES (1811-92), a native of St. Johnsbury, Vermont, moved with his family to Caldwell County in 1836 and was one of those imprisoned at the time of the fall of Far West. In 1844 he was ordained the senior member of the fourth quorum of seventy in Nauvoo. He died in Provo, Utah.

Mary Snow GATES (1813-91), sister to Erastus Snow, was born in St. Johnsbury, Vermont, and married Jacob Gates in 1833. Both were baptized the same year. Mary's name appears in the Far West Record in connection with the trial of Elder John Murdock in 1838.

Thomas GATES (1776-1851) was born in Hennica, New Hampshire, and became a member of the Church in 1833. At a conference in Kirtland in 1835, Gates, as assistant president of the deacons quorum, was called on to testify to the truthfulness of the soon-to-be-published Doctrine and Covenants. He later moved to Utah.

Jesse GAUSE (also *Gauss*) (?-?) was a Shaker before joining the Church in 1831. He was a member of the presidency of the high priesthood and traveled to Jackson County, Missouri, with Joseph Smith in 1832. However, later that year he fell away and was excommunicated.

Luman GIBBS (?-?), a native of Vermont, was among those arrested in Far West in 1838. He turned state's evidence, however, and was later excommunicated at a special meeting of the Apostles on April 26, 1839.

Alpheus GIFFORD (1793-1841) was born in Adams, Massachusetts, and joined the Church in 1831. He gathered with the Saints in Jackson County, Missouri, in 1833, relocating with them in Clay County after their expulsion and also in Far West a few years later. He died in the Morley settlement in Illinois in 1841.

Algernon Sidney GILBERT (?-1834) was baptized in Ohio in 1830. He was a partner with Newel K. Whitney in a mercantile business in Kirtland. He was called to operate the Church store in Jackson County, Missouri, and was arrested with other leaders at the time of the expulsion from that county. He died of cholera in 1834 at the time of the visit of Zion's Camp to Clay County.

Cornelius GILLIAM (?-1848) professed to be a minister of the gospel. He was a Missouri state senator from 1838 to 1844. He led one of the militia groups that harassed the Saints in Caldwell and Daviess Counties in 1838.

Thomas C. GORDON (?-?) was chosen to serve on the high council of Adam-Ondi-Ahman in 1838. He was among those who filed a petition to the government for redress from the persecutions in Missouri.

George D. GRANT (1812-76), a native of Windsor, New York, joined the Church with his brother, Jedediah M. Grant, in New York. He moved with the Saints to Utah in 1848 and later served as an officer in the state militia during the Indian wars.

Joshua GRANT (1778-1865), a native of Stonington, Connecticut, was the father of George and Jedediah Grant. Although he was present with the Saints in Missouri, it is not known whether he was baptized.

Alphonzo GREEN (1810-75) was born in Brookfield, New York, and was baptized in 1840. He afterward moved with his family to Nauvoo, Illinois. He migrated to Utah in 1847.

Harvey GREEN (1806-?), a native of Lake Pleasant, New York, was married to Sally who died in Jackson County. He later married Ann Rich, a sister to Charles C. Rich. He migrated to Utah in 1848.

Younger GREEN (?-?) was listed as Doctor Green and was a counselor to William Law in Law's apostate church, founded near the time of Joseph Smith's death. Green was excommunicated in 1844.

John Portineus GREENE (1793-1844) was born in Herkimer, New York, and married Rhoda Young, the sister of Brigham Young. He was baptized in 1832 and moved to Kirtland, Ohio. In 1838 he moved his family to Far West, but was forced to flee back to Illinois soon after. Greene served as marshal and was the officer in charge of the destruction of the *Expositor* press in 1844. He became ill shortly thereafter and died.

John GREG (?-?) was a property owner in Caldwell County. He was excommunicated April 26, 1839, in Far West.

William GREGORY (?-?) was a member of the Church living in Caldwell County, Missouri, and was among those who signed the covenant to assist the poor in the Church's removal from the state.

Selah J. GRIFFIN (1792-?) was called on a mission with Thomas B. Marsh in 1831. He lived in Jackson County, Missouri, and later in Caldwell County. He was a blacksmith.

Hiram GRIFFITH (?-1845) was an early member in Ohio and was among those who left that state in the fall of 1837 with the "poor camp." He died in Nauvoo, Illinois.

Thomas GROVER (1807-86), a native of Whitehall, New York, joined the Church in 1834. He was a member of the high council in Kirtland, Far West, and Nauvoo. He migrated to Utah in 1847.

Elisha H. GROVES (1797-1867), a native of Kentucky, was baptized in 1832. He was sustained a member of the Far West high council in 1837. He migrated with the Saints to Utah, settling in Washington County.

Thomas GUYMAN (also *Guymon*) (1781-1855) was born in Stokes County, North Carolina. He migrated to Utah in 1850, settling in Springville.

Isaac HAMBLIN (1776-?), a native of Yarmouth, Massachusetts, was acting president of the deacons quorum in Far West at the conference held there July 6, 1838.

Levi W. HANCOCK (1803-82) was baptized by Parley P. Pratt in November 1830. He was a member of Zion's

Camp and was afterward a president of the First Quorum of Seventy. He also marched with the Mormon Battalion. He died in Washington, Utah.

Solomon HANCOCK (1793-1847), a native of Springfield, Massachusetts, was baptized in 1830 and was called on a mission to Missouri in 1831. He moved with his family to Jackson County in 1832. He was later a member of the high council in Clay County.

Emer HARRIS (1781-1869), the brother of Martin Harris, was born in Cambridge, New York. He joined the Church and became an elder in 1831. He moved to Kirtland that same year, and in 1839 moved his family to Nauvoo. He died in Logan, Utah.

George W. HARRIS (1780-1857), a native of Lanesborough, Massachusetts, was baptized in 1834. He was a member of the high council in Far West and Nauvoo. He did not migrate west. He died in Council Bluffs in 1857.

Martin HARRIS (1783-1875) was born in Easttown, New York, and served as a scribe to Joseph Smith during the translation of the Book of Mormon. He was one of the Three Witnesses. He was excommunicated in 1837 but was rebaptized in 1842. He left the Church again and joined with the Strangites, but migrated to Utah in 1870 and was baptized once again.

Peter HAWS (1796-?), a native of Canada, was a member of the Nauvoo Agricultural and Manufacturing Association. He was sent on a mission to collect funds for the Nauvoo House and the temple in 1843. He located in western Iowa in 1846. His children joined the Reorganized Church.

Norval (also *Norvil*) *HEAD* (1815- ?) was born in Missouri. He was ordained an elder in Far West. He migrated to Nauvoo, where he received his endowment in 1846.

George HEARTLY (?-?) testified before the conference in Randolph County, Indiana, December 6, 1831, about his difficulties with Oliver Walker.

James HENDRICKS (also *Hendrix*) (1808-70), a native of Kentucky, joined the Church in 1836 and moved first to Clay County and then Caldwell County, Missouri. In 1838 he was wounded at the battle of Crooked River and was crippled for the rest of his life. He journeyed to the Great Basin, arriving in 1847 with the Jedediah M. Grant company.

Alonzo HERRICK (?-?) lived first in Jackson County, then in Clay County, and finally in Far West, Missouri, where he attended the school taught by John Murdock. He was called upon to testify in the case involving his classmates, March 24, 1838.

Elias HIGBEE (1795-1843) was born in Galloway, New Jersey. He was baptized in 1832 and moved to Missouri in 1833. He was a member of the high council in Clay County and Far West. He later traveled with Joseph Smith to Washington to present grievances to congress. He died of cholera in Nauvoo.

Isaac HIGBEE (1797-1874), brother of Elias and a native of New Jersey, joined the Church in 1832 and located in Jackson County, Missouri. In 1835 he was ordained a high priest while residing in Clay County. He was later a bishop in Nauvoo and a justice of the peace. He died in Provo, Utah.

John S. HIGBEE (1804-77), brother of Isaac and Elias Higbee and a native of Tate, Ohio, was baptized in 1832 with the rest of his father's family. He was arrested at the time of the fall of Far West. He settled in Toquerville, Utah.

George M. HINKLE (1801-61), born in Kentucky, joined the Church as early as 1832 and moved to Missouri. In Far West he operated a store. During the fall of Far West he allegedly turned Joseph Smith and other Church leaders over to General Lucas. Most of the Saints felt that he betrayed the Prophet. He was excommunicated in 1839.

Jesse HITCHCOCK (1801-?), a native of North Carolina, was one of the early Mormon settlers in Jackson County. He was ordained a high priest in Clay County in 1834. He was appointed to the Missouri high council in 1836. He was cut off from that body in 1837, but retained membership in the Church.

Chandler HOLBROOK (1807-89), a native of New York, was baptized in 1833. He was among those arrested at the fall of Far West, but he was released within a few days. He emigrated with the Saints to the Great Basin, settling in Fillmore, Utah.

Joseph HOLBROOK (1806-86), born in Florence, New York, and brother of Chandler, was baptized in 1833 and marched with Zion's Camp in 1834. He later returned to Missouri, settling in Caldwell County. He followed the Saints to the Rocky Mountains, eventually settling in Bountiful, Utah.

Charles HULET (1790-1863) was born in Lee, Massachusetts, and joined the Church in 1831. He moved to the Prairie Branch in Jackson County, Missouri, in 1832. He and his family went through the sufferings of Clay County and Far West and eventually settled in Nauvoo. He came to Utah in 1850, settling in Springville.

Sylvester HULET (1800-?), brother of Charles and a native of Massachusetts, joined the Church in 1831 and removed to Jackson County, Missouri. In Clay County he married Anne Schott Whitmer, widow of Christian Whitmer, shortly after Whitmer's death. He moved to the Salt Lake Valley in 1847.

Solomon HUMPHREY (1775-1834) was converted by Don Carlos Smith and was ordained an elder by 1831. He assisted in laying the foundation stone of the Kirtland Temple in 1833. He was a member of Zion's Camp. He died in Clay County, Missouri, in September 1834.

Jefferson HUNT (1803-79), a native of Kentucky, joined the Church in 1834 and moved to Clay County, Missouri. Later, in Nauvoo, he served as a major in the Nauvoo Legion. He was also a captain in the Mormon Battalion. He settled in Ogden, Utah.

Dimic (also *Dimick*) *B. HUNTINGTON* (1808-79) was baptized in 1835. He served in various political positions in Nauvoo, including constable and coroner, and he was also drum major in the Nauvoo Legion military band. He served with the Mormon Battalion as well. He died in Salt Lake City.

Heman T. HYDE (1812-42) was born in Stratford, Vermont, and was baptized in 1834. Although his parents voiced opposition to his conversion, they joined the Church a month later and became the nucleus of the Freedom Branch.

Orson HYDE (1805-78), a native of Oxford, Connecticut, and a former Campbellite, converted to the Church in 1831. He was ordained an Apostle in 1835, but was dropped from the Twelve in 1838. In 1841, after his repentance, he was sent to Jerusalem to dedicate land for the gathering of the Jews. He later published the *Frontier Guardian* in Kanesville, Iowa. He died in Spring City, Utah.

James R. IVIE (1802-66) was born in Georgia and baptized in 1832. He marched with Zion's Camp in 1834. He journeyed to the Great Basin with the Saints, eventually settling in Springville, Utah. In 1853, Ivie's interference in a quarrel among the local Indians caused the Walker War.

James IVINS (?-?), a convert to the Church from New Jersey, was a prominent property owner in Nauvoo. His brother, Charles, was among those involved in the *Nauvoo Expositor* incident. He settled in Keokuk, Iowa.

Albert JACKMAN (1812-91), the son of Levi Jackman, was born in Stillwater, New York. He married Lucinda Stone. He died in Salem, Utah, in 1891.

Levi JACKMAN (1797-1876), a native of Vermont, was converted by Harvey Whitlock in 1831. He moved to Jackson County, Missouri, in 1832, and to Clay County in 1833. He was a member of the high council in Clay County. He was a justice of the peace in Far West. He labored on the temple in Nauvoo, leaving for the Great Salt Lake Valley in 1846.

Henry JACKSON (?-?) was ordained an elder in Far West in 1837. His wife, Sarah, was involved in a high council trial in Far West in April 1838.

Sarah JACKSON (?-?), the wife of Henry Jackson, was involved in a high council trial in Far West in April 1838.

Aaron JOHNSON (1806-77) was born in Haddam, Connecticut, and was baptized in 1836. He was among the families that moved from Kirtland to Far West in the spring of 1838. He served on the high council in Nauvoo and was a lieutenant in the Nauvoo Legion. He headed a company of Saints, arriving in Utah in 1850.

Benjamin Franklin JOHNSON (1818-1905), a native of Pomfret, New York, moved with his family to Kirtland in 1833, although he wasn't baptized until 1835. He moved with the Kirtland Camp to Missouri in 1838. He settled in Adam-Ondi-Ahman, but was soon driven out and arrested. Later, in Nauvoo, he was chosen as a member of the Council of Fifty. He died in Gila Bend, Arizona.

Edward JOHNSON (1809-90), was born in Morristown, New Jersey. He married Matilda Archer in 1833.

James JOHNSON (?-?) was listed as a property owner in Caldwell County, Missouri, in 1837.

Joel Hills JOHNSON (1802-82) was born in Grafton, Massachusetts, and was baptized in 1831. His removal to Missouri was apparently late in the Far West period, and he was forced out soon after. He established himself in Ramus, Illinois, where he served as president of the short-lived Ramus Stake. He came to Utah with the Willard Richards company in 1848.

Luke S. JOHNSON (1807-61), a native of Pomfret, Vermont, was baptized in 1831 and ordained a high priest the same year. He was a member of the Kirtland high council and of Zion's Camp. In 1835 he was ordained an Apostle, but he was disfellowshipped in 1837 and excommunicated in 1838. He was rebaptized in Nauvoo in 1846 and migrated to Utah in 1847.

Lyman E. JOHNSON (1811-56), brother of Luke Johnson and a native of Vermont, was baptized in 1831 and was a member of Zion's Camp. He was ordained an Apostle in 1835, but, like his brother, was excommunicated in 1838. He, however, did not return to the Church. He was killed in a drowning accident in the Mississippi River in 1856.

Orson JOHNSON (?-?) was an elder present at the special conference held at the Big Blue settlement in Jackson County, Missouri, in 1832. He served with Zion's Camp and on the high council of Kirtland.

David JUDA (also *Judah*) (?-?) fought at the battle of Crooked River in 1838. He served as a missionary in the Joseph Smith campaign in Illinois in 1844.

John KILLIAN (1796-1858), a native of North Carolina, was baptized in 1831. He served as a captain of the Caldwell County militia (Mormon) during the "Mormon War" at Far West. He later emigrated to Utah.

Heber C. KIMBALL (1801-68), born in Sheldon, Vermont, was baptized in 1832 and moved to Kirtland 1833. He was ordained an Apostle in 1835. He served missions to Great Britain in 1837 and 1839. He moved to Missouri in 1838 and aided the Saints during the expulsion from Far West. Later, in Utah, he served as a member of the First Presidency.

Samuel KIMBALL (?-?) was one of the witnesses who testified against the Church in Missouri in November 1838.

Newel KNIGHT (1800-1847) was born in Marlborough, Vermont, and was baptized in May 1830. He was leader of the Colesville Branch in New York and led that group to Jackson County, Missouri, as the first Mormon settlers there. He lived through all the Missouri depredations. His wife, Sally Coburn, died in Clay County. He later married Lydia Goldthwait. He died in Nebraska territory.

Vinson KNIGHT (1804-42), a native of Chester, New York, was ordained a high priest and counselor to Bishop Whitney in Kirtland in 1836. He later became bishop at the settlement at Adam-Ondi-Ahman. As a Church land agent, he assisted in purchasing thousands of acres of land from Isaac Galland in Iowa. He also served as a bishop in Nauvoo.

Isaac LANEY (1815-73) was born in Franklin, Kentucky, and was baptized in 1838. He was among the survivors of the raid at Haun's Mill. He migrated to Utah in 1847, settling in Salt Lake City.

Thomas LAPLESH (?-?) was an elder of the Church living in Jackson County, Missouri. He was present at a conference there on September 27, 1832.

Edward LARKEY (1809-?) testified against Lyman Wight in a trial held June 29, 1838, at Far West.

Francis LEE (1811-66), a native of Wilmington, Ohio, married Jane Vail Johnson in 1835 in Clay County, Missouri. After migrating with the Saints to the Great Basin, Lee settled in Panaca, Nevada.

Elizabeth LEGG (?-?) was presumably a younger woman attending the Murdock school in Far West. She was called to testify in the high council trial on March 24, 1838.

William LEGG (1805-35) was a sailor, and his occupation apparently brought him to America from England and eventually to the Church. He died at Liberty, Missouri, July 29, 1835.

William J. LEMANS (?-?) was ordained an elder in Far West on November 10, 1837.

Lyman LEONARD (1793-1877), a native of Springfield, Massachusetts, was baptized in 1832 and moved to Jackson County, Missouri. He accompanied the Saints to Clay County, Far West, Nauvoo, and finally to Utah.

Joshua LEWIS (1795-1835) resided in Jackson County at the time the Mormon settlements were established there. He converted to the Church in the winter of 1830-31. He died in 1835 in Clay County, Missouri.

Adam LIGHTNER (1810-85) was born in Liberty, Missouri, and married Mary Elizabeth Rollins in 1835. His wife was sealed to Joseph Smith in 1842 but never sealed to Lightner, since he was never baptized. Lightner operated a store at Far West, Missouri.

Cornelius P. LOTT (1798-1850), a native of New York City, received his endowment in Nauvoo and left for the Great Basin, arriving in the fall of 1847.

Daniel E. LOVELAND (?-?) was called on a mission to Massachusetts in the spring of 1844.

John LOWRY (also *Lowrie*) (1799-1867) was born in Nashville, Tennessee. His first wife, Susan Groom, died in Missouri. He came to Salt Lake City with the John Taylor company in 1847.

Samuel D. LUCAS (?-1868) located in Jackson County, Missouri, as early as 1826. He was a general in the Missouri State Militia. He led the forces against the Mormons in Jackson County, and he later led forces against Far West, arriving ahead of General Clark. He took Joseph Smith prisoner and ordered him shot, but Alexander Doniphan refused to carry out the order.

Amasa Mason LYMAN (1813-77) was born in Lyman, New Hampshire, and joined the Church at age eighteen. He was ordained a high priest in 1833. He marched with Zion's Camp and later moved his family to Missouri, only to be expelled in 1838. In 1842 he was ordained an Apostle. He was excommunicated in 1870 for denying the atonement of the Savior.

Aaron LYON (also *Lyons*) (?-1839) converted to the Church in 1831-32. He worked on the Kirtland Temple and settled Salem, Missouri. He died at Bear Creek, Hancock County, Illinois.

Roxana Palmer LYON (?-1836) died August 23, 1836, in Caldwell County, Missouri.

John LYTLE (1803-92), a native of Turbet, Pennsylvania, was baptized in May 1836 and moved to Missouri. Later, in Nauvoo, he served as a police officer and was among those arrested for the destruction of the *Expositor* press. He later migrated to Utah.

William MARKS (1792-1872), a native of Rutland, Vermont, became prominent in the Church late in the Kirtland period, serving there on the high council. He was stake president in Nauvoo from 1839 to 1844. He was also an alderman for the city. After Joseph Smith's death, he joined with the reorganization and became a leading figure in that movement.

Thomas B. MARSH (1800-1866) was born in Acton, Massachusetts, and joined the Church in September 1830. He was appointed physician to the Church. He moved to Missouri and became a member of the high council in Clay County. In 1835 he was ordained an Apostle. In 1838 he became one of the "dissidents" who disagreed with Church leadership. He was excommunicated, but returned to be rebaptized in 1857.

Moses MARTIN (?-?) was a member of Zion's Camp and of the First Quorum of Seventy. He also served a mission to New York. He settled in Lee County, Iowa, in 1839.

Silas MAYNARD (1787-?) was among those arrested at Far West, but he was released shortly thereafter.

Dr. James McCORD (?-?) served on the high council at Far West until his excommunication in 1838.

William E. McLELLIN (also *Mc.lellin, Mclellin, McClellin,* and *M'Lellin)* (1806-83), a native of Tennessee, was baptized in August 1831. He was a member of the high council in Clay County, Missouri, and became an Apostle in 1835. He left the Church in 1838 and became an enemy of the Prophet.

Daniel S. MILES (1772-1845) was born in Sanbornton, New Hampshire, and was called as a President of the First Quorum of Seventy in 1837. He moved to Missouri in 1838 and was expelled with the rest of the Saints. He died in Illinois in 1845.

Eleazer MILLER (1795-1876), born in Coeymans, New York, was baptized in 1831. He served in Zion's Camp in

1834. During the exodus from Illinois, he served on the committee to expedite the removal of the Saints.

George MILLER (1783-1837) was a priest in the Shalersville, Ohio, Branch. He was silenced at a conference held September 12, 1831, in Kirtland. He is not the same man as the Bishop George Miller of the Nauvoo period.

Henry William MILLER (1807-85), a native of Lexington, New York, became a convert in 1839. He served as stake president in Freedom, Illinois, during the Nauvoo period. He migrated to Utah in 1852.

William MITCHELL (?-?) was baptized and ordained an elder before June 1833. He lived in the Kirtland area.

James MORE (?-?) was a member of the Church in Indiana. His license was taken from him at a conference held in Randolph County, Indiana, December 6, 1831. He was accused of abusing his family.

George MOREY (also *Moery*) (1803-?), born in Pittstown, New York, served on the high council in Far West and was appointed as a constable in Nauvoo. He was ordained a high priest in 1841. Morey did not leave Nauvoo with the main body of the Church. He later joined the reorganization under Joseph Smith III.

Isaac MORLEY (1786-1865), a native of Montague, Massachusetts, was baptized in November 1830 and was ordained a high priest in 1831. He suffered with other Church leaders through the persecutions in Jackson County, Missouri, in 1833. He was a patriarch in Far West, Missouri, in 1837. He played important roles in Nauvoo and in Utah.

Arthur MORRISON (?-?) was called on twice to testify at high council courts in Far West. One source identifies Morrison as accompanying George Hinkle under the flag of truce to come to terms with General Lucas during the siege of Far West. He died in Keokuk, Iowa.

Justus MORSE (1809-87) was born in Chester, Massachusetts, and joined the Church in 1833. He died in 1887 in Pleasanton, Iowa.

John MURDOCK (1792-1871) was born in Kortwright, New York, and joined the Church in November of 1830. He was a member of Zion's Camp. He, with George Hinkle, settled DeWitt, Missouri, in 1838, but was soon expelled. He served as a bishop in Nauvoo. He died in Beaver, Utah.

Samuel MURICH (1804-?), a native of Virginia, is listed as living in Jackson County in 1833, in Clay County in 1834, and in Far West in 1838. In Nauvoo, Murich was ordained an elder.

Emanuel MURPHEY (1809-71) was born in Union, South Carolina, and was baptized in 1836. He came to Utah in 1860 and died in Millcreek, Salt Lake County.

Samuel MUSICK (1804-?), a native of Virginia, owned a store in Far West, Missouri. He located in Nauvoo, where he was ordained an elder and later a seventy. He was endowed in the Nauvoo Temple in 1846.

James NEWBERRY (1791-1884) was born in New York and was held at the fall of Far West, but he was released soon afterwards. He helped the other Saints leave the state. He eventually united with the reorganization.

John S. NOAH (1800-?), a native of Pennsylvania, was a farmer and resident of Mentor County, Ohio. He never gathered with the Saints.

Chauncy ODLE (?-?) had his license taken away in Ohio at a conference held in Amherst, September 29, 1831.

John OUTHOUSE (1786-?) and his son, Joseph, were witnesses in the Murdock/Newberry schoolroom trial in Far West, March 24, 1838. He later moved to Nauvoo, where he was ordained a high priest in 1844.

Joseph OUTHOUSE (1820-?), a native of Illinois, attended the school of John Murdock in Far West. This led to his involvement in the trial of Murdock before the high council. He became a seventy in Nauvoo. After the prophet's death, the younger Outhouse joined the reorganization.

Jonathan T. PACKER (1817-89) was born in Perry, Ohio, and was baptized in 1836. He died January 29, 1889, at Safford, Arizona.

Ebenezer PAGE (1807-?), a native of Waterville, New York, ordained his brother, John E. Page, to the office of elder in 1833. He was among the prisoners taken at the fall of Far West.

Hiram PAGE (1800-1852), a native of Vermont, joined the Church in April 1830. He moved to Missouri in 1832, but left the Church in 1838. He was one of the Eight Witnesses.

John Edward PAGE (1799-1867) was born in Trenton, New York, and joined the Church in 1833. After a lengthy and successful mission in Canada, he moved to Missouri. His wife and two of his children died in Far West. He became a member of the Quorum of Twelve Apostles in 1838. He later became disaffected with the Church and was excommunicated in 1846.

Lorin PAGE (1813-?), the brother of John Edward Page, was born April 12, 1813, at Waterville, New York.

Sylvester PARKER (?-?) was a member of the Church in Ohio. He is listed as having left the Church.

Ezra PARRISH (1804-83) was born in Brownsville, New York, and served as an alternate high councilor in Nauvoo. He migrated to the Great Basin in 1850.

Warren PARRISH (?-?) was a member of Zion's Camp and the First Quorum of Seventy in Kirtland. He served as a scribe to Joseph Smith from 1835 to 1837. He renounced his membership in 1837.

Thoret PARSONS (1802-?), a native of New York, was ordained a seventy in Nauvoo in 1844.

Edward PARTRIDGE (1793-1840) was born in Pittsfield, Massachusetts, and was baptized in December 1830. He was the first bishop of the Church, serving as leader of the Saints in Jackson County, Missouri, from the time of the first settlement there. After living through all the trials of the Saints in Missouri, he died in Nauvoo.

Charles PATTEN (1811-?), a native of New York, was ordained a high priest in Nauvoo in 1844. He later served on a committee to aid the destitute of that city.

David W. PATTEN (1799-1838) was born in Theresa, New York, and joined the Church in 1832. He was ordained an Apostle in 1835. He was mortally wounded at the battle of the Crooked River in Ray County, Missouri, just before the fall of Far West.

John PATTEN (1787-1847), a native of New Hampshire, served on the high council in the Iowa Territory during the Nauvoo period.

Hezekiah PECK (1782-1850) was born in Vermont and was baptized a few months after the organization of the Church, in the summer of 1830. As a member of the Colesville settlement, he was one of the first Mormon settlers in Jackson County, Missouri. He served as a bishop in Nauvoo and died near St. Joseph, Missouri.

Joseph PENNOCK (?-?) was a resident of Nauvoo involved in a high council case held June 15, 1844.

William C. PERRY (1813-?) was born in New York and joined the Church in 1835. He left Kirtland for Missouri in the spring of 1838 with the Kirtland Camp. He later moved with the Saints to Nauvoo. There he served as an alternate member of the high council.

Ziba PETERSON (?-1849) was baptized in April 1830. He was ordained an elder soon after and was one of the four missionaries to the Lamanites later that year. He later left the Church, however, and in 1833 he was excommunicated.

David PETTIGREW (1791-1863), a native of Weatherfield, Vermont, joined the Church in 1832 and moved to Jackson County, Missouri. He was driven out of both Clay County and Caldwell County with the body of the Saints. He was jailed at the time of the fall of Far West. He was later a member of the Mormon Battalion, and died in Salt Lake City.

Ethan PETTIT (1810-84), a native of Hempstead, New York, was baptized in 1840 and soon after moved to Nauvoo. He migrated to Utah in 1848.

Albert PETTY (1795-1869) was born in Kentucky and joined the Church in 1835. He served as justice of the peace in Far West. He followed the Saints to Illinois and eventually to the Great Basin.

Burton H. PHELPS (1806-85) was born in Chenango County, New York. He received a "re-baptism" in 1863. He died in Payson, Utah.

Morris PHELPS (1805-76), a native of Northhampton, Massachusetts, was baptized in 1831, settling in Missouri that same year. He was one of the Saints imprisoned after the fall of Far West. He reached Illinois and settled in Ramus, where his wife died. He moved to Utah in 1851.

William W. PHELPS (1792-1872) was born in Hanover, New Jersey, and was baptized in June 1831. He was appointed printer for the Church. He was a member of the presidency of the Church in Missouri from 1834-1838. He helped to found the city of Far West. He was excommunicated in 1838, but was received back into the Church in 1841. He died in Salt Lake City.

George PITKIN (1801-73), born in Hartford, Vermont, served as the sheriff of Portage County, Ohio, at the time of his baptism by Joseph Smith in 1831. In Far West, he was elected sheriff of Caldwell County. His first wife, Amanda Eggleston, died in 1847 in Iowa, during the exodus from Illinois. He later settled in Cache County, Utah.

Chauncey Warriner PORTER (1812-68) was born in Holland, New York, and married Emma Summer in 1833 while living in Clay County, Missouri. He migrated with the Church to the west, settling in Centerville, Utah.

Sanford PORTER (1790-1873) was born in Brimfield, Massachusetts, and joined the Church in 1831. By 1833 he had moved to Jackson County, Missouri. He migrated to the west in 1847 with the Charles C. Rich company.

Orson PRATT (1811-81) was born in Hartford, New York, and joined the Church in 1831. He was a member of Zion's Camp and of the high council in Clay County, Missouri, 1834. He was ordained an Apostle in 1835. He was excommunicated in 1842, but was rebaptized in 1843 and returned to his apostleship. He died in Salt Lake City.

Parley P. PRATT (1807-57), brother of Orson and a native of Burlington, New York, was baptized and ordained an elder in September 1830. He was ordained a high priest the next year. He was one of the great early missionaries of the Church, his missions including the Lamanite mission to Missouri in 1830-31. He became an Apostle in 1835. He was assassinated in 1857 while on a mission in Arkansas.

Allen RATHBURN (?-?) was proposed to be ordained a deacon at the conference in Far West on July 6, 1838. He was a property owner in Ray County, Missouri, in 1837. He testified for the state in the trial of Church leaders following the fall of Far West.

Robert RATHBURN (?-?) was among the Saints in Jackson County, where he operated a blacksmith shop. He is listed as one of the survivors of the Haun's Mill massacre.

David Harvey REDFIELD (?-?) was a resident of Kirtland. He traveled with the "poor camp" to Missouri in 1838. He was among those involved in the destruction of the *Expositor* press in Nauvoo in 1844.

Levi Harlow REDFIELD (1801-66), a native of North Madison, Connecticut, served on the Kirtland high council. He migrated to Utah in 1850.

Calvin REED (1821-95) was born in Ackworth, New Hampshire, and was baptized in 1833. He died at St. David, Arizona, in 1895.

Charles C. RICH (1809-83) was born in Kentucky and was baptized in 1832. He was a member of the Nauvoo high council and stake presidency. He led one of the early companies to the Great Basin. He became an Apostle in 1849. He helped colonize California and Cache County, Utah.

Leonard RICH (?-?) was a prominent member of the Church in Kirtland. He was a president of the First Quorum of Seventy. He became a dissenter, however, and was identified as a member of the mob that persecuted Joseph Smith and members remaining in Nauvoo as late as 1845.

Ezekial RIDER (?-?) was an early convert of the Church in Ohio and was tried before a bishop's court in Kirtland for slandering Bishop Whitney.

Sidney S. RIGDON (1793-1876) was born in St. Clair, Pennsylvania, and joined the Church in November 1830. He served as a member of the First Presidency from 1832 to 1844. He was jailed with Joseph Smith and other leaders in the Liberty Jail in the winter of 1838-39. He attempted to lead the Church after the Prophet's death. He was excommunicated in 1844.

Burr RIGGS (1810-60), a native of New Haven, Connecticut, was baptized and ordained an elder before June

1831. He was ordained a high priest later that year, but in 1833 he was excommunicated. He was baptized again by 1834 and marched with Zion's Camp. He later resided in Far West.

Alanson RIPLEY (?-?) was an early member of the Church in Ohio. He served in Zion's Camp in 1834 and later removed to Missouri. He was held for trial at the time of the fall of Far West. The high council directed him to serve as a bishop in Iowa in 1839, but this was reversed in 1841 when the conference failed to sustain him in that position. He was appointed surveyor for Nauvoo in 1841.

Ebenezer ROBINSON (1816-91) was born in Floyd, New York, and was baptized in 1835 by Joseph Smith. He lived in Ohio until 1837, when he moved to Far West, and later moved to Nauvoo. He became a member of the Reorganized Church after the death of the Prophet.

Lewis ROBINSON (1811-?), a native of Ohio, presented himself to the council meeting on August 6, 1834, in Clay County, Missouri, as being called on a mission. He was ordained a seventy in Nauvoo.

Orrin Porter ROCKWELL (1813-78), a native of Belcher, Massachusetts, was baptized on the day of the organization of the Church when only seventeen. He settled in Jackson County, Missouri, in 1831 and lived through all the Missouri expulsions. In Nauvoo he became a personal bodyguard to Joseph Smith. He was accused of the attempted murder of Lilburn W. Boggs, former Missouri Governor, but he was never actually tried on the charge. He died in Salt Lake City.

Shadrack ROUNDY (1788-1872) was born in Rockingham, Vermont, and was baptized in 1831. He was a prominent leader in Kirtland, Far West, and Nauvoo. He migrated to the Salt Lake Valley, where he served as a bishop.

Isaac RUSSELL (1807-44) was successful in founding a number of branches of the Church in his native England during the establishment of the English mission. However, he became disaffected with the Church during the difficulties in Far West. He was excommunicated in 1839.

Simonds RYDER (1792-1870), a native of Hartford, Vermont, joined the Campbellite movement in 1828 and was among the members of that group who joined the Church in 1831. His name was misspelled in a revelation calling him on a mission. His disillusionment over the misspelling led to his apostasy. He helped tar and feather Joseph Smith in 1832.

Henry Harrison SAGERS (1815-86) was born in Leroy, New York, and joined the Church in 1833. He served on the high council in Adam-Ondi-Ahman. He was charged with teaching "spiritual wifery" in Nauvoo, but apparently came west with the body of the Church.

William SCOBEY (1811-33) joined the Church in his native Fayette, New York, around 1831. He died while visiting relatives in Pontiac, Michigan, in 1833.

John SCOTT (1811-76) was a convert from Ontario, Canada. A member of the Nauvoo Legion, he died at Millcreek, Utah.

Absalom SCRITCHFIELD (?-?) was a member of the Church, first residing in Jackson County, then Clay, and finally in Far West, Missouri. He was charged with riot in the trials following the fall of Far West.

Daniel SHEARER (1791-1874), a native of Saratoga, New York, was among those arrested at the fall of Far West, but he was soon released. He was ordained a high priest in Iowa in 1847. He subsequently joined the Reorganized Church.

Jacob SHERMAN (?-?) was a priest in the Church in Ohio. He was present at the conference held June 3, 1831, in Geauga County. His name appeared in the Kirtland tax records for 1834-37.

Lyman SHERMAN (1804-39) was born in Monkton, Vermont, and was baptized in 1832. He moved to Kirtland in 1833 and was a member of Zion's Camp the next year. He was ordained as a President of the First Quorum of Seventy in 1835 and was in the high council in Kirtland and Far West. He was called to be an Apostle but was never ordained. He died in February 1839 in Far West.

Henry G. SHERWOOD (1785-1862), a native of Kinsbury, New York, was ordained an elder in 1832. He was a member of the high council in Kirtland and Nauvoo. He migrated to Utah in 1848.

Henry SHIBLEY (?-?) was an elder in the Church in Ohio and was a member of Zion's Camp in 1834. He was among those called to the First Quorum of Seventy in 1835.

Luman Andros SHURTLIFF (1807-84) was born in Montgomery, Massachusetts, and was baptized in 1836. During the Nauvoo period, he served in the Nauvoo Legion, and at the time of the exodus he was chosen to be captain of a company.

Roxana SLADE (?-?), the wife of Benjamin Slade, testified against Samuel Brown in the Hulet trial. Her husband was among the disaffected at Far West who testified for the state against the Church.

Albert SLOAN (?-?) was a member of the Church in Caldwell County, Missouri. He was ordained an elder in 1838.

Don Carlos SMITH (1816-41), a native of Norwich, Vermont, was brother to Joseph Smith. He was baptized in June 1830 and was ordained president of the high priests quorum in 1836. He took charge of the *Elders' Journal* in Kirtland and edited the *Times and Seasons* in Nauvoo. He was a member of the Nauvoo city council. He died in Nauvoo in 1841.

Emma SMITH (1804-79) was born in Harmony, Pennsylvania, and married Joseph Smith in 1827. She was baptized in June 1830 and was appointed to prepare a hymnal for the Church. She became the first president of the Relief Society in 1842. She married Lewis C. Bidamon in 1847, after the Prophet's death.

Hyrum SMITH (1800-1844), born in Tunbridge, Vermont, was the elder brother of Joseph Smith. He was one of the Eight Witnesses. He became the assistant counselor in the First Presidency in 1837 and then Second Counselor to Joseph Smith later that same year. He was called to the office of Patriarch in 1841. He was killed with the Prophet in 1844.

Jackson Osborne SMITH (1815-80) was born in North Carolina and served in Zion's Camp in 1834. He moved with the Church to Nauvoo and later to the Great Basin.

John SMITH (?-?) was an older man at the time he was baptized by Lyman Wight in 1831. He was ordained a high priest in 1831 but was disfellowshipped in 1833 for exercising his priesthood authority after his license had been demanded from him.

Joseph SMITH, Jr. (1805-44) was born in Sharon, Vermont, translated the Book of Mormon, and was the founder of the Church. He received the priesthood from heavenly messengers. He presided over the Church during the Kirtland, Missouri, and Nauvoo periods. He was killed in Carthage, Illinois, in 1844.

Joseph SMITH, Sr. (1771-1840), born in Topsfield, Massachusetts, was father of Joseph Smith, the Prophet. He was one of the Eight Witnesses. He became Patriarch of the Church in 1833. He was a member of the Kirtland high council and was appointed assistant counselor to the First Presidency in 1837. He died in Nauvoo in 1840.

Joshua SMITH (1788-1845), a native of Nobleborough, Maine, was baptized in 1836. He served as an alternate high councilor in Nauvoo. He died in Carthage, Illinois, where he had been summoned to attend court. Suspicion of poisoning by the militia of Carthage was confirmed by the post mortem examination.

Samuel H. SMITH (1808-44), a native of Tunbridge, Vermont, was a younger brother of Joseph Smith. He was one of the Eight Witnesses. He is traditionally recognized as the first missionary of the Church. He served as a member of the Kirtland high council. He participated in the battle of Crooked River in 1838. He died in Nauvoo in 1844.

Sylvester SMITH (ca. 1805-?) was baptized before June 1831. He was ordained a high priest in 1831, and in 1834 he was a member of Zion's Camp and is known for his heated arguments with the Prophet during the march. He was a member of the Kirtland high council, but became disaffected from the Church and was excommunicated by 1838.

William SMITH (1811-93), a younger brother of Joseph Smith, was born in Royalton, Vermont. He was ordained a high priest in 1833. He became a member of the Quorum of Twelve Apostles in 1835. He edited the *Wasp* in Nauvoo. He was excommunicated in 1845, following Joseph's death.

Willard SNOW (1811-52), a native of St. Johnsbury, Vermont, joined the Church after his two brothers, William and Erastus, in 1833. He marched with Zion's Camp and afterward was a member of the First Quorum of Seventy. He lived through the difficulties in Far West and Nauvoo, eventually settling in Salt Lake City.

William SNOW (1806-79), a native of St. Johnsbury, Vermont, was baptized in 1832. William served in the first legislature of the Utah territory.

Leonard SOBEY (?-?) served on the Nauvoo high council from 1841 to 1844, when he was disfellowshipped for following Sidney Rigdon.

Daniel STANTON (1795-1872), a native of Manlius, New York, was baptized by Parley P. Pratt in November 1830. He became a high priest in 1831. In 1840 he was ordained president of the Quincy, Illinois, Stake.

David STEPHENS (1819-99), the son of Alexander Stephens, was born in North Carolina. He married Rebecca Kimball.

Urial (also *Uzziel*) *STEVENS* (?-?) was brother-in-law to John E. Page. He was ordained an elder in 1835.

Levi STEWART (1812-76) was born in Edwardsville, Illinois, and joined the Church in 1837. Soon after, he moved to Missouri. He followed the Church to Nauvoo, and then to the West.

Calvin W. STODDARD (1801-36), a native of Palmyra, New York, married Sophronia Smith, sister of Joseph Smith. Stoddard was involved in many of the initial events of the organization of the Church. He died in 1836, presumably in Kirtland, Ohio.

Michael STOKER (1805-?), the son of Michael Stoker and Ana Barbara, was born in North Carolina. He married Martha McDavid.

Robert STONE (1777-?) was born in England. He received a patriarchal blessing in 1846. He served as an alternate high councilor in Nauvoo.

Hosea STOUT (1810-89), a native of Kentucky, married Surmantha Peck and gathered with the Saints in Missouri, although he was not baptized until 1838. He had to flee from Far West at the time of the fall of that city. He became clerk of the high council in Nauvoo and entered minutes in the Far West Record. He was also a captain of the police force. He later migrated to Utah.

Stephen STRONG (?-?), a Church member in Orange, Ohio, was ordained a priest in 1831.

Jonathan SUMNER (1774-?) was an elder of the Church in Missouri. His son, Josiah, was the subject of mob attacks during the violence in Jackson County.

Josiah SUMNER (1807-?) was born in Virginia and baptized in December 1830. He was whipped by a mob during the expulsion of the Saints from Jackson County. He was later ordained a seventy, but he left the Church before the end of the Nauvoo period.

John TAYLOR (1808-87), a native of Milnthorpe, England, was baptized in 1836 in Toronto, Canada. He became an Apostle in 1838. He edited the *Times and Seasons* and the *Nauvoo Neighbor.* He was seriously wounded by the mob that killed the Prophet at Carthage Jail. He survived and eventually served as President of the Church from 1880 to 1887.

Ezra THAYER (1790-?) was born in Randolph, Vermont, and was a bridge builder. He was baptized in October 1830, and became a high priest the next year. He joined with the Reorganized Church after the Prophet's death.

Robert B. THOMPSON (1811-41), a native of England, joined the Church in 1836 and moved to Kirtland the next year. He moved to Far West in 1838, only to be forced out soon after. He served with the Nauvoo Legion and was associate editor of the *Times and Seasons.* He died in Nauvoo.

Samuel THOMPSON (1813-92) was born in Pomfret, New York, and was baptized in 1833 by Brigham Young. He marched with Zion's Camp, and later became a seventy. He eventually migrated west with the main body of the Church.

Alva TIPPETS (1809-47) was born in Lewis, New York, and was baptized in 1832. He died in 1847 at Winter Quarters, Nebraska.

TUBB (?-?) was perhaps Amos Tubbs, a member in Jackson County and, later, Caldwell County.

Theodore TURLEY (1801-71), a native of England, was baptized in Ontario, Canada. He moved from there to Missouri and then to Nauvoo, eventually settling in Beaver, Utah.

Thomas TURNER (?-?) was ordained a seventy at Far West in July 1838.

Elizabeth VAN BENTHUSEN (?-?) married Sidney Gilbert. She was baptized with her husband in the winter of 1830-31 in Kirtland, Ohio. In spite of her husband's death in Missouri, she migrated with the Saints to Utah.

Truman WAIT (1810-?), a native of Vermont, was baptized before 1833, when he was called on a mission to the eastern states with Larkins Salisbury. In 1844 he lost his elder's license for running a grog shop.

Oliver WALKER (1782-1843) was born in New York and married Nancy Cressy in 1803. He died in 1843. His widow was subsequently sealed to Brigham Young.

George WALTERS (1796-?) was born in Norfolk, Connecticut, and was baptized in 1834. He was one of the large landowners in Caldwell County, Missouri. During the difficulties at Far West he left the Church and remained in Missouri when the body of Saints was forced out.

Elias F. WELLS (?-?) was a member of Zion's Camp and was approved for an advancement in the priesthood in 1834 in Clay County, Missouri.

Micah B. WELTON (1794-?) was born in Watertown, Connecticut, and was baptized in 1831 in Ohio. He was ordained a priest that same year. He received his endowment in the Nauvoo Temple in January 1846.

Nathan Ayres WEST (1808-?) was born in Hubbard, Ohio. He was involved in the Hulet Branch trial in Clay County in 1834.

Brother WHEELER (1814-?) was possibly Henry A. Wheeler, born August 29, 1814, in Benton, New York.

Harvey WHITLOCK (1809-?), a native of Massachusetts, was ordained a high priest in 1831. He located in Missouri that year. He was disfellowshipped about 1834 and excommunicated in 1838.

Christian WHITMER (1798-1835), a native of Pennsylvania, was baptized in April 1830. He was one of the Eight Witnesses. He moved to Missouri, where he was ordained a high priest. He was a high councilor in Clay County, where he died in full fellowship in 1835.

David WHITMER (1805-88), a native of Harrisburg, Pennsylvania, was one of the first members of the Church and one of the Three Witnesses. In 1834 he was ordained President of the Church in Missouri and successor to Joseph Smith. However, in 1838 he apostatized from the Church and was excommunicated.

Jacob WHITMER (1800-1856), born in Pennsylvania, was baptized in April 1830 and became one of the Eight Witnesses. He was driven from Jackson County, Missouri, in 1833 and followed the Church to Clay and then Caldwell County. He severed his connection with the Church in 1838.

John WHITMER (1802-78), a native of Pennsylvania, was an early member of the Church. He became an elder in June 1830. He was appointed Church historian in 1831 and was a member of the Presidency of the Church in Missouri from 1834 to 1838. He, like his brothers, was excommunicated for apostasy in 1838.

Peter WHITMER (1809-36), son of Peter Whitmer, Sr., and a native of Fayette, New York, was one of the Eight Witnesses. He served with the early Lamanite mission in 1830. He was appointed a member of the Clay County high council in 1836. He died in full fellowship in 1836.

Newel K. WHITNEY (1795-1850) was born in Marlborough, Vermont, and was baptized in November 1830. He was appointed bishop in Kirtland in 1831. He operated the Church store in Kirtland and was an intimate associate of the Prophet from 1831 until Joseph Smith's death. He died in Salt Lake City.

Lyman WIGHT (1796-1858), a native of Fairfield, New York, was baptized in November 1830 and was ordained a high priest in 1831. He became an Apostle in 1841 after having served as a military leader and valiant defender throughout the Missouri difficulties. After the Prophet's death, he led a group that settled in Texas. He was eventually cut off from the Church.

John WILKINS (1800-1890), born in Saratoga, New York, signed the agreement to help the poor leave Missouri in 1839. He eventually settled in Provo, Utah.

Thomas WILLES (1810-36) died in Tomkins, New York, only twenty-six years old.

Alexander WILLIAMS (1803-76), a native of Georgia, moved to Utah in 1848 and settled in Provo where he served as a counselor in a bishopric and as sheriff of the county.

Frederick G. WILLIAMS (1787-1842) was born at Suffield, Connecticut, baptized in November of 1830, and ordained a high priest the following year. In 1833 he became a counselor in the presidency of the high priesthood. He was dropped from the First Presidency in 1837 and was excommunicated in 1839.

Eleazer WILLIS (?-?) was a member in Tompkins, Ohio, and was ordained a priest at a conference at Orange, Ohio, in October 1831.

Calves WILSON (?-?) was baptized before October 1831. He was ordained a priest in 1831. He served a mission to Cincinnati, Ohio, in May 1832.

Lewis Dunbar WILSON (1805-56) was born at Milton, Vermont, and joined the Church in 1836. He became a member of the Nauvoo high council, serving from 1839 to 1846. He migrated to Utah in 1853.

Zecherriah WILSON (?-?) was a member of the Church who lived near Adam-Ondi-Ahman. He served as temporary member of the high council in Far West. He removed with the Saints to Illinois, serving a mission to southern Illinois in 1840.

Stephen WINCHESTER (1795-1873), a native of Vermont, joined the Church in 1833 and marched with Zion's Camp the following year. He removed, with his family, to Caldwell County, Missouri. At his home near Far West, David Patten died after being shot at Crooked River. Following his expulsion from Missouri and Illinois, he migrated to Utah.

Solomon WIXOM (1809-79) was born in Hector, New York, and was baptized in 1832. He was a member of the Pleasant Grove Bank in western Illinois along with Charles C. Rich. He migrated to Utah in 1850.

John WOODARD (1805-?), a native of Vermont, was baptized and ordained an elder in 1831. He was silenced by a conference of the Church held at Orange, Ohio, in September 1831.

Wilford WOODRUFF (1807-98) was born in Farmington, Connecticut, and was baptized in 1833 in New York. He became a member of Zion's Camp in 1834. He was ordained an Apostle in Far West in 1839, and served a mission to England soon after. He was President of the Church from 1889 to 1898.

Brigham YOUNG (1801-77), a native of Whitingham, Vermont, was baptized in 1832 and was a member of Zion's Camp in 1834. He served as an Apostle from 1835 to 1847. He was the central figure in leading the migration of the Saints to the Great Basin. He served as President of the Church from 1847 until his death in 1877.

Phineas Howe YOUNG (1799-1879), a native of Hopkinton, Massachusetts, and brother to Brigham Young, was baptized in 1832 and soon moved to Kirtland, Ohio. He migrated west in the first company, led by his brother. He was a printer by trade.

Henry ZABRISKIE (1788-1857), a native of Pennsylvania, joined the Church in 1832. After the fall of Far West, he was arrested, but was released shortly afterward. He migrated to Utah, eventually settling in Provo.

Lewis ZABRISKIE (1817-72) was born in Hamilton, Ohio, and was baptized in 1836. In 1839 he married Mary Higbee. He was expelled from Missouri and Illinois with the rest of the Saints. He migrated to Utah, settling in Spring City.

Date Index

Name and Subject Index